13 50

NARCOTICS

UNIVERSITY OF CALIFORNIA
MEDICAL EXTENSION SERIES—Los Angeles

Editorial Committee

Thomas H. Sternberg, M.D., *Chairman*
Morton H. Maxwell, M.D., *Department of Medicine*
Franklin L. Ashley, M.D., *Department of Surgery*

Published

Barker SURGICAL TREATMENT OF PERIPHERAL VASCULAR DISEASE
Brown and Pearson CLINICAL USES OF ADRENAL STEROIDS
Maxwell and Kleeman CLINICAL DISORDERS OF FLUID AND
ELECTROLYTE METABOLISM
Mellinkoff THE DIFFERENTIAL DIAGNOSIS OF ABDOMINAL PAIN
Mellinkoff THE DIFFERENTIAL DIAGNOSIS OF DIARRHEA
Sharpe MANAGEMENT OF MEDICAL EMERGENCIES
Sternberg and Newcomer THE EVALUATION OF THERAPEUTIC
AGENTS AND COSMETICS
Sternberg and Newcomer MODERN DERMATOLOGIC THERAPY
Tallman TREATMENT OF EMOTIONAL PROBLEMS IN
OFFICE PRACTICE
Turner OFFICE UROLOGY
Tyler STERILITY: OFFICE MANAGEMENT OF THE
INFERTILE COUPLE
Weinstein and Beutler MECHANISMS OF ANEMIA

NARCOTICS

EDITED BY

Daniel M. Wilner, Ph.D.

Professor of Public Health,
School of Public Health
University of California, Los Angeles

Gene G. Kassebaum, Ph.D.

Associate Research Sociologist,
School of Public Health
University of California, Los Angeles

The Blakiston Division
McGRAW-HILL BOOK COMPANY
New York   Toronto   Sydney   London

NARCOTICS

Library of Congress Catalog Card Number: 64-8421

70638

CONTRIBUTORS

Francis A. Allen, A.B., LL.B., J.D. (Hon.)   University Professor in the Law School and the School of Social Service Administration, University of Chicago, Chicago, Illinois

Leon Brill, M.S.   Project Director, Washington Heights Rehabilitation Center, New York, New York

Isidor Chein, Ph.D.   Professor of Psychology, New York University, Washington Square, New York, New York

Charles E. Dederich   Executive Director, Synanon Foundation, Inc., Santa Monica, California

Nathan B. Eddy, M.D., D.Sc.   Executive Secretary, Committee on Drug Addiction and Narcotics, National Academy of Sciences–National Research Council; Consultant on Narcotics, National Institutes of Health, Bethesda, Maryland

Alfred M. Freedman, M.D.   Professor of Psychiatry, New York Medical College, New York, New York

Harris Isbell, M.D.   Professor of Medicine, Section on Clinical Pharmacology, Department of Medicine, University of Kentucky Medical Center, Lexington, Kentucky

Louis Lasagna, M.D.   Associate Professor of Medicine, and Associate Professor of Pharmacology and Experimental Therapeutics, The Johns Hopkins University School of Medicine, Baltimore, Maryland

Alfred R. Lindesmith, Ph.D.   Professor of Sociology, Indiana University, Bloomington, Indiana

Richard A. McGee, M.A.   Administrator, Youth and Adult Corrections Agency, State of California, Sacramento, California

James F. Maddux, M.D.   Medical Officer in Charge, Public Health Service Hospital, Fort Worth, Texas; Clinical Associate Professor, Department of Psychiatry, Southwestern Medical School, Dallas, Texas

Harold Meiselas, M.D. Director, Division of Narcotics, Department of Mental Hygiene, State of New York, Manhattan State Hospital, New York, New York

John A. O'Donnell, Ph.D. Associate Director, Addiction Research Center, National Institute of Mental Health, Public Health Service Hospital, Lexington, Kentucky

E. Leong Way, Ph.D. Professor of Pharmacology and Toxicology, San Francisco Medical Center, University of California, San Francisco, California; and Visiting Professor and China Medical Board Research Fellow, University of Hong Kong (1962–63), Hong Kong

Abraham Wikler, M.D. Professor of Psychiatry, University of Kentucky College of Medicine, Lexington, Kentucky

Charles Winick, Ph.D. Director, Narcotics Addiction Program, American Social Health Association, New York, New York

Leslie T. Wilkins Reader in Social Survey Methods, Royal College of Science and Technology; and formerly Deputy Director Research, Home Office Research Unit, London

Lewis Yablonsky, Ph.D. Professor of Sociology, San Fernando Valley (California) State College, Northridge, California

FOREWORD

In writing a foreword for this volume, I find it difficult adequately to define narcotic addiction. It is not a specific disease entity but rather a set of interrelated processes which combine to present a complicated medical problem. In many instances motivation to use drugs stems from a psychiatric problem, but inadvertent addiction is not unknown. While addiction involves physical dependence on drugs, merely eliminating withdrawal symptoms does not result in permanent abstinence from renewed addiction.

Narcotic addiction in the United States is further complicated in that it involves violations of the law, both because possession of narcotics is a crime under our law, and because theft is often committed in order to buy expensive illegal drugs. It is not possible to study the medical problem—and particularly the treatment problem—without also considering innumerable legal problems involving user and law enforcement.

The faculty was selected with the hope that all important knowledge relative to this subject could be aired, including contributions from medicine, the law, sociology, psychology, and corrections. Above all, the aim was to bring contending points of view into mutual contact in these meetings. I believe that the conference succeeded in this respect and that the contents of this volume will prove of value to those who must deal with one of the more serious problems in modern urban life.

Thomas H. Sternberg, M.D.
Assistant Dean in Charge of
Postgraduate Medical Education

PREFACE

In April, 1963, a national Narcotics Conference was held on the campus of the University of California, Los Angeles. This volume brings together the major papers presented during the several days of the proceedings which summarized contemporary epidemiologic and therapeutic viewpoints regarding the perplexing problem of narcotics use. The drugs principally under discussion are the morphine derivatives and synthetics, with major attention concentrated on heroin, the narcotic in wide and illegal use.

Participating in the conference were some five hundred professional people, including many persons charged with the responsibility of coping with established narcotics habits of thousands of addicts the country over. The purpose of the conference was to provide for these professionals a forum both for the review of the more secure knowledge in the area and for the debate of a number of critical issues in this complex field of inquiry and action.

What are the facts of addiction, its incidence and extent? Discussion of the incidence and prevalence of narcotics use in the United States is offered principally in Chapts. 1 (Winick) and 7 (Chein). Comparative information on general epidemiology of drug use is also touched on in Chapt. 9 (Wilkins on the situation in England) and in Chapt. 17 (Way on events in Hong Kong). These chapters taken together review some of the basic problems of estimating the extent of narcotics use in the United States. Information on incidence and prevalence of narcotics use originally derived from either medical or legal sources, but as the problem has grown over the years, increasing reliance has been placed on police accounting of arrests and formal legal charges. Careful reading of the analyses of Chapts. 1 and 7 will arm the reader with guides for the assessment of numerical data on the number of drug users in the United States.

How extensive is present knowledge of the basic chemistry and pharmacology of narcotics? The discussion in at least three chapters shows that this knowledge, while not complete, is considerable. Chapter 5 (Eddy) traces the challenging history of attempts to identify pain relievers which are at the same time nonaddicting. It would appear that we now know of analgesics largely free of addicting characteristics, although they are yet generally untried in clinical practice. In Chapt. 6 (Wikler), there is presented a detailed theory of the psychophysiology of addiction and relapse, resulting from more than a decade of study and experimentation in addiction in animals and of observation of human addiction. Chapter 3 (Isbell) provides a stimulating review of current broad research activities in all subareas of the addiction problem, with particular emphasis on pharmacologic aspects.

What do we know about treatment and relapse of narcotics users? Chapter 10 (Maddux) reviews the experience at the Federal Public Health Service Hospitals at Lexington, Kentucky, and Fort Worth, Texas; characteristic clinical treatment modes are discussed in some detail, and an accounting is given of the 3,400 admissions at both hospitals in the year 1962. Chapter 11 (Freedman) describes the philosophic and theoretical premises and objectives of a treatment program operated in a voluntary metropolitan hospital. Chapter 13 (Brill) summarizes the qualitative experience of an effort to provide aftercare and rehabilitation to almost 1,000 persons released from the Public Health Service Hospital at Lexington in the period 1957–1962. Chapter 14 (O'Donnell) reviews in detail the relapse rates from the major follow-up studies of the past 25 years.

Chapter 12 (Yablonsky and Dederich) describes a substantial innovation in the rehabilitation of narcotics users: the voluntary banding together of narcotics users in open society for the purpose of resisting relapse to narcotic drugs.

What are new developments in official governmental programs for the rehabilitation of drug users? Chapter 15 (Meiselas) tells of the New York Department of Mental Hygiene program underwritten by the Metcalf-Volker Act. This act codifies several previously existing procedures for commitment of confirmed drug users and adds a decidedly new practice: the civil commitment of users—with certain disqualifiers—from police and court channels to the facilities of the Department of Mental Hygiene for treatment for a maximum period of 36 months. Chapter 16 (McGee) describes the provisions of California legislation directed toward the same general ends with provision for much longer periods of confinement and parole. In California the general rehabilitation program, including principles of civil commitment, are carried out directly by the Department of Corrections in a number of special facilities. Recent broad trends in narcotics legislation are reviewed in Chapt. 2 (Allen). Attention is given to the status of use of drugs as a matter of police rather than medical concern, and a number of questions are raised about the legal character of civil commitment.

Three papers contain contributions to the general social psychology of the narcotics problem, and a fourth may be considered an essay on the topic from the perspective of social medicine. Chapter 8 (Lindesmith) recapitulates a theory of addiction that depends on the existence of a "cognitive conditioning process," in which the addicted person "defines himself as an addict because he realizes that he is one." Such a theory places little reliance on more traditionally accepted characterologic motivations for the onset of drug use and seriously disputes the role of euphoria as an inciting lure for continued use. Chapter 9 (Wilkins), while commenting on differences in the use of drugs in the United States and the United Kingdom, offers some social-psychologic hypotheses for the difference in drug practices between the two countries. These hypotheses include reliance on the perceptual basis of much of social behavior and on social feedback mechanisms that do much to define deviant and nondeviant behavior and to maintain a deviant subculture. The suggestion is that the two countries differ sharply in what is considered deviant.

Chapters 7 (Chein) and 4 (Lasagna), in addition to the commentaries already mentioned, have set as their tasks the reduction of what is considered social and medical mythology regarding narcotics, their use, and users. Chapter 7 suggests that to regard narcotics addiction as "contagious" is misleading, that addicts are persons with serious psychosocial problems, and that the particular nature of the spread of addiction "reflects unsolved problems that are focused on limited segments of society." This chapter also reminds us that despite some possible characterologic similarities among addicts, no two addicts are alike and that narcotics laws that ignore these differences are doomed to failure. Finally in Chapt. 4, it is suggested that medical practice is preoccupied with exaggerated fears of addictive possibilities of drugs in legitimate practice and that the supposed "pernicious" properties of heroin as a drug, per se, are difficult to document. The chapter calls for broad reconsideration of existing points of view regarding "criminality" of the drug user for the use of drugs alone.

This brief synopsis only hints of the controversy that pervades the discussion in many of the papers. Is the use of narcotic drugs harmful per se to the individual and society? Is the user of narcotic drugs a debased criminal for that fact alone, in the commonly accepted connotations of the term? Or is the user a criminal because of the criminal acts many drug users commit to obtain funds necessary to purchase illegal drugs once addiction has been established?

Is successful treatment in the United States possible in the present medicolegal framework? Can we implant in drug users who are in legal or even medical custody the seeds of resistance to relapse once they are free of custody? Or are we dealing with a social, psychologic, pharmacologic, and legal complex that almost certainly ensures relapse to drugs, granted that personal and social factors leading to initial addiction remain the same, and granted that the only access to drugs is through illicit channels of supply?

There would seem to be at least three kinds of solutions to this grave problem. All three are given visibility in these proceedings. The first is to continue by and large as before, searching for treatment schemes that might be effective *within the present legal status* of narcotics addiction. This means learning more about the drugs in question, trying out treatment modes in all legal-medical combinations possible, with the hope of hitting on some that inhibit dependence and habituation to drugs. The second does not seek to alter society's conviction that narcotics use is itself reprehensible, but seeks to provide protection from relapse in a complex of group activities and cognitions of drug users themselves—the Synanon approach. The third— echoed in several papers—suggests that the very premise of reprehensibility of drug use is not in keeping with the best medical evidence and that control of drug use is best accomplished by first reappraising the extraordinary status that drug use has assumed and by redefining it as a purely medical problem.

Many persons and agencies assisted in making the conference possible and in making it better than it would have been without their help.

Funds for the conference derived from Grant No. OM-1012, National Institute of Mental Health. Dr. Carl Anderson, of that Institute, was helpful at all stages in the development of the conference, from the earliest consideration of topics and speakers to encouragement to get the proceedings in print.

Many persons at the University of California, Los Angeles, played significant roles. Thomas H. Sternberg, M.D., Assistant Dean, and Mrs. Betty Minifie of UCLA Postgraduate Medical Education developed the original plans for a narcotics conference at UCLA. Their extension staff, headed by Mrs. Betty Gifford, made arrangements for speakers and participants a model of thoughtful and considerate efficiency.

A steering committee helped decide the tenor of the conference: on the one hand, to provide an opportunity for an interdisciplinary audience of administrators, researchers, and other professional persons concerned with narcotic addiction to share knowledge of the etiology, epidemiology, and treatment of illegal narcotic use; and, on the other hand, to provide a forum for the debate of the many unresolved issues by participants from many fields. The steering committee was under the chairmanship of Lenor S. Goerke, M.D., Dean, UCLA School of Public Health, and of Dr. Sternberg. Committee members for the UCLA campus included Walter C. Bailey, Ph.D. (Social Welfare), Keith S. Ditman, M.D. (Psychiatry), Donald J. Jenden, M.B. (Pharmacology), James L. Malone, LL.B. (Law), and Lewis Yablonsky, Ph.D. (Sociology). Committee members from California state agencies included Lester Breslow, M.D. (Public Health), Elmer F. Galioni, M.D. (Mental Hygiene), and J. Douglas Grant, M.A. (Corrections).

Conceptualizing the conference topics fell to the program committee consisting of Rosabelle Price Walkley and David A. Ward, Ph.D., both of the UCLA School of Public Health, and the editors. This notice is, at best, inadequate acknowledgment of the imaginative contribution of Mrs. Walkley and Dr. Ward for the substance and format of the conference program.

Finally, a considerable debt must be acknowledged to actual program participants whose remarks do not appear in these pages. Opening the conference were remarks by Dr. Sternberg; Richard C. Maxwell, Dean, UCLA School of Law; John Field, Ph.D., Associate Dean, UCLA School of Medicine; and Stanley Mosk, Attorney General, state of California. Chairing various sessions were John A. Clausen, Ph.D., Director, Institute of Human Development, University of California, Berkeley; Dr. Eddy; Dr. Lindesmith; Daniel Lieberman, M.D., Chief Deputy Director, California Department of Mental Hygiene; and Lester Breslow, M.D., Chief, Division of Preventive Medical Services, California Department of Public Health.

All concurrent sessions of the conference included panel discussions. Discussants not otherwise presenting formal papers included Keith S. Ditman, M.D., Lecturer and Research Psychiatrist, and Director, Alcoholism Research Clinic, UCLA Department of Psychiatry; Harold B. Bradley, M.A., Associate Superintendent, California Rehabilitation Center, Corona; Walter C. Bailey, Ph.D., Lecturer, UCLA School of Social Welfare; Dr. Clausen; Ernest G. Reimer, M.S.W., Chief, Correctional Program Services Division, California Department of Corrections; and Samuel Levine, District Supervisor, Bureau of Narcotics, United States Treasury Department.

Editorial assistance was provided by Mrs. Elaine Linden. Stenographic assistance was provided by Mrs. Geraldine Shaffer and Mrs. Marion Ellinthorpe.

Daniel M. Wilner, Ph.D.
Gene G. Kassebaum, Ph.D.

INTRODUCTION

Gene G. Kassebaum and Daniel M. Wilner

AT THE TIME these papers were assembled for publication, the press was headlining the release of the U.S. Surgeon General's committee report on the health risks of cigarette smoking.[1] It was official recognition of the ubiquitous cigarette as a factor of consequence in the mortality and morbidity of the nation.

Today, smokers may be heard to argue the relative deprivations of a shorter and sicker life with cigarettes versus a longer and jittery life without them, and many evidently do not blanch at the prospect of possible cancer as the price of continued smoking. Even those persons who try to quit report the persistence of strong craving, tension, nervousness, and other symptoms of withdrawal so uncomfortable that they are sometimes driven to relapse. It is apparent that a substantial proportion of the population of the United States is involuntarily habituated to a practice now widely known to be linked to fatal diseases.[2]

Let us consider another practice, that of drinking alcoholic beverages. After a number of years of active campaigns of "temperance" (really abstinence) societies, the United States amended its Constitution to prohibit the manufacture and sale of fermented and spirituous liquors. For a decade, many millions of otherwise more-or-less law-abiding citizens found the appeal of drinking so strong that the elaborate special agencies

---

[1] "Smoking and Health," *Report of the Advisory Committee to the Surgeon General of the Public Health Service,* U.S. Government Printing Office, 1964.

[2] Cigarette smoking may fit Wikler's definition of addiction: "For clinical purposes, 'drug addiction' in general may be defined as the compulsive use of chemical agents which are harmful to the individual, to society, or to both." Wikler, Abraham: "Opiate Addiction: Psychological and Neurophysiological Aspects in Relation to Clinical Problems," p. 3, Charles C Thomas, Publisher, Springfield, Ill., 1963.

created for the suppression of drinking were notoriously unable to effectively stop this practice.

It is not entirely fanciful to speculate on what might be the situation if a smoking-abstinence movement were to achieve a tobacco prohibition to decrease the health risks of cigarettes—which in any analysis would appear to be as grave as the social evils of beer—and the Federal government were to create a corps of agents to enforce the law. Is there any reason to suppose that law violation would be less frequent than in the Dry Era? Is it not well within the realm of the possible that, as smoking became penalized, smokers might be driven to clandestine indulgence, law enforcement might become correspondingly more vigorous, and regulatory personnel more numerous in efforts to detect and suppress? In such a sequence, as the penalties increased, the expenses of protection and the possibility of profit would add to the cost of deviance, and smoking would soon become, not merely illegal, but criminal.

Of course, it is unlikely that cigarettes in the 1960s will go the course of beer in the 1920s. Smoking is currently regarded as a medical matter and a public health problem, and so long as it remains so defined, the regulation and reduction of tobacco consumption will probably be achieved through such devices as proper labeling, propaganda, and education of young presmokers. However effective or ineffective these measures should prove to be, they are unlikely in themselves to produce a caste of criminal smokers, incarcerated ex-smokers, and syndicate of tobacco pushers and a wave of repressive laws against the habituated and recalcitrant smoker.

It is apparent from the papers in this symposium that the narcotic addict is in something approaching a class by himself. Not as numerous as the drinker or smoker, he has neither the votes nor the consumer power to merit direct consideration. Saddled with an appetite which increases with each sating, tied to a craving which is qualitatively more compelling than tobacco and more habituating with casual indulgence than either tobacco or alcohol, and victimized by high prices for drugs, the addict lives an underground existence looking for drugs, dodging the law, and periodically spending years of his life behind bars in jails, hospitals, asylums, and prisons. Where the precancerous chain smoker and the troublesome alcoholic can avail themselves of private medical aid, the physician who recognizes a drug addict in his examining room in most cases rejects him as a patient.

The narcotics user holds a peculiar status legally, medically, and socially. No other form of deviant indulgence receives so much unsought attention or is dealt with so severely by the state; no other sickness is barred from any medical treatment not imposed by the court. The full weight of public opinion, legal statute, and police power is brought down upon the drug user in an effort to either bring him to heel or drive him from sight.

Whatever may be the arguments for and against the ethics or justification of such strenuous measures, the chapters in this book make it apparent that they have thus far not been successful in removing narcotic addiction from the list of public problems. The matter is a proper subject for study and has prompted, in recent years, a number of organized efforts to examine available data and indicate areas for immediate inquiry into the mechanisms, epidemiology, treatment, and control of narcotics addiction.

In what ways is drug use popularly regarded as different from other forms of extreme dependence? There has, surprisingly, not yet been published a truly adequate explanation of why opiate use is regarded not merely as a self-limiting or incapacitating habit (such as excessive drinking) but as a heinous, almost dehumanizing depravity. The social significance of drug addiction to the nonaddict has not been systematically investigated. It can scarcely be averred that society's repugnance of drug use stems from the effect of the drug per se. Thirty-four years ago Wallace wrote: [3]

In carefully planned and carried out studies made at Philadelphia General Hospital and repeated in part at Bellevue Hospital it was

[3] Wallace, George B.: The Rehabilitation of the Drug Addict, *J. Educational Sociol.*, 4(6):347, 1931.

shown that continued taking of opium or any of its derivatives resulted in no measurable organic damage. The addict when not deprived of his opium showed no abnormal behavior which distinguished him from a non-addict. Further, the most careful examination of his body functions failed to show any damage which could be directly attributed to the narcotics.

Thus, while by no means an argument *for* drug use, the physical or mental state of the drug user with ample legal supplies does not seem in itself a sufficient explanation for the reaction of the nonuser. A carefully conducted inquiry into the psychologic basis of feelings of nonusers toward drug users would seem desirable.

Such an inquiry could serve other than purely academic purposes, since the distinctive characteristic of the "narcotics problem" in the United States is the manner in which this social repugnance is codified in law.

The Harrison Act of 1914 created the basic machinery for regulation of the illegal drug traffic in the United States; through its implementation by the Federal Bureau of Narcotics, it quickly became a means for the prohibition of all use of opiates for nonmedicinal purposes. One of the most far-reaching of its effects has been to remove the treatment of narcotics addicts from the purview of the private physician and civilian hospital and place it within the exclusive jurisdiction of the courts, and state and Federal correctional agencies. In a comparison of British and U.S. programs, Schur[4] states "... the practical effect of the Narcotics Bureau's interpretation [of the Harrison Act] has been to deter almost all individual practitioners from attempting to treat addict patients." Schur goes on to quote Judge Ploscowe, who explains that although the language of the law permits prescribing to an addict in good faith as part of a treatment, this in practice is determined after the fact, by trial and jury. The prudent physician may perhaps be excused for demurring, in most instances, from laying himself open to the publicity and possible consequences of such proceedings. Indeed, recently the

[4] Schur, Edwin M.: "Narcotic Addiction in Britain and America," Indiana University Press, Bloomington, Ind., 1962.

President's Commission speculated that fear of Federal harassment might even discourage researchers from becoming too closely connected with narcotics users. "There is some fear of prosecution under Federal narcotics laws among medical researchers," they state. "The fear grows out of past disagreements between physicians and those charged with enforcement of the Federal narcotic laws over the legitimate extent to which a physician may dispense or prescribe narcotic drugs in the treatment of addiction. This fear although unjustified [sic] nonetheless deters researchers." [5]

The legal developments since 1914 are commented upon extensively by Professor Allen in this book. The general effect of the laws pertaining to sale, possession, and use has been to define control of the narcotic user as either a penal or state hospital responsibility. In many cases, legislative acts have given both a large custodial assignment and a broad mandate to departments of corrections and prison administrators, with little secure knowledge of treatment techniques and, indeed, not very much in the way of either discretionary latitude or resources for improving such techniques. As a result, it is not unfair to say that in most prisons, the narcotic user is subject to no treatment other than that available to the burglar, the forger, or the child molester. Like the town drunk tank for the chronic inebriate petty offender, the prison yard has a "revolving door" for the drug user. Recidivism rates for paroled narcotic users are high; in the prison system more pessimism is openly expressed about the parole chances of a heroin addict than about any other offender.

Owing in part to the manifest failure of simple incarceration as a means of reducing drug use, state and Federal agencies have in recent times inaugurated clinical and quasi-clinical treatment programs. Several of the most important of such programs will be discussed in Part 4, by administrators charged with the responsibility for their conduct. There have been many new developments in the past decade. In California, for example, the limitation on control and intervention of the laws governing

[5] President's Advisory Commission on Narcotic and Drug Abuse, 1963, p. 27.

narcotics use has been radically extended by two developments: the passage in 1962 of legislation providing for the involuntary civil commitment of known or suspected drug addicts or those in imminent danger of addiction, and the utilization on a wide scale of the Nalline test as a chemical means of detecting recent opiate use. The first of these widens the scope of the state's jurisdiction to include persons on whom there is not evidence of a felony; the second makes it more difficult to evade detection of narcotics use on parole. Civil commitment is yet unproven in its effects: it is still under judicial review in the courts, with test cases likely in the next few years, and it has not run long enough for data on treatment outcome to accumulate. If retained, however, the provisions for custody and parole supervision of thousands of narcotics users, coupled with the Nalline testing program on parole, offer unique opportunities for empirical research on relapse and abstinence after in-service treatment.

What directions might this research take? It seems a warranted conclusion from the papers in this symposium that more data and more theoretical integration are needed everywhere: in the areas of histologic processes, the addiction mechanisms, epidemiology, treatment outcome, and relapse. But one area in particular is quite poorly explored. This is the study of the behavior of the addict in the community, and the forms of social relations and groups relevant to that behavior. Howard Becker has stressed the difficulties of explaining deviant behavior without detailed accounts of noninstitutionalized deviants living their own lives.[6] He has pointed out that when personal deviance serves to make a person a member of a deviant group, his conduct becomes subject to positive sanctions and becomes in turn more resistive to change in the direction desired by the agencies of social control. The group membership of the narcotic addict is as yet imperfectly charted. An article by Ray outlines the cycle of drug use, abstinence, and relapse as it is monitored by the addicts' involvement in a drug-using subculture, the experience of disparities between self-image as user

[6] Becker, Howard: "Outsiders," The Free Press, Chicago, Ill., 1963.

and a developing discontent with that image, and the experience of difficulties of acceptance of a new social image by non-users which frequently leads to relapse into drug use.[7] It is in a somewhat similar manner that Volkman and Cressey analyze the success of the Synanon organization in maintaining a considerable number of former addicts in a drug-free life for long periods of time.[8] More such work is necessary if the prevailing stereotype of the "junkie" is to be reduced to a set of differentiated empirical types. The pariah status of the narcotic user is a prime factor in the ignorance of clinical and academic disciplines. The moral exclusion of the drug user has effects not only on the treatment of the disease but on the very apprehension of the phenomenon. The papers in the last section of this book direct critical attention to both the clinical and epistemological consequences of a continued repressive program to narcotic addiction.

[7] Ray, Marsh: The Cycle of Abstinence and Relapse Among Heroin Addicts, *Social Problems,* 9:132 (Fall, 1961).

[8] Volkman, Rita, and Cressey, Donald R.: Differential Association and the Rehabilitation of Drug Addicts, *Am. J. Sociol.,* 69:129 (1963).

CONTENTS

Part 1

BASIC ISSUES IN NARCOTICS USE

Charles Winick | **1**

EPIDEMIOLOGY OF NARCOTICS USE

How MANY DRUG USERS are there, where are they, and what kinds of persons are they? The extent to which drug use is illegal in our society and has quasi-criminal overtones makes it difficult to get descriptive data of the quality that exists in the case of analogous conditions. The relative paucity of published data on epidemiology and recidivism in the narcotics addiction field is striking in view of the stringency of laws and penalties that have presumably facilitated the collection of data from institutions that receive drug addicts, like prisons. However, on the basis of studies that have been conducted over the years, it is possible to develop some impressions of the epidemiology of the use of opiates, which can be pragmatically defined as drugs, whatever their origin, with morphinelike properties. Heroin is the opiate that is most likely to be used by American addicts today.

INCIDENCE

A logical question in determining the importance of opiate use in America is: How many persons are involved? The only agency keeping systematic records of the number of opiate users in the United States is the Federal Bureau of Narcotics. Its annual reports list the number of violations of the narcotics law and the

number of persons who otherwise come to the attention of the
Bureau as addicts, and such information has been regularly reported in the annual statements of the Bureau. The collection of
this information relies on a pyramidal structure, with small areas
that report to larger areas that report to the Bureau. The Bureau
listings only cover the opiates. Although persons may be arrested
for the use or possession of drugs that do not produce physical
dependence but the abuse of which has serious consequence, like
cocaine and marihuana, the Bureau does not include them.

Some idea of trends in incidence may be obtained from annual
reports of the Bureau. In its report for 1931, the Bureau noted
that 4,534 persons violated the Federal narcotics law.[14] Separate
figures were cited for violations of various state laws. The Bureau
reported there were 4,742 Federal cases in 1934.[15] Beginning in
1953, the Bureau introduced a machine-coded system for inven-
torying by name all cases reported to it by local and other agencies, placing the data on IBM cards. Every attempt is made to
avoid duplication, to drop addicts who are known to have died
or to have received extensive prison sentences, and in other ways
to keep the files up-to-date. Accepting the medical tradition of
a period of 5 years as the period during which a chronic illness
is likely to have run its course, if there is no recurrence of symptoms, the Bureau keeps a user in its "active" file for 5 years after
he has been reported. If he has not subsequently been reported,
his name is dropped into the inactive list after 5 years, and he no
longer figures in Bureau reports on the number of users. If he is
reported subsequent to the initial report, the date of his activity
is reckoned from the most recent date on which he is reported to
have used drugs.

The Bureau's records have an either-or quality, in that they
do not permit gradation of degree of use of drugs, so that all
references made by the Bureau to its records are to "addicts."
Another consideration in assessing the Bureau's coverage is that
the different agencies that execute the standard report form supplied by the Bureau may interpret their instructions in varying
ways, and thus the definition of the kind of case reported may not
be standard throughout the United States. The shortcomings in
the data collection procedures of the Bureau have been docu-

mented by Eldridge, who feels that statistics on addiction are so unreliable that there is uncertainty in regard to the scope of the narcotics problem as well as the results of our procedures for coping with the problem.[6] Some voluntary agencies and other non-law enforcement groups may be reluctant to submit the names of users who come to their attention, because of their feeling that the Bureau is a law enforcement agency that may ultimately cause the arrest of a person whose name is reported. The Bureau, which has been charged with inadequate record keeping as in the paper by Chein (Chap. 7), has responded that it can hardly be expected to have complete records if there are agencies not submitting information on users.

The Bureau records are the only national figures on the incidence of opiate use and do suggest trends in the number of users in the United States. In the reports of the first several years after 1953, there were probably many persons who had begun drug use before 1953. The large numbers of such users whose names were submitted during the first few years of the new record-keeping procedure made it likely that many older users were reported during this period. By 1955, many of the previous users had been reported, and there were 10,882 new users for the year.[16] The first year in which there had been enough time for the first group of users who had become inactive to be dropped from the rolls was 1958, when there was a national total of 46,266 users reported.[17] By the end of 1962, there were 47,489.[18,19]

From such figures, what can be said about the number of persons taking opiates in the United States during the last few years? The likelihood is that most confirmed users will come to the attention of the authorities within perhaps 2 years. The theft in which a male user engages to get money for illegal drugs, which has been estimated to cost the community over $250 million a year, is practically impossible to conceal, when it is done on an almost daily basis. A woman user can engage in prostitution to raise money to buy drugs and is more likely to continue without detection for a longer period of time. Many police jurisdictions are also less enthusiastic about arresting prostitutes than they are about arresting thieves. In addition to such modal users, there are doubtless some white-collar workers and entertainers or others with substantial incomes who have been able to obtain opiates without coming to the attention of the authorities. It is difficult to estimate the number of such users, but they are probably not very numerous.

Let us assume that the average male or female user comes to the attention of the authorities in 2 years after onset of the use of opiate drugs. Over the years 1958–62, the Federal Bureau has reported an average of 6,840 new users each year, with a range from 5,690 to 7,626.[19] This figure of 6,840 may be a reasonable approximation of the number of persons who actually do begin opiate use every year, even though we do not know the frequency of their use. As of the end of 1962, there is a minimum of 47,489 persons reported to be users by the Bureau during the preceding 5-year period. In addition, let us assume that there are twice 6,840, or 13,680, persons who had begun drug use during 1961 and 1962 but had not yet come to the attention of the authorities. This would mean a total of 61,169 persons using opiates as of the end of 1962. The relative constancy in the number of new users reported annually suggests that the incidence of drug abuse in America has reached a certain stability, with a fairly constant number entering the new-user population each year and a fairly stable proportion becoming inactive.

Although the actual number of new users will probably remain constant over the next few years, it is likely that there may be an apparent decrease in their incidence as one result of a 1963 Supreme Court decision on search and seizure practices of police. This decision raised questions about the right of a police officer to arrest a narcotics user without legally sufficient "probable cause." It led to a sharp decrease in arrests of opiate users in early 1963. This decrease does not, however, necessarily mirror an actual decline in the incidence of users but only the greater difficulties of police officers in "making a case."

AGE

How old are opiate users? A number of different reports over the last few decades present a fairly clear picture of their age. Of 1,660 persons violating the narcotics laws during 1929, 47% were under 24 and 19% between 25 and 29. Three-fifths were between 20 and 34.[13] Of 1,592 users in the Chicago area during the early 1930s, 14.4% were under 19, 31% between 20 and 24, 27.5% between 25 and 29, and 14.1% between 30 and 34. Fourteen per cent were over 35.[4] Of 1,036 patients admitted to the Lexington Hospital during 1936 and 1937, 44.6% were under 24, 25.1% between 25 and 29, and 14.2% between 30 and 34. There were 15.8% over 35.[12]

The decline in the age of drug users that has alarmed so many parents in the last decade was documented by Zimmering. He found not one admission of an adolescent user to Bellevue Hospital in New York from 1940 through 1948, but six in 1950 and 84 during the first two months of 1951.[26] A similar phenomenon was identified in a Chicago study which found one-third of known drug users in 1952 to be under 21, while one-tenth in 1943 and only one-fiftieth in 1932 were under 21.[9] The relative youth of so many drug users has led to community as well as scientific concern. Such concern has led to special facilities like Riverside Hospital in New York, which provided services to addicts under 16 for a decade before it closed in 1963, and to a thorough study of juvenile drug use in New York, probably the most intensive yet conducted of any group of opiate users.[3]

Nationwide data from the Federal Bureau include an average of 1,013 new users under 21, 3,827 between 21 and 30, 1,456 between 31 and 40, and 542 over 40 for years 1958–1962. As of the end of 1962, there was a total of 1,619 users under 21, 23,087 between 21 and 30, 17,583 between 31 and 40, and 5,200 over 40.

Opiate users today are primarily young adults. Inasmuch as drug users in the 1930s and in 1953, when the Bureau began its current record-keeping procedure, were mainly also young adults, why are there comparatively few older users? Some may die from infections caused by the circumstances under which they take narcotics, like unsterilized hypodermics. Others may die of overdoses, of inadvertently taking the wrong drug, and of indirectly related causes: fires, traffic accidents, etc. Some may suffer malnutrition and thus lower the resistance of their bodies to other infections. It is relatively difficult to get precise data on these causes of death in drug users, but there is reason to believe that the number of users is underreported in such circumstances.

In order to clarify why there are apparently so few older addicts, the hypothesis of "maturing out" of opiate addiction has been developed.[24] Data have been reported suggesting that a majority of narcotics users cease taking drugs by their 30s, and it has been suggested that they no longer need the satisfactions that drugs were providing for them in the years from adolescence to early adulthood. The typical drug user begins using in adolescence or his mid or late teens. The maturing-out hypothesis suggests that this is because he is facing urgencies of vocational decision, school, and starting a family. Taking opiates replaces these other decisions. It gives him something to do, a special vocabulary, and provides him with an ingroup. It absorbs aggression and sex, the manifestation of which might be very troubling, and meets a number of other needs.

By the early mid-30s, such needs are less urgent, and the person seems to drift away from drug use, with longer and longer periods of abstention before return to drug use. The pressures of the authorities and of law enforcement seem to make themselves felt with more than usual salience to the user by his early and mid-30s, and the user's periods of contact with drugs become briefer. After a while, the theory concludes, he has matured out. The phenomenon is similar to that observed by the Gluecks in their studies of juvenile delinquents, which found that the delinquent was ready for more normal living by his 30s.[8] It is also similar to a number of studies of psychopaths, many of whom seem to return to normal society by their 30s.[14]

The typical user of opiates uses them for a mean of 8.6 years, although some are known to have been taking drugs for as long as 56 years. The earlier in life drug use begins, the longer it is likely to continue. According to one estimate, for every year that the user delays the onset of drug use, the length of the period of drug use is shortened by one-eighth to one-ninth of a year.[25] At any given time, the number of users can thus best be expressed in terms of the number of users at the various stages of the cycle of addiction. A minority (7.26%) of users take opiates for 15 years or more and do not mature out; 15 years appears to be the period beyond which forces that are countervailing to maturing out make themselves felt.

SEX

There are today several times more men than women users. Of 1,660 users in 1929, 1,317 were men and 276 were women.[13] Several thousand users in the Chicago area in the early 1930s consisted of 73% men and 27% women.[4] For 1955, the Federal Bureau reported that 77% of its recorded users were men and 23% women.[16] As of the end of 1962, the Bureau reported 38,654 men and 8,835 women.[19] This is a ratio of almost one woman to every five men. Other estimates have suggested that there may be one woman user for every three men users.[21] It is possible that the very nature of drug use and the kinds of persons it attracts have changed in the last several decades. Before the Harrison Act, women traditionally used opiates for relief of pain. Women seem to have found other substances to ease their pain, and men seem to have increased their drug use in the years since 1914.

ENVIRONMENT

During the last several decades, large cities with minority-group populations seem to have had a growing proportion of the opiate users. The reports of the Federal Bureau in the 1930s often mention New York City, Los Angeles, Detroit, and Chicago as frequent locales for opiate use. By 1958, the Bureau reported that 45% of its users were in New York State, 14% in Illinois, and 13% in California.[17] As of the end of 1962, 46.4% were in New York, 15.6% in California, 14.8% in Illinois, and 3.8% in Michigan.[19]

As early as the late 1920s, there were several times as many users born in urban areas as in both suburban and rural areas combined.[13] In Chicago in the early 1930s, 82.6% of the users were from urban areas,[4] and over half the patients at Lexington in the 1930s had come from deteriorated sections of urban areas.[12] All the cases of heroin addiction seen by Zimmering in the early 1950s came from a New York City slum area.[26]

There can be little question about the concentration of opiate users in slum areas of large cities, where the minority group population is high. The economically depressed environment in which drug use is spawned and flourishes has been far more intensively studied than have the host and agent, of the traditional epidemiological triad of host, agent, and environment. A large number of users is currently concentrated in a few large cities; as of the end of 1962, the Federal Bureau reported that 21,566 were in New York City, 6,972 in Chicago, 3,183 in Los Angeles, 1,780 in Detroit, 918 in the District of Columbia, 655 in San Francisco, 652 in Newark, 615 in Philadelphia, 482 in Oakland, and 477 in San Antonio.[19]

A number of the cities and states in which there are large numbers of users are also very populous. They may have a large number of users because they have a large number of people. In order to evaluate this relationship, the Federal Bureau's count of known opiate users as of December 31, 1961, was divided by the total population of the state as derived from the 1960 census data, and expressed as a rate per 100,000 of population. Table 1-1 gives the rate per 100,000 of the states in the Union, with the states divided into four groups in decreasing prevalence of addiction.

ETHNIC FACTORS

Considerable data have been accumulated on the race and national origin of opiate users. Of 318 users admitted voluntarily to New York's Bellevue Hospital in the late 1920s, 310 were white and 8 Negro.[11] A large sample of users of the same period consisted of 1,024 white, 242 Negro, and 326 Oriental.[13] In 1935, a sample of California addicts was 59% white, 14% Negro, and 16% Oriental.[2] In Chicago in the early 1930s, 77% were white, 17% Negro, and 6% Oriental.[4]

By the early 1950s, it had become necessary for record-keeping agencies to subdivide their white category more fully, as an increasing number of Puerto Ricans began to use opiates. Whereas only 1.8% of the new users reported by the Federal Bureau in 1953 were Puerto Ricans, by 1957 the figure had risen to 9.8%

Table 1-1 PREVALENCE OF OPIATE USE BY STATE, 1961 *

(Over 20 users per 100,000)		(10–20 users per 100,000)		(5–10 users per 100,000)		(Less than 5 users per 100,000)	
State	Rate	State	Rate	State	Rate	State	Rate
New York	130.0	New Jersey	16.8	Delaware	9.9	Virginia	5.0
District of Columbia	101.8	Arizona	15.1	Nevada	9.5	Oklahoma	4.1
Illinois	68.7	New Mexico	12.4	Louisiana	8.6	Wisconsin	3.7
California	48.3	Maryland	12.3	Oregon	7.8	Ohio	3.5
Michigan	25.2	Texas	11.3	Massachusetts	7.1	Minnesota	3.3
Missouri	20.3	Colorado	10.1	Hawaii	7.1	Florida	3.0
				Indiana	6.8	Alabama	2.9
				Washington	6.4	Kentucky	2.7
				Pennsylvania	5.5	Montana	2.1
				Connecticut	5.4	Tennessee	1.9
						Georgia	1.9
						Kansas	1.8
						Mississippi	1.5
						Nebraska	1.5
						Arkansas	1.4
						North Carolina	1.3
						South Carolina	1.3
						Iowa	1.2
						Wyoming	1.2
						Idaho	1.1
						Rhode Island	0.9
						Vermont	0.8
						West Virginia	0.7
						New Hampshire	0.7
						Maine	0.5
						South Dakota	0.4
						North Dakota	0
						Alaska	0
						Utah	0

* Denominators for rates are from 1960 U.S. Census of population. SOURCE: U.S. Treasury, Bureau of Narcotics: Traffic in Opium and Other Dangerous Drugs for the Year Ended December 31, 1961 (1962).

and by 1962, to 11.9%. Also among the white, Mexicans are listed separately, accounting for 2.3% of new users reported in 1953, 6.5% in 1957, and 7.6% in 1962. As of the end of 1962, the Federal Bureau reported 54.9% to be Negro, 10.9% to be Puerto Rican (white), 7.2% to be Mexican (white), 25.9% other white, and all other groups to constitute only 1.1%.[19] This 1.1% includes such groups as the Oriental, which loomed much larger in the incidence of opiate use in the United States in the 1920s and 1930s, but which have ceased to do so as the older generation died off and relatively few members of the next generation were involved in drug use.

The proportion of users with foreign-born parents is not and has not in the last few decades been significantly different from that of the general population.

OCCUPATION

A considerable variety of occupations has been reported for various user groups in the past. In New York City in the late 1920s, the most frequently reported occupation was relatively un-skilled laborer,[11] and many male users were regularly employed.[7] In Chicago in the early 1930s, three-fifths of the female and one-fourth of the male users were engaged in domestic and personal service work.[4] Over one-third of the men and one-twentieth of the women worked in manufacturing industries, and over one-fourth of the men and one-seventh of the women worked in trades. One-fifth had no occupation. Approximately 4% of both men and women worked in occupations connected with recreation and amusement. At Lexington in the 1930s, 30.9% of the users worked in the domestic and personal service field, 21.7% in manufactur-ing industries, 12.9% at trades, 9.3% at semiprofessional or pro-fessional tasks, 8.3% in transportation, 7.1% in clerical work, 4.7% in agricultural work, and only 1.5% had no occupation.[12] Most recently, it can be speculated that the typical user of the last 15 years probably has no established vocation, although there has been no large scale study of vocation of users.

Occupational groups studied include jazz musicians, physicians, and nurses. One study of 409 jazz musicians in the New York City area reported that, during the mid-1950s, 24% were described as occasional and 16% as regular users of heroin, with the corresponding figures for marihuana 54% and 23%, respectively.[22] The attraction of drugs to the 5,000 jazz musicians in New York was attributed to a combination of several factors: jazz being a music of protest and deviation, the surroundings in which such music is played, the ownership by some of the same people who control the drug traffic of some of the nightclubs in which jazz was played, the great fame of a few very famous jazz musicians who were addicts as well as being enormously talented, the history of association between jazz lyrics and drug use, and a cyclical relationship between the type of drug used at any given time by musicians, their feelings of acceptance by the larger society, and the very quality of the music they played. Although the incidence of drug use by musicians is not nearly so great as the sensational press frequently claims, there is no doubt that it has contributed consistently to the drug problem in the United States, especially from the 1930s through the early 1950s.

It has been estimated by former Commissioner of Narcotics Anslinger that approximately 1% of the more than 200,000 physicians in the United States are addicted to opiates.[10] A study of 98 physician opiate addicts concluded that factors such as role strain, underlying passivity, their own feelings of omnipotence and capacity to control a medication which they prescribed for patients, as well as the specific effects of the drug combine to lead physicians to become addicts.[23] The high proportion of physician users is surprising in view of the extremely high status enjoyed by physicians in our society and the nature of the physician's work, which makes it necessary for him to undergo considerable training and to defer gratifications, while exhibiting continuing mastery of a series of skills. Such characteristics are not frequently found in the majority of users.

The American Nursing Association receives reports each year from state licensing boards on nurses who have lost their licenses, temporarily or permanently, as the result of using opiates illegally. In 1961, 74 lost their licenses temporarily or permanently for this reason.[1] An interview study by the author with 120 nurses who had been or were opiate users found that a variety of personality factors, disaffection in personal life, work unhappiness, and a low frustration tolerance were among the factors that contributed to nurses' beginning opiate use. The figures available on nurse opiate users are probably less reliable than those on physicians, since it is relatively easier for a nurse to conceal her drug use than it is for a physician. Physicians and nurses have unique access to drugs and syringes and are familiar with their effects, although only a small minority uses its access and familiarity to become addicts.

SOCIOECONOMIC STATUS

Practically all reports suggest that socioeconomic status is a crucial contributor to opiate use in America. In the 1920s, irregular employment in marginal occupations characterized the great majority of a large sample (2,407) studied.[13] Users in Chicago in the early 1930s had largely marginal economic status (78.6%).[4] Well over half (57.3%) the parents of the early patients at Lexington had marginal economic status.[13] The report by Chein in the present volume makes it clear that the spread of drug use is connected with conditions of "human misery." Mistrust, negativism, and defiance, found in the high-addiction areas in New York City, are traditionally associated with low socioeconomic status. A number of other investigations have made it quite clear that the slum minority-group teen-agers, living in an overcrowded area, are potential candidates for opiate use. Major institutions of society that engage in socialization, like the school, appear to be relatively unable to reach this group. However it be called, it is clearly this group at the bottom of the socioeconomic status continuum that is most likely to see people taking drugs, as well as discussing them. Living in a highly congested minority-group area in a large city, the opportunities for hearing and knowing about narcotics are immeasurably multiplied. The adolescent who becomes an opiate user is likely to grow up in a subculture in which there already is an atmosphere of acceptance of stimulants and intoxicants. This is as true in Los Angeles as it is in Chicago and New York or Detroit. Ecologically, he is growing up in an environment in which there is an established interest in stimulants and intoxicants and in experimenting with drugs.

The more typical young users appear to have engaged in delinquent activity either before or during their concern with drugs.[9] There is no consistent relation of predrug nondeviant behavior to deviance as a direct outcome of opiate use. The need for money to buy drugs may lead to an increase in the incidence but not in the type of criminal activity.

SOME PARAMETERS

The dimensions of the problem of opiate addiction in the United States thus seem to be reasonably definable, in terms of the traditional criteria of epidemiology. This is so in spite of the many difficulties of collecting data. The problem has become a relatively stable one, with roughly the same number of persons entering the known user population every year, and with a fairly consistent number either maturing out or otherwise not remaining in the active user category.

Even more detailed information may eventually be obtained. For example, the Village Aid and Service Society in the Greenwich Village area of New York City conducted an actual census of users in its area. Independently, the local police precinct conducted its own census. Both groups used specific names of users, in order to avoid duplication. Both the police group and the voluntary agency came up with almost precisely the same number of users in the Greenwich Village area.[20] A census was also conducted in the East Harlem area of New York City, by the East Harlem Protestant Parish.[5] It surveyed the area within a four-block radius of its office, which is in the heart of a high-density drug use area. The census was able to locate 558 opiate users. This kind of local augmentation of larger-scale data collection efforts may be invaluable in providing spot checks on areas of heavy incidence and prevalence. These are the areas which spawn new users and which can profit most from programs for remedial action.

Like any other social problem, opiate addiction is described differently by persons working in each of the disciplines that are in contact with the problem. This difference in vocabulary often makes it difficult to see the many similarities in points of view. Whatever one's point of view and theoretical orientation, there can be little disagreement on the desirability of establishing the number and the kinds of persons who are involved in drug use today and over the last several decades. Perhaps it would help to calm some of the many debates that are largely hortatory if the word "addict" were no longer used, and a more generalized word like "user" be employed. The tendency of a number of scientific groups to suggest that we are dealing with a problem of "drug abuse" provides another guidepost for the future.

The opiate user of the 1920s and 1930s differs from more recent users in several ways, in addition to the racial, occupational, and age differences noted. The earlier user paid from $25 to $40 for an ounce of heroin that was about 87 per cent pure. He would mix 1 part heroin with 2 parts of sugar of milk and inject it into the flesh of his arm or leg. The Second World War led to a decline in the supply of illegal drugs, so that from 1948 to 1953 the typical user would pay $2 or $2.50 for a packet of 30 to 40 per cent pure heroin. He would inject the drug directly into a vein in order to maximize its effect. The contemporary user pays an average of $5 for heroin that is perhaps 2 per cent pure and that he injects into the vein. The steady decrease in the purity of the drug, which is probably a function of the greater risks in its smuggling and distribution, has thus led to a continuing diminution in the strength of the "habit" of opiate users over the decades since the Harrison Act.

Users today, in addition to having a milder habit, are more likely to include experimenters with polysubstances than were users of a generation ago. There are more products available today than before, and some users of polysubstances have discovered the opportunities for delaying or trying to avoid addiction by using different substances. Such a person might use heroin, barbiturates, tranquilizers, codeine, and marihuana on successive days.

Although it is difficult to document such an assertion, there is reason to believe that opiate users today are more sociable and spend more time with one another than users of earlier decades. This may be a function of the concentration of users in specific areas in a few large cities and among some minority groups.

The future will surely see an increase in the use of barbiturates, nonbarbiturate sedatives, and phenyl alkamines. California has taken the lead in designating such substances as "dangerous drugs." State regulations on these substances vary so radically that it is impossible to make even a guess on the number of persons who are involved in abuse of these substances. But there is no doubt that it is in the hundreds of thousands. The next step in any serious study of the epidemiology of drug use would involve a study of the demography of rates of abuse of these other substances—the newer dangerous drugs.

There is a growing demand for better epidemiologic data on both the opiates as well as the dangerous drugs, and it is to be hoped that the growing articulation of this demand will ultimately lead to the kind of better data that are needed.

REFERENCES

1. American Nurses' Association: "Current Practices in Regard to Disciplinary Action," Exhibit II–C, The Association, New York, 1962.
2. California Senate Interim Narcotic Committee: "A Report on Drug Addiction in California," State Printing Office, Sacramento, 1936.
3. Chein, I., Gerard, D. L., Lee, R. S., and Rosenfeld, E., with the collaboration of Daniel M. Wilner: "The Road to H: Narcotics, Delinquency, and Social Policy," Basic Books, Inc., Publishers, New York, 1964.
4. Dai, B.: "Opium Addiction in Chicago," The Commercial Press, Shanghai, 1937.
5. East Harlem Protestant Parish Narcotics Committee: Unpublished report, New York, 1963.
6. Eldridge, W. B.: "Narcotics and the Law: A Critique of the American Experiment in Narcotic Drug Control," New York University Press, New York, 1962.
7. Fishman, J. F., et al.: The Real Narcotic Addict, *Am. Mercury*, 25:100 (1932).
8. Glueck, S., et al.: "Juvenile Delinquents Grown Up," The Commonwealth Fund, New York, 1940.
9. Illinois Institute for Juvenile Research: "Drug Addiction among Young Persons in Chicago," The Institute, Chicago, 1953.
10. Interview with Hon. Harry J. Anslinger, *Modern Med.*, 25:170 (1957).
11. Lambert, A. et al.: Report of the Mayor's Committee on Drug

Addiction to the Hon. R. C. Patterson, Jr., Commissioner of Corrections, *Am. J. Psychiat.*, 433:471 (1930).

12. Pescor, M. J.: A Statistical Analysis of the Clinical Records of Hospitalized Drug Addicts, *Public Health Repts.*, U.S., Suppl. 143 (1943).

13. Treadway, W. L.: Further Observations on the Epidemiology of Narcotic Drug Addiction, *Public Health Rept.*, U.S., 95:541 (1930).

14. U.S. Treasury Department, Bureau of Narcotics: Traffic in Opium and Other Dangerous Drugs for the Year Ended December 31, 1931 (1932).

15. U.S. Treasury Department, Bureau of Narcotics: Traffic in Opium and Other Dangerous Drugs for the Year Ended December 31, 1934 (1935).

16. U.S. Treasury Department, Bureau of Narcotics: Traffic in Opium and Other Dangerous Drugs for the Year Ended December 31, 1955 (1956).

17. U.S. Treasury Department, Bureau of Narcotics: Traffic in Opium and Other Dangerous Drugs for the Year Ended December 31, 1958 (1959).

18. U.S. Treasury Department, Bureau of Narcotics: Traffic in Opium and Other Dangerous Drugs for the Year Ended December 31, 1961 (1962).

19. U.S. Treasury Department, Bureau of Narcotics: Traffic in Opium and Other Dangerous Drugs for the Year Ended December 31, 1962 (1963).

20. Village Aid and Service Society: Unpublished report, New York, 1963.

21. Winick, C.: Narcotics Addiction and Its Treatment, *Law and Contemporary Problems*, 22:9 (1957).

22. Winick, C.: The Use of Drugs by Jazz Musicians, *Social Problems*, 7:240 (1959–60).

23. Winick, C.: Physician Narcotic Addicts, *Social Problems*, 9:174 (1961).

24. Winick, C.: Maturing Out of Narcotic Addiction, *Bull. Narcotics*, U.N. Dep. Social Affairs, 14:1 (1962).

25. Winick, C.: The Life Cycle of the Addict and of Addiction, *Bull. Narcotics*, U.N. Dep. Social Affairs, in press.

26. Zimmering, P. et. al.: Heroin Addiction in Adolescent Boys, *J. Nervous Mental Disease*, 114:19 (1951).

Francis A. Allen | **2**

CURRENT TENDENCIES IN AMERICAN
NARCOTICS LEGISLATION

IN THE UNITED STATES narcotic addiction and the distribution of narcotic drugs continue to present fundamental issues of public policy. In some respects this fact may constitute the most telling commentary on the current situation. For it is a remarkable circumstance that a half century after the Federal government embarked on its active efforts to control the narcotics traffic, we are still in contention as to what the basic assumptions of our policy ought to be. The importance of public policy in this area is likely to be conceded even by many whose professional concerns are ordinarily not focused on problems of law making and law enforcement. Indeed, it is the medical and behavioral disciplines that are among the most directly and profoundly affected by narcotics law; for, surely, one of the central issues of public policy in this area relates to the freedom of these professional groups to engage in inquiry, experimentation, and therapy. But this issue, important as it is, involves only one of a range of vital concerns affected by the law and its policy. The problems clustering around the phenomenon of narcotic addiction provide serious challenges for the legal order. Are we doing what can most effectively be done to minimize the incidence of addiction? And what of the costs, human and financial, of the measures we have taken? In short, the problems presented provide a prime test of the capacity of the legal order to respond to challenge and to create and administer sound public policy.

This paper does not undertake the ambitious task of resolving these fundamental issues or of engaging in a comprehensive appraisal of the policy of American narcotics law. I shall not, for example, consider the frequently expressed allegations that attempts to control distribution of narcotics principally through the agencies of criminal justice increase, rather than diminish, the incidence of crime.[4,14] Not only do the limitations of time dictate a more modest effort, but the absence of reliable data on the most basic and elementary aspects of the narcotics problem precludes full and objective policy evaluation.[8] This paper undertakes, first, to survey the principal features of American narcotics legislation and to identify recent tendencies and trends in the statutory law. Study of the statutes indicates the wisdom of giving greater emphasis to state, rather than Federal, legislation, both because state legislation has received less attention in the literature and because state laws may reveal more of the problems requiring consideration. Next, an effort will be made to identify the principal assumptions upon which the statutory law is based and to consider some of the characteristic and recurring problems associated with it. Obviously, any discussion focused on the statutory law is subject to serious limitations. That the law in the books is not the same as law in action is an observation familiar to all students of the legal order; and to understand what American narcotics law is, in fact, requires data relating to enforcement policies and practices that cannot be supplied by the language of legislation. Nevertheless, much can be learned from a careful consideration of the laws, and these insights have sometimes been overlooked in studies of the narcotics problems. Statutory analysis and a consideration of the problems so revealed constitute indispensable first steps toward an adequate appraisal of the law and the policy it expresses.

There is no question of the general constitutional power of the states to control the manufacture, distribution, or possession of narcotic drugs.[24] This is not to deny that particular kinds of statutory regulation may run afoul of the constitutional limitations; and one such problem will be considered at a later point in this paper. Nor is it to deny that certain enforcement practices, such as those relating to arrest and search or to the use of informers, may sometimes pose constitutional issues of genuine urgency. But the general power of the state to regulate the narcotics traffic and to employ penal sanctions in the regulatory effort cannot seriously be doubted. We are for the most part, therefore, concerned with issues of legislative policy, not of constitutional law. The struggle to achieve sound and sensible policy must be fought primarily in the legislative arena and not in the courts.

American legislative intervention in the narcotics area possesses a longer history than is often supposed.[13] As early as 1862 California enacted a statute dealing with the administration of drugs with intent to facilitate commission of a felony.[27] The first state law seeking to control the use and distribution of narcotics is said to be that enacted in Nevada in 1877.[28] The first legislation specifically authorizing institutional commitment of addicts was apparently that of Connecticut in 1874.[29] The nineteenth-century legislation was sporadic, however, and cannot be taken as evidence of any general or widespread perception of a "narcotics problem." Indeed, the evidence appears to point in the opposite direction. One commentator may be substantially correct when he observes: ". . . until the turn of the twentieth century, the use of opium and its derivatives was generally less offensive to Anglo-American public morals than the smoking of cigarettes." [9]

The legislative basis of twentieth-century narcotics policy in the United States is provided principally by two series of enactments, one at the Federal level and the other in the states. In 1912 the United States adhered to the Hague Opium Convention and thereby undertook to control domestic production, distribution, and use of opium and coca products.[36] In part to comply with these commitments, Congress in 1914 passed the Harrison Act, or (more accurately) three Harrison Acts, the most important of which provides the legal foundation for Federal activity relating to domestic distribution of narcotic drugs.[30] The provisions

of the Act of December 17, 1914, are familiar to all persons concerned with the American narcotics problem and public efforts to
control the distribution of narcotics. However, we may note that
the administrative interpretation of the statutory phrases, "legitimate medical uses" and "professional practice only," continue to
produce one of the major controversies in the field.[10,23]

The second series of legislative enactments requiring attention
are those passed by the American state legislatures. The passage
of the Harrison Act by Congress apparently did not immediately
prompt a rash of new state laws.[5] In the years following the First
World War, however, increasing interest in narcotics legislation
developed in the state legislatures. The most significant manifestation of this concern was the drafting and adoption of the Uniform Narcotics Act by the National Conference of Commissioners
on Uniform State Laws in 1932.[26] According to the most recent
survey, the Uniform Act has now been adopted in some form by
47 states, Puerto Rico, and the District of Columbia—by all the
states, that is, except California, New Hampshire, and Pennsylvania.[12] The uniformity of state legislation is impressive but
should not be overstated. Variations in matters of detail abound.
Moreover, the Uniform Act makes no provision for civil commitment of addicts, and hence such provisions lack a common source.
Most important of all, the Uniform Act contains no recommendations for penalties, and the state laws are thus characterized by
significant variations in the criminal sanctions provided.

As one surveys the state legislation in this field, he quickly
observes the strongly prohibitive character of the regulations.
Moreover, the ultimate sanctions relied on are criminal penalties.
Thus, although the legislation makes provision for familiar techniques of administrative regulation, such as licensing, control of
labeling, record keeping, and requirements of written orders, it
can be said with substantial accuracy that, in the final analysis,
the task of control of the distribution and possession of narcotics
has been delegated to the system of criminal justice. Section 7
of the Uniform Act and similar provisions in many state laws
permit a doctor "to prescribe, administer, and dispense narcotic
drugs . . . in good faith and in the course of his professional

practice only." [26] The question of whether a prescription is in good faith and in the course of professional practice is thus made not only a question of law but a question of criminal law. It is, of course, true that American narcotics legislation sometimes makes provision for devices other than criminal sanctions, such as authorization of civil commitment of addicts, presumably for therapeutic purposes. There is evidence, however, that even these provisions are often intended to serve and advance the purposes of law enforcement or are, at least, not conceived of as weakening the legislative commitment to criminal-law enforcement as the principal instrumentality of control. This tendency is clearly revealed in a statement appearing in the report of a congressional subcommittee. "It should be noticed," the report observed, "that these recommendations for treatment and rehabilitation are not intended as a substitute for criminal confinement and punishment of those addicts who are convicted of law violation. They should pay their debt to society the same as non-addicts. . . ." [20]

A second general conclusion derived from a survey of state narcotics legislation relates to the penalties provided. It will be observed not only that the penalties are in most cases severe but that they have become progressively more severe in the period since the Second World War. In Illinois the present penalty for selling or furnishing narcotics is a term of imprisonment from 10 years to life for the first offense and a mandatory life term for subsequent offenses. In Pennsylvania penalties for the same crime range from a fine up to $5,000 and imprisonment from 5 to 20 years for the first offense to a fine up to $30,000 and imprisonment for life for a third offense. The threat of capital punishment is incorporated in some of the state statutes. Thus in 1957 the Texas Legislature, without one opposing vote being cast, followed the lead of the Federal Congress and made provision for the death penalty in certain cases of sales to minors.[31,32] A press report indicates that the Colorado Legislature has recently taken similar action. While not all states have authorized penalties so extreme, maximum penalties from 20 to 30 years for the offense of selling are not unusual. In many of the states provision for high maximum terms is accompanied by substantial mandatory minimum

terms. Furthermore, many of the states have made convicted narcotics offenders ineligible for probation, suspended sentence, and
sometimes, parole.[32] Another element to be taken into account
when estimating the severity of these penalties is the possibility
of multiple sentences for technically distinct offenses arising out
of the same transaction. It is true that the Uniform Act provides
that no person shall be prosecuted for violation of a state law who
has been tried for the same act or omission under the applicable
provisions of the Federal law.[26] But the Federal law, itself, has
so defined the criminal offenses as to make it possible for the
offender to violate three or more Federal criminal provisions by
a single illegal sale of narcotics.[6] In such cases the Supreme Court
of the United States has upheld the authority of the Federal
courts to impose cumulative sentences for all the offenses so committed. Such a result, said the Supreme Court, is consistent with
the "determination of Congress to turn the screw of the criminal
machinery . . . tighter and tighter." [21]

As suggested above, a study of penalties discloses not only that
sanctions are severe but that in the postwar era there has been
a strong tendency to provide penalties of ever-increasing severity.
Investigation reveals that in each of eight states, including most
of those generally regarded as presenting the most serious narcotics problems, penalties have been altered since the close of the
Second World War, and, with minor exceptions, these changes
have all been in the direction of increased severity.[32] That a similar tendency is revealed in Federal legislation during the same
period is well known. Although the laws of a few other states
suggest some deviations from this pattern, it can fairly be reported
that the tendency of American narcotics legislation has been overwhelmingly in the direction of increased severity of criminal sanctions and that the end of this tendency is not yet clearly in sight.

Enough has been said of the specific content of American narcotics legislation to demonstrate that it presents some highly
remarkable features. Perhaps the most striking aspect of these
statutes is the consistency with which the problems dealt with are
conceived as problems for the police agencies. In an area of
natural concern to a wide range of professional groups the legis-

lation establishes the hegemony of law enforcement and its in-strumentalities. That the law of narcotics limits professional dis-cretion in the practice of medicine has been frequently noted.[10] What is perhaps more remarkable is the degree to which the nar-cotics legislation deprives officials within the legal order, itself, of ordinary powers of decision making. This is nowhere more clear than in the exercise of the sentencing function. Limited by high mandatory minimum sentences and deprived of the power to make use of probation, the judge's ability to control dispositions is severely limited, unless he elects to nullify the law through the various *sub rosa* devices within his command.[14] So also, the judg-ment of correctional officials is rendered inoperative when, as is frequently the case, the statute defines the narcotics offender as unparolable. American narcotics legislation thus demonstrates the conviction of lawmakers that the problems of the area are, in many ways, unique. The problems are conceived principally as matters for penal regulation; but in many respects they are treated differently from other problems of law enforcement.

Any public posture taken in the presence of important social issues involves certain costs and consequences. Frequently the consequences include those that are unintended and unantici-pated.[11] Since we have had much experience with the criminal process as the instrumentality of social control, it should be pos-sible, without elaborate empirical inquiry, to identify some of the costs and consequences of the current measures being applied in the narcotics area.

First, it is clear that the way in which the distribution of nar-cotics and narcotic addiction is viewed by the legal order tends to influence the nature of the narcotics problem. Among other things, it tends to define the segments of the population that will display a high incidence of addiction. For, as others have observed, if the distribution of narcotics is, in general, attended by severe criminal consequences, such distribution will, in general, be undertaken by criminal groups and organizations.[14] Since addiction must in some degree be related to access and availability of drugs, it follows that patterns of highest incidence of addiction are likely to be displayed in those areas in which persons have relatively freer access to the criminal underworld. Thus, the legal order strongly influences the distribution of addiction among the various groups and subcultures that constitute our society. Without in any way speculating about the superior efficacy of alternative legal approaches, it may safely be concluded that the particular problems we face are defined to a significant degree by the nature of the law's response to these problems.

Second, the decision to view the American narcotics problem as primarily one of criminal-law enforcement involves other implications. Any system of regulation presupposes that certain minimal conditions will be satisfied in order that the system may function and maintain itself. Thus, American narcotics law abounds in measures intelligible only as devices necessary, or believed to be necessary, for effective law enforcement. This phenomenon is by no means peculiar to the narcotics area. For example, when legislatures decide to delegate to the criminal law the task of attaining certain objectives of economic regulation, there is a strong tendency to alter the fundamental character of the criminal law to get the job done more readily.[7] It has been discovered, for example, that in certain kinds of economic crimes it is particularly difficult to obtain evidence of criminal purpose on the part of defendants. Hence, there is a strong propensity to define these crimes in such fashion as to dispense with proof of criminal purpose, not because purpose is ordinarily irrelevant to an estimate of the social dangerousness of the behavior, but because requiring such proof is thought to impose burdens on the prosecution that may imperil the effectiveness of the regulatory effort. So also in the narcotics area, the exigencies of law enforcement have played a crucial role in the definitions of the drug offenses. This is well illustrated by the problems surrounding the offense of unlawful possession of narcotics, which will be considered briefly at a later point in this discussion. Another example of the same tendency is provided by the so-called "status crimes," those that make the fact of drug addiction criminal.

Whatever motivations may underlie the enactment of such statutory offenses, it can hardly be doubted that among the primary considerations are the supposed necessities of law enforcement. Thus the definition of addiction as a crime may in some cases expand police powers of arrest and detention and, perhaps more importantly, provide the police with the leverage of a threat of prosecution to induce the addict to reveal the sources of his drug supply.[8] The criminal law is the heavy artillery of organized society. A decision to rely on it as the principal means of control represents, wittingly or unwittingly, a decision to accept the assumptions and requirements of criminal-law enforcement.

Third, the point last mentioned leads to a broader observation. Intervention of the legal order in any area of human activity involves costs, and this is surely true whenever the organized community elects to employ the criminal-law processes as the mode of intervention. This observation, of course, does not demonstrate that intervention is unwise: for costs may also be involved in nonaction; and, in any event, the gains from legal intervention may be worth the price. It appears entirely responsible to assert, however, that too often in this country we have rushed into programs of penal regulation with too little calculation of the costs involved and that our public policy has suffered in consequence.

One of the areas of possible costs in the administration of the American narcotics statutes relates to police practices and the legal norms intended to contain and regulate the powers of law enforcement agencies. While abuse of police authority may, of course, occur in connection with any law enforcement effort, instances of such illegality appear to occur with unusual frequency in certain areas, such as those involving gambling, liquor and narcotics offenses, prostitution and sexual immorality—in short, the typical "vice-squad" crimes.[3] Indeed, this phenomenon is sufficiently visible to warrant the following generalization: In almost every area in which the law calls upon the enforcement agencies to stamp out conduct that involves a willing seller and a willing buyer—or, more fundamentally, conduct in which the "victim," if there be one, is a willing victim—a tendency toward illegal police behavior is revealed.[2] It is not difficult to understand why this should be true. Such enforcement areas present problems of extreme difficulty to the police agencies. No victim or his family is likely to announce the commission of the offense or volunteer information or assistance to the police in apprehending the offender. The nature of these offenses is such that detection invites violations of individual privacy. Confronted by unusual difficulties of detection and apprehension, the enforcement agencies are likely to protest the traditional limitations on police authority, even those established by constitutional command, and, under the stress of pressure and temptation, to ignore and violate them. Thus these are areas in which issues of illegal arrest, unlawful search, and improper use of undercover agents are most likely to arise.

These tendencies can be roughly demonstrated. In the years between 1946 and 1962, 50 cases went to opinion in the Supreme Court of the United States, involving issues of unlawful arrest and search, entrapment, and wiretapping. In over half, the convictions were reversed because of the police practices revealed. Of the total 50 cases at least 30 involved prosecution of what I have called "victimless" crimes or crimes involving willing victims. Sixteen, or approximately one-third of the total, arose out of prosecutions of narcotics offenses. The point being made should be clearly understood. It is not that all or most enforcement in the narcotics area is or must inevitably be in violation of the legal limitations on police behavior. I do suggest, however, that a tendency toward unsanctioned police practices has characterized much narcotics-law enforcement and that there appear to be no sufficient reasons to doubt that this tendency will persist in the future.

Let us turn now to some of the particular problems associated with existing narcotics legislation and current proposals for reform. Of necessity, I can hope to do little more than identify the nature of the problems and present brief suggestions for further consideration.

One of the classic problems in the drafting of narcotics law relates to the application of provisions punishing possession when the offender is an addict. In short, what special provision can and should be made with reference to possession of drugs by one who intends to make personal use of them? Whether viewed from the standpoints of culpability, social dangerousness, or treatment, such possessors present problems for public policy different from other offenders. Yet, not only do most statutes fail to draw such distinctions, but the rigidities introduced into the sentencing structure by recent legislation impede, if not prevent, appropriate recognition of different types of offenders at the disposition stage. The failure of the substantive law to make these important discriminations cannot be explained by their irrelevancy to social policy. The failure can only be explained by a fear that their introduction into the statutes would render unmanageable the law enforcement problem. In a few states efforts have been made to reconcile the requirements of intelligent policy with the demands of enforcement. In New York, for example, a 1956 amendment draws a distinction between possession and possession with intent to sell, the latter intent being presumptively established by possession of drugs of a given quantity or weight. Moreover, in this same statute, no distinctions are made in the penalties for the offenses of sale and possession with intent to sell.[33] Although the New York provisions have been criticized by law enforcement personnel, a persuasive case against such legislative innovation has not clearly been made out.[8] If the New York experiment does not represent an acceptable approach to these problems, the fact merely emphasizes the need for greater ingenuity and creativity in the drafting of narcotics laws.

A second problem area of much current interest involves provisions creating the so-called status crime by which the fact of being an addict is made criminal. I speculated earlier on some of the considerations that may have induced approximately one-third of the states to enact such laws.[16] Some of the provisions are remarkably severe. In Louisiana an adult convicted of being an addict may be sentenced from 20 to 30 years at hard labor. If he has not previously been convicted of a narcotics offense, his sentence may be suspended and he may be placed on probation upon condition that he agree to enter a Federal hospital and remain there until "certified by the medical officer in charge as being cured."[34] The Uniform Act defines no status crime, and state laws creating such offenses reveal considerable variation. In view of the recent decision of the United States Supreme Court

in *Robinson v. California,* however, the need for detailed analysis
of these various provisions is less urgent.[25] That decision announced the proposition that the states lack constitutional power
to subject persons to criminal, as contrasted to civil, sanctions for
the sole reason that they are addicted to narcotic drugs. The
rationale of the decision appears to be that addiction is an illness
in the same sense that mental disorder is an illness. Just as an
effort to punish insanity would run afoul of the constitutional
limitations, so also criminal prosecution of addiction is to be conceived as "cruel and unusual punishment."

Although the *Robinson* decision seems clearly to invalidate
state statutes which directly impose criminal penalties on addicts
because they are addicts, the full scope of the opinion and the
ultimate reach of its principle are much less clear. Putting aside
the lawyer's interest in whether "cruel and unusual punishment"
is the correct articulation of the constitutional ground of decision,
other, and perhaps more practical, questions arise. The Court
sharply distinguished between criminal provisions punishing acts,
such as purchase and sale, and those punishing a status or condition. The distinction produces problems of analysis. For if addiction is an "illness" and cannot constitutionally be punished, what
is the source of state authority to punish acts of purchase and
possession which are necessarily and unavoidably associated with
the illness? Whatever logical projections might be made from the
holding, however, it appears likely that the Court is not prepared
to invalidate the state laws defining the traditional offenses of
purchase, use, and possession. In this respect, it can reasonably
be anticipated that in subsequent cases, the *Robinson* holding
will be given rather narrow application.

It may be expected, however, that one of the consequences of
the *Robinson* decision will be the giving of additional impetus to
the current movement for compulsory civil commitment of addicted persons. Almost gratuitously, the opinion of the Court
observes: "In the interest of discouraging violation of such laws,
or in the interest of the general health or welfare of its inhabitants,
a State might establish a program of compulsory treatment for
those addicted to narcotics. Such a program of treatment might

require periods of involuntary confinement. And penal sanctions might be imposed for failure to comply with compulsory treatment procedures." [25] There is already some evidence of the kind of impact the *Robinson* decision is likely to have on state practices. In a case recently decided by the California Supreme Court, the addict had been proceeded against criminally under the statute subsequently invalidated in *Robinson.* Before conviction and sentence, however, the criminal proceedings were suspended; and, following a nonjury civil proceeding, the defendant was committed as an addict to a state facility for treatment. The commitment was upheld by the California court. It was conceded that the civil proceedings had certain "criminal overtones": for example, persons are committed to the director of corrections rather than to the director of mental hygiene, and the period of commitment is limited by minimum and maximum terms. Nevertheless, said the California court, the commitment was civil, not criminal, and hence valid under the ruling of the *Robinson* case.[22]

Modern interest in civil commitment procedures must be recognized as one of the striking and significant legislative developments in the narcotics area. Manifestations of this interest are widespread. It may be observed in the proceedings of the White House Conference on Narcotic and Drug Abuse and in the very recent Interim Report of the President's Advisory Commission.[18,19] It has revealed itself in state practice, as in California, and in new legislation, such as the notable recent provisions in New York authorizing commitment as an alternative to criminal prosecution in certain cases.[35] It would not be far wide of the mark to refer to this interest and its results as the civil commitment movement.

It is not difficult to understand the enthusiastic support for procedures thought to present a sound alternative or a valuable supplement to traditional American techniques of narcotics control. The seriousness and the intractibility of the underlying problems make a search for alternatives both desirable and inevitable. It should be recognized, however, that civil commitment proposals are not new and that we have acquired an extensive fund of experience from the use of such procedures outside the nar-

cotics area.[15,17] Prudence would seem to dictate that this experience be carefully consulted before new legislative proposals are
advanced or adopted. American experience with civil commitment
in the form of sexual-psychopath laws, defective-delinquent laws,
and others, presents recurring problems. Obviously no generalizations derived from such wide and varied experience are infallible;
but the main tendencies can probably be identified with reasonable accuracy.

It should be recognized, first, that to the extent our problems
in the narcotics area stem from the lack of scientific understanding
of addiction and the absence of adequate therapeutic techniques,
such knowledge and such skills are not supplied by statutes
authorizing compulsory hospitalization. This is true even if it be
hoped that research carried on in connection with institutions of
commitment will lead to new knowledge. Experience with other
forms of civil commitment suggests that when there are deficiencies in knowledge and techniques, or when public authority fails
to supply adequate facilities and personnel, such commitments,
despite hopes and public assurances to the contrary, will perform
essentially an incapacitative, rather than a rehabilitative, function.[1] The very numbers of addicts in many of our states suggest
that unless commitments are relatively few and highly selective,
the size of the patient population may virtually guarantee that
the function performed will be largely incapacitative in character.
Even if it be urged that incapacitation is a legitimate objective of
public policy, it cannot readily be assumed that the conditions
under which persons civilly committed are confined will represent
improvement over prison conditions. In many American states
persons committed under the sexual-psychopath laws are confined
in institutions which are prisons in all but name and which, in
some cases, provide conditions of detention inferior to those furnished persons convicted of crimes. Moreover, such statutes, while
subjecting the individual to an essentially punitive regimen, may,
through manipulation of the terms "civil" and "criminal," deprive
him of essential procedural rights.

It is, of course, true that we are not necessarily condemned to
repeat the errors of the past. And with effort and good will some

of the gross deficiencies of earlier commitment programs may be avoided in the narcotics area. But the prior experience is surely relevant as evidence of the characteristic tendencies of the civil commitment device. One may suspect that, here again, proposals in the narcotics area have not been tested against the totality of our relevant experience.

I shall conclude by reference to one further problem in American narcotics legislation. This is a problem by no means peculiar to the narcotics area. It is fair to say that one of the most serious deficiencies of the American legislative process is the failure to provide machinery for the routine collection of data adequate for evaluation of existing regulatory measures and the consideration of new proposals. Nowhere are the consequences of these deficiencies more serious than in the area of narcotics control. For two generations we have engaged in a program of penal regulation profoundly affecting the lives and liberties of persons and involving public interests of great importance without reliable data on a host of matters indispensable to any sound audit of what we have been doing and to sound judgment as to what we should be doing.[8] A growing awareness of the essential absurdity of this situation constitutes one of the most encouraging tendencies in the narcotics field. Several states, notably California, have begun to fulfill these responsibilities. Private research and investigation may be expected to reach more impressive proportions. If these tendencies persist and strengthen in the years ahead, the formulation of rational policy may yet be achieved.

REFERENCES

Books and Articles

1. Allen, Francis A.: Criminal Justice, Legal Values and the Rehabilitative Ideal, *J. Criminal Law, Criminol. Police Sci.*, 50:226 (1959).
2. Allen, Francis A.: The Borderland of the Criminal Law: Problems of "Socializing" Criminal Justice, *Social Service Rev.*, 32:107 (1958).
3. Allen, Francis A.: Federalism and the Fourth Amendment: A Requiem for Wolf, *Supreme Court Rev.*, 1961:1 (1961).

4. American Bar Association and American Medical Association, Joint Committee on Narcotic Drugs: "Drug Addiction: Crime or Disease?", Indiana University Press, Bloomington, Ind., 1961.
5. Anslinger, Harry J.: The Reason for the Uniform Narcotic Legislation, *Georgetown Law Journal*, 21:52 (1932).
6. Comment: Multiple Offenses and Multiple Penalties under the Federal Narcotics Laws, *Univ. Chicago Law Rev.*, 28:308 (1961).
7. Edwards, L. Ll. J.: "Mens Rea in Statutory Offences," Macmillan & Co., Ltd., London, 1955.
8. Eldridge, William B.: "Narcotics and the Law," American Bar Foundation, Chicago, 1962.
9. King, Rufus: Narcotic Drug Law and Enforcement Policies, *Law and Contemporary Problems*, 22:113 (1957).
10. King, Rufus: The Narcotics Bureau: Jailing the Healers and the Sick, *Yale Law Journal*, 62:735 (1953).
11. Merton, Robert K.: "Social Theory and Social Structure, Rev. ed., The Free Press of Glencoe, New York, 1957.
12. National Conference of Commissioners on Uniform State Laws: "Handbook," Chicago, 1962.
13. Prosser, William L. (ed.): The Narcotics Problem, *U.C.L.A. Law Rev.*, 1:405 (1954).
14. Schur, Edwin M.: "Narcotic Addiction in Britain and America," Indiana University Press, Bloomington, Ind., 1962.
15. Sutherland, Edwin H.: The Sexual Psychopath Laws, *J. Criminal Law, Criminol. Police Sci.*, 40:543 (1950).
16. Yockey, Diane F.: Constitutional Law—Criminal Sanctions against the Narcotics Addict, *Tulane Law Rev.*, 37: 119 (1962).

Official Documents

17. New Jersey Commission on the Habitual Sex Offender: "The Habitual Sex Offender," Trenton, 1950.
18. President's Advisory Commission on Narcotic and Drug Abuse: "Interim Report," Apr. 1, 1963.
19. *Proceedings, White House Conference on Narcotic and Drug Abuse,* Washington, Sept. 27–28, 1962.
20. Senate Committee on the Judiciary: *Treatment and Rehabilitation of Narcotic Addicts,* 84th Cong., 2d Sess., S. Rept. 1850 (1956).

Judicial Decisions

21. *Gore v. United States,* 357 U.S. 386 (1958).
22. *In re* De La O, 31 L. W. 2421 (1963).

23. *Linder v. United States,* 268 U.S. 5 (1925).
24. Minnesota *ex rel. Whipple v. Martinson,* 256 U.S. 41 (1920).
25. *Robinson v. United States,* 370 U.S. 660 (1962).

Statutes

26. National Conference of Commissioners on Uniform State Laws: "Uniform Narcotics Act," *Handbook,* 324 (1932).
27. Original Penal Code of California §222, adopted by California Stat. 1872.
28. Nevada Stat. 1877, p. 69.
29. Connecticut Laws 1874, p. 256.
30. Act of December 17, 1914, 38 Stat. 785, as amended 26 U.S.C. §§4701–4736 (Supp. III, 1956).
31. 70 Stat. 571 (1956), 21 U.S.C. §176(b) (1958).
32. California Health and Safety Code, §§11000–11797.
    Illinois Stat. Ann. ch. 38, §§22-1–22-54.
    Massachusetts Stat. Ann. ch. 94, §§197–217E.
    Michigan Stat. Ann. §§18-1121–18-1127.
    New York Penal Law §§1747-b–1747-e, 1751–1752a.
    Ohio Rev. Code §§3719.01–3719.99.
    Pennsylvania Stat. Ann. ch. 35, §§821–871.
    Texas Penal Code art. 725b–725d.
33. New York Penal Law §§1751.1–1751.3.
34. Louisiana Rev. Stat. §40:981.
35. New York Mental Hygiene Law §§208–215.
36. "Convention between the United States and Other Powers for Suppression of Abuse of Opium and Other Drugs," 38 Stat. 1912 (1912).

Harris Isbell | **3**

PERSPECTIVES IN RESEARCH ON
OPIATE ADDICTION

In RESEARCH it is often useful to review what has been done in order to pick out gaps in our knowledge and to select the most urgent and promising lines of future investigation.

The present paper will be limited to research on opiate addiction. Although intoxication with marihuana, cocaine, the amphetamines, and the barbiturates is important, so little information is available on these addictions that our knowledge here is rudimentary, and there is little to say except that they deserve a great deal more study.

Opiate addiction is a complex process in which pharmacologic, psychologic, physiologic, biochemical and socioeconomic factors play interdependent roles. In addition, these various factors have to impinge on the individual at a critical time in his life cycle, most often in adolescence or in early middle life. In order to understand opiate addiction completely, it is necessary to carry on research in all of these fields. Facts developed in the various areas of study have already been useful in the prevention of addiction, and research in any of these fields may produce new knowledge which may enable us to improve therapeutic and preventive programs.

BROADNESS OF RESEARCH IN ADDICTION

Most scientists are inclined to regard the study of addiction as a very limited and narrow field. From the foregoing remarks, it is apparent that this is not true; rather, the study of addiction is very broad. In order to understand addiction, we must not only work in a variety of fields, but we must also study basic problems in each of these fields. For example, we are trying to understand such fundamental problems as biologic adaptation to foreign chemicals in the environment. We must deal with basic problems of personality formation and function. We must study basic problems in the biochemistry and physiology of the central nervous system, and we must try to unravel how drugs alter these processes. New knowledge developed from the study of addiction will certainly have broad applications to other problems.

PHARMACOLOGIC PERSPECTIVES

The oldest and best developed approach to the study of addiction—the pharmacologic attack—has been reviewed by Nathan Eddy (see Chap. 5), but, for reasons of balance, it must also be covered in this paper. Systematic pharmacologic investigation of the problems of addiction began in 1929, when the Committee on Drug Addiction and Narcotics of the National Research Council [1] initiated a program designed to develop new derivatives of morphine which would have the pain-relieving and other useful effects of morphine but which would be either less addictive than morphine, or not addictive at all. In order to implement the program, the committee set up a chemical laboratory at the University of Virginia under the direction of Lyndon F. Small; a pharmacologic laboratory at the University of Michigan under Nathan B. Eddy; and, with the cooperation of the U.S. Public Health Service, a clinical unit for drug testing was established at the U.S. Penitentiary at Leavenworth, Kansas. Later the clinical unit was transferred to the Public Health Service Hospital at Lexington, Kentucky, when that hospital was opened in 1935. Several hundred derivatives of morphine were developed and tested in animals, and the most promising of these compounds were studied in addicted patients. Definite principles relating chemical structural changes in potency, type of action, and addictiveness which held for the drugs of the morphine group were discovered.[2] However, little was achieved in dissociating the useful properties of morphine from the addictive properties.

In 1939, meperidine (Demerol), a synthetic compound with a different chemical structure from that of morphine, was accidentally discovered to have morphinelike properties. This initiated the era of the synthetic analgesics. Shortly thereafter methadon was synthesized, and at present a dozen different distinct chemical families of drugs that have pain-relieving properties are known. Originally it was felt that the discovery of these new chemical structures gave more hope for the development of a drug that would be a potent analgesic without addictive qualities. Unfortunately, despite the diversity of molecular structures, all these various chemical types have been addictive, and, in general, addictiveness has paralleled potency for pain relief.[3] For a time it seemed possible to see unifying chemical principles relating structure to action, even in diverse chemical structures.[4] However, exceptions have been discovered, and, at the moment, all of the chemical theories relating structural action are of little use.

In reviewing the situation on a previous occasion, the writer [5] pointed out that all of the synthetic analgesic drugs had been developed in two different ways—both of which automatically selected drugs with morphinelike properties: (1) by synthesis of a chemical structure closely related to the one already known, and (2) by accident. Examples of the first kind of compounds are the morphinans, which resemble morphine in chemical structure, and the nexamethyleneimines, which resemble meperidine. Examples of drugs discovered accidentally are meperidine, methadon, and the diethylthiambutenes. These latter drugs were synthesized for other purposes, but in routine pharmacologic screening they were found to induce the Straub reaction (a characteristic morphinelike effect) in mice. On further examination, these drugs were shown to be analgesics by the available animal tests—they sedated dogs, excited cats, etc. In short, the compounds similar to morphine were being selected either chemically or biologically. Thus the dice were being loaded in favor of addictiveness being associated with analgesia.

In that same review it was suggested that the chemical pharmacologic approach to addiction should be altered. Most of the molecular manipulation in known groups of analgesic drugs should be stopped. When a new chemical group of analgesics was discovered and the prototype proved to be addicting, further chemical modifications should not be made without very cogent and pressing reasons. When any substance was shown to have a full pattern of biologic effects resembling those of morphine in animals, there was no great point in investigating it clinically. Agents that have chemical and biologic resemblances to morphine should be avoided; rather, analgesic drugs with patterns of effects different from the pattern of effects of morphine should be sought.

At the time, one lead existed. Nalorphine (Nalline), the first of the morphine antagonists, had a biologic spectrum of activity distinctly different from that of morphine. Even though nalorphine was a very weak analgesic by the standard animal tests, it proved to be as potent as morphine in relieving postoperative pain in humans.[6] Moreover, nalorphine did not cause physical dependence in either monkeys or man. Thus, in a sense, the nonaddicting analgesic had been found. Unfortunately, nalorphine was not a practical analgesic because it induced disturbing mental effects in a considerable proportion of patients, and this led to the synthesis of other antagonists in the morphine, morphinan, and phenazocine series. As a result, two very interesting compounds are now under study. One of these, N-dimethylallylphenazocine, is reported to be approximately one-half as potent as morphine as a clinical analgesic, does not seem to induce disturbing mental effects in most patients, and is not an addictive compound.[7] Another nonaddictive antagonist, N-cyclopropylmethylphenazocine, is 40 times as potent an analgesic as morphine in postoperative patients and does not seem to induce Nallinelike side effects in analgesic doses.[8] As yet, data on chronic use of these compounds under clinical conditions are not available.

The phenothiazine tranquilizers may present still another opportunity. Chlorpromazine is known to potentiate the analgesic effects of morphine in animals. More recently, methotrimeprazine (levomepromazine) has been reported to be an analgesic in postoperative patients,[9] and it certainly does not induce morphinelike addiction on continued administration. Methotrimeprazine creates postural hypertension, and repeated doses cause excessive sedation so that it may not be a practical agent for chronic use. Nonetheless further exploration of possibilities in the phenothiazine group is indicated.

Thus we seem closer than ever before to the development of a nonaddicting analgesic. If we achieve this object, what would be the effect on the addiction problem in the United States? Probably very little. Such an agent should reduce or eliminate addiction arising from chronic therapeutic use. The illicit traffic in opium, morphine, and heroin would still exist, and susceptible individuals would still experiment with these drugs and become addicted.

PHYSIOLOGIC PERSPECTIVES

Physiologic research in addiction has necessarily been concerned primarily with the problems of tolerance and physical dependence on the opiates. These phenomena have definitely been shown to be due to physiologic alterations which are independent of symbolic (psychologic) factors. Furthermore, physiologic studies have shown that addiction involves primarily the central nervous system. Changes occurring in other organ systems are largely secondary to the physiologic alterations within the central nervous system. Most of our knowledge of these processes is traceable to the pioneering researches of Dr. Abraham Wikler.[10,11] He has shown that tolerance and physical dependence are associated with the development of hyperirritability in multineuron arcs at all levels of the central nervous system, including the spinal cord, the midbrain, hypothalamus, and the cerebral cortex. The neuronal pathways that become hyperirritable are those that are depressed by morphine. As hyperexcitability develops, more and more morphine is required to counteract the excessive activity in these neurons, thus accounting for tolerance. When morphine is stopped, the hyperirritability is unmasked, thus accounting for the withdrawal symptoms. Thus the signs of abstinence are opposite in direction to the acute effects of morphine.

Many problems still remain. All the neuronal circuits involved in tolerance and dependence have not been traced. It is known that tolerance and dependence develop more rapidly at supraspinal than at spinal levels. Furthermore, nothing is known of the nature of the change in the individual neurons which must underlie the development of these phenomena. Further neurophysiologic investigations must be undertaken to settle these questions.

BIOCHEMICAL PERSPECTIVES

Biochemical investigations have shown that there are no basic alterations in the way in which morphine or similar drugs are catabolized, distributed within the body, or excreted during cycles of addiction.[12] Also, there is no evidence that a toxic metabolite of morphine accounts for tolerance or dependence; in fact, the latter idea is now nearly inconceivable because of the great diversity in chemical structures of drugs with morphinelike addictive properties.

Perhaps the most striking general biochemical change has been the demonstration that, in man, maintained addiction to morphine causes significant depression in the excretion of 17-ketosteroids [13] and 17-hydroxycorticosteroids.[14] Since the adrenals and the gonads are still responsive to specific stimulation with ACTH and gonadotropin during maintained addiction, these changes are probably due to depression of anterior pituitary activity, probably secondary to hypothalamic depression. These observations are important in that they show that the decline in sexual drive and activity consistently reported by addicts has a definite physiologic basis.

We know very little about the changes in the biochemical activities of neurons during cycles of addiction. Morphine seems to have very little effect on the respiration of resting nervous tissue, and, in pharmacologic concentrations, seems to have no appreciable effects on the classic enzymatic pathways for the metabolism of glucose. Recently Takemori [15] has reported that morphine depresses the stimulation of respiration of brain slices from nontolerant rats brought about by the addition of potassium to the medium. Stimulated respiration of brain tissue of animals made tolerant to morphine is inhibited to a lesser degree. Takemori may have made the first demonstration of "biochemical" tolerance at the cellular level. Unfortunately other workers have had difficulty in confirming Takemori's results.

Recently great interest has been manifested in studying tissue levels of possible neurohumoral transmitters in the central nervous system. Gunne [16] found that during chronic administration of morphine the brain level of noradrenalin in rats was increased, whereas the brain level of serotonin was unaltered. When the drugs are withdrawn from the rats, the brain levels of norepinephrine fell to, but not below, normal. In dogs, Gunne found no change in norepinephrine, dopemine, or serotonin during chronic administration of morphine. When morphine was discontinued or when abstinence was induced with nalorphine, norepinephrine levels were reduced in all parts of the brain. Maynert and Klingman had similar results in dogs.[17] At the moment the significance of these findings relative to norepinephrine is obscure.

Obviously the need for biochemical research in addiction remains very great. Despite the paucity of information and despite the lack of good leads, one can postulate on theoretical grounds that the changes underlying the phenomena of physical dependence and tolerance must have a biochemical basis. A continuing strong effort to determine what the changes are at the cellular level should be carried on. When biochemical mechanisms are known, we should be in a much better position to plan a therapeutic attack on the problems of addiction.

PSYCHOLOGIC PERSPECTIVES

An enormous body of literature on the psychologic and psychiatric aspects of addiction exists. It has been shown that opiate addicts in the United States are, on the average, normal in intelligence. Very few addicts are psychotic. In this country addiction is most often associated with sociopathic and neurotic personality traits. These traits seem to precede and to be important in the genesis of addiction. They are, however, obviously not specific, since the number of people with such traits who become addicted is relatively small as compared with the numbers of such persons with similar personality structures who do not become addicted.

There have been three main psychologic formulations of the addiction process. The first of these is the symptomatologic, or psychobiologic, theory.[18] In this hypothesis, specific personality reaction patterns are supposed to develop because of specific mental stresses arising from the individual's environment. Such stresses cause "anxiety" in neurotics, who use the opiates to allay the anxiety. This type of use is referred to as "negative pleasure." Individuals with sociopathic traits, on the other hand, use drugs not to suppress anxiety but to obtain an elated state called "positive pleasure" or "euphoria." "Normal" persons become addicted only as a result of therapeutic use of drugs to relieve physical pain. In the psychobiologic formulation, the choice of the particular drug of addiction—marihuana, alcohol, cocaine, or opiates—is an accident and is largely dependent on the particular drug available in the environment. The development of physical dependence is regarded as a complication which is entirely undesirable from the point of view of the user and important in the total process only insofar as it tends to keep the addiction continuous. After the development of tolerance and dependence, drugs are used only to prevent the appearance of abstinence. Relapse after treatment is attributed to the original personality problem.

Psychoanalysts regard addicts as individuals whose psychosexual development has been arrested or has undergone regression to infantile or even more primitive levels.[19] In infancy and early childhood a strong consistent father figure has generally been lacking, whereas the mother has been overindulgent and rejecting in an inconsistent way. The child, as a consequence, has been unable to learn that all his wants cannot be fulfilled in reality and has commonly regarded other persons, particularly the mother or mother substitutes, as objects to be used for self-gratification. Because of the arrested psychosexual development "oral cravings" have become paramount, whereas genital pleasures are devoid of interest. Since such wants can never be fulfilled in reality, frustration results, and the narcissistic, oral-dependent individual reacts with hostility often toward the mother or other women. Drugs are taken because of this conflict. Predisposition to use drugs is regarded as present before addiction begins. Addictive use of drugs is ascribed to the predisposition itself and to the contrast between the elated state induced by the drugs and the disillusionment which ensues when such effects wear off.

Both of the above formulations are not completely satisfactory, and neither is testable in a strictly scientific sense. It is known that the number of persons who have such psychologic traits and are not addicts far exceeds the number of persons with such traits who are addicts. Further, it is known that under conditions of equal exposure to alcohol, opiates, and marihuana, some persons will choose alcohol, others opiates, and others, none of these drugs. For these reasons, Wikler and his coworkers [20,21] have developed a "pharmacodynamic formulation" which is independent of theories of personality structures and which emphasizes the specificity of drug actions and the psychologic importance of physical dependence on drugs. Different classes of drugs are regarded as having different effects on motivations of a "primary" and "secondary" nature. Opiates depress the primary drives of pain, sex, hunger, and thirst. Thus an individual whose chief source of anxiety is related to pain, sexuality, or repression of aggressive drives will obtain specific relief from morphine. On the other hand, alcohol releases behavioral controls and in this sense enhances sexual and aggressive drives. Therefore, in individuals who characteristically "act out" anxiety-provoking conflict, alcohol would be the preferred drug. In short, opiates take away the need for the solution of emotional problems, whereas alcohol prevents direct aggressive action against the source or symbols of the emotional conflict.

Furthermore, the development of physical dependence on drugs creates a new biologic need comparable to hunger or thirst. Satisfaction of this need is directly and highly pleasurable, just as is satisfaction of hunger, thirst, or sexual gratification. Note that this concept is opposite to the concept of negative pleasure and that it presupposes that one of the chief gratifications of being an addict is to be dependent, or "hooked," so the new biologic need can be gratified.

Wikler [21] postulates that abstinence symptoms can be "conditioned" and may appear in response to conditional stimuli of various sorts long after withdrawal of drugs has been accomplished and all classic manifestations of physical dependence have vanished.

Thus the development of physical dependence creates a continuous cycle of alternating drug-induced biologic need and gratification of that need by obtaining the drug. Each dose of the drug reinforces behavior in which the addict must engage in order to obtain the drug by reduction of the drive produced by the previous dose.

The attraction of the pharmacodynamic formulation of Wikler is that it can be tested with currently available techniques, and some of the experimental work relating to this hypothesis is presented in this group of papers (see Chap. 6). In brief, making use of etonitazene, a drug which is 5,000 times as potent as morphine, researchers have shown that addicted rats will drink much larger amounts of etonitazene than nonaddicted rats. Conditioning of abstinence phenomena can be developed in addicted rats, and such conditioned abstinence persists for months after discontinuation of opiates. Furthermore addicted rats show a high tendency to "relapse" to the drug (will drink more of the opiate than water) when placed in situations in which they have "conditioned" symptoms of abstinence and a free choice of drinking either the opiate or water.

The importance of these observations is very great. Relapse occurs so frequently that it is almost a part of the definition of opiate addiction. If relapse can be induced at will in experimental animals, we have a powerful tool for studying how to prevent it. Secondly, if the conditioning hypothesis is correct, our current treatment systems are wrong, since simple withdrawal of the drug does not extinguish the conditioned response. Therefore we must try to devise ways to extinguish these conditioned responses and apply these methods of extinction therapeutically.

In the United States most addicts are classified as being sociopaths or psychopaths.[22] The personality patterns of opiate addicts are strikingly similar to those of alcoholics or to those of non-addicted criminals.[23] Even though sociopathy is a vaguely defined term, the high incidence of these traits in opiate addicts suggests that prevention and management of addiction may be dependent on advances in knowledge of sociopathy.[24] In fact, it may be that in the United States addiction is simply another manifestation of delinquent or antisocial behavior. Some measurable correlates of this condition that would sharply distinguish sociopaths are badly needed. We need instruments to sort the sociopaths into subgroups since we are dealing not with a homogenous condition, but rather with a group of disorders. Many other suggestions concerning research on sociopathy could be made. The problem is difficult but so important that a strong attack on the problems of social deviance is required.

SOCIOLOGIC PERSPECTIVES

Through the efforts of the Bureau of Narcotics,[25] of state enforcement agencies, and of sociologists,[26-28] we now have a fairly clear picture of the epidemiology and ecology of addiction in the United States. It is known that opiate addiction is not a "large problem" as compared with alcoholism, schizophrenia, etc.; there are probably fewer than 60,000 addicts in the United States. Addiction is limited chiefly to certain areas of a few large cities (New York, Chicago, Los Angeles). Most addicts are between the ages of 20 and 30 years, are members of minority groups, and come from the lower socioeconomic classes. The areas in which large concentrations of addicts exist are the most deprived areas of the cities. In these areas incomes are the lowest, the incidence of crime highest, and family ties the most tenuous. Obviously these socioeconomic factors associated with addiction are not specific, since they are associated with all kinds of other social and medical problems.

One of the most pressing needs that we have at the moment is to learn in detail the natural history of opiate addiction in the United States. Everyone who has studied addiction has been impressed by the age distribution. Most addicts are relatively young, with the majority being found in the age range of 20 to 30. After the age of 35 there is a sharp "drop-off" in the number of addicts by ages.[29] The same phenomenon was true 20 or 30 years ago. The reasons for the decline are probably several—the death rate of addicts is probably quite high; many addicts may receive very long prison terms and are out of circulation; some may become so adept at evading the law that they do not come to attention; and, hopefully, a significant proportion of addicts may mature out of addiction. However, we do not know that the last is true. If it is, it is an important fact that would indicate that perhaps the most important therapeutic tool we have is long-continued supervision until addicts have had sufficient time to develop more mature controls of behavior. A follow-up study of addicts from Kentucky is presented in Chap. 14, and indicates that in Kentucky a considerable proportion of addicts do manage to remain abstinent from drugs after treatment.

So far sociologists have been largely concerned with describing the epidemiology and social conditions associated with addiction in cities with a high incidence of addiction. They have paid very little attention to "controls." Studies of the ecological differences between cities with high and low rates of addiction might be quite informative. Studies on individuals who are exposed to the same environmental pressures as are addicts, but who do not become addicts, might also be quite revealing. We also need information on differences in addictions in different cultures.

RESEARCH ON METHODS OF TREATMENT

Perhaps the greatest deficiency in the study of addiction has been the lack of any well-designed and well-executed therapeutic trials. There are various reasons for this. These include the great expense, the physical difficulty of supervising and maintaining contact with addicts after treatment has been carried out, the division of responsibility between the different levels of government, and the lack of research orientation on the part of physicians in charge of the treatment. For this reason we still do not know whether our present system of managing addicts is useful, or possibly even harmful.

The need for research on treatment methods is now more acute than ever. All persons who have studied the problem have been impressed that the most obvious deficiency in treatment has been the lack of long-continued postinstitutional supervision and assistance. It is now being tacitly assumed that if these deficiencies can be remedied the results of treatment will improve markedly, and the problem of addiction will be solved. Obviously, this view is naive. We cannot guarantee that supplying postinstitutional services and supervision will be any more successful than those currently employed. We have no idea of what the most useful postinstitutional services and techniques will be. For what length of time should supervision be given? Does intensive parole supervision have an effect on relapse rate? Do Nalline tests or chemical tests for narcotics in the urine actually contribute to a lower relapse rate? Are halfway houses necessary, or even useful?

For these reasons, any new treatment systems that are set up should have built into them an evaluation system, and the laws and regulations governing management of addicts should be sufficiently flexible to permit controlled therapeutic experimentation. Otherwise we shall not know whether our efforts are meeting with success, and we will not know in what ways the treatment systems should be altered in the future.

REFERENCES

1. White, W. C.: Report of Committee on Drug Addiction, National Research Council, and collected reprints, Washington, D.C., 1941.
2. Small, L. F., Eddy, N. B., Mosettig, E., and Himmelsbach, C. K.: Studies on Drug Addiction. With Special Reference to Chemical Structure of Opium Derivatives and Allied Synthetic Substances and Their Physiological Action, *Public Health Rept., U.S.,* Suppl. 138 (1938).
3. Eddy, N. B., Halbach, H., and Braenden, O. J.: Synthetic Substances with Morphine-like Effect. Clinical Experience: Potency, Side Effects, Addiction Liability, *Bull. World Health Organization,* 17:569 (1957).
4. Eddy, N. B., and Braenden, O.: Synthetic Substances with Morphine-like Effect, *Bull. World Health Organization,* 14:353 (1956).

5. Isbell, H.: Trends in Research on Opiate Addiction, *Trans. Studies Coll. Physicians Phila.*, 24:1 (1956).
6. Lasagna, L., and Beecher, H. K.: Effectiveness of Nalorphine and Nalorphine-Morphine Combinations in Man, *J. Pharmacol. Exp. Therap.*, 112:356 (1954).
7. Keats, A. L.: Personal communication.
8. DeKornfeld, T. J., and Lasagna, L.: Win 20740, a Potent New Analgesic Agent, *Federation Proc.*, 22:248 (1963).
9. Lasagna, L., and DeKornfeld, T. J.: Methotrimeprazine—a New Phenothiazine Derivative with Analgesic Properties, *J. Am. Med. Assoc.*, 178:887 (1961).
10. Wikler, A.: Recent Progress in Research on the Neurophysiologic Basis of Morphine Addiction, *Am. J. Psychiat.*, 105:329 (1948–49).
11. Wikler, A.: Opiates and Opiate Antagonists: A Review of Their Mechanisms of Action in Relation to Clinical Problems, Public Health Monograph no. 52, *Public Health Service Publication* no. 589, Government Printing Office, Washington, D.C., 1958.
12. Way, E. L., and Adler, T. K.: The Pharmacologic Implications of the Fate of Morphine and Its Surrogates, *Pharmacol. Rev.*, 12:383 (1960).
13. Eisenman, A. J., Fraser, H. F., Sloan, J., and Isbell, H.: Urinary 17-Ketosteroid Excretion during a Cycle of Addiction to Morphine, *J. Pharmacol. Exp. Therap.*, 124:305 (1958).
14. Eisenman, A. J., Fraser, H. F., and Brooks, J. W.: Urinary Excretion and Plasma Levels of 17-Hydroxycorticosteroids during a Cycle of Addiction to Morphine, *J. Pharmacol. Exp. Therap.*, 132:226 (1961).
15. Takemori, A. E.: Studies on Cellular Adaptation to Morphine and Its Reversal by Nalorphine in Cerebral Cortical Slices of Rats, *J. Pharmacol. Exp. Therap.*, 135:89 (1962).
16. Gunne, L-M.: Catecholamines and 5-Hydroxytryptamine in Morphine Tolerance and Withdrawal, *Acta Physiol. Scand., Suppl.* 204, 58:91 (1963).
17. Maynert, E. W., and Klingman, G. I.: Tolerance to Morphine: I. Effects of Catecholamines in the Brain and Adrenal Glands, *J. Pharmacol. Exp. Therap.*, 135:285 (1962).
18. Kolb, L.: Pleasure and Deterioration from Narcotic Addiction, *Mental Hyg.*, 9:699 (1925).
19. Rado, S.: The Psychoanalysis of Pharmacothymia (Drug Addiction), *Psychoanalyt. Quart.*, 2:1 (1933).

20. Wikler, A., and Rasor, R. W.: Psychiatric Aspects of Drug Addiction, *Am. J. Med.*, 14:566 (1953).
21. Wikler, A.: On the Nature of Addiction and Habituation, *Brit. J. Addict.*, 57:73 (1961).
22. Hill, H. E., Haertzen, C. A., and Glaser, R.: Personality Characteristics of Narcotic Addicts as Indicated by the MMPI, *J. Gen. Psychol.*, 62:127 (1960).
23. Hill, H. E., Haertzen, C. A., and Davis, H.: An MMPI Factor Analytic Study of Alcoholics, Narcotic Addicts and Criminals, *Quart. J. Studies Alc.*, 23:411 (1962).
24. Hill, H. E.: The Social Deviant and Initial Addiction to Narcotics and Alcohol, *Quart. J. Studies Alc.*, 23:562 (1962).
25. Federal Bureau of Narcotics: Statistics on Narcotic Addicts (mimeographed), available by years 1957–1962.
26. Clausen, J. A.: Social and Psychological Factors in Narcotic Addiction, *Law and Contemporary Problems*, 22:34 (1957).
27. Chein, I., and Rosenfeld, E.: Juvenile Narcotics Use, *Law and Contemporary Problems*, 22:52 (1957).
28. Finestone, H.: Narcotics and Criminality, *Law and Contemporary Problems*, 22:69 (1957).
29. Winick, C.: Maturing Out of Narcotic Addiction, *Bull. Narcotics, U.N. Dep. Social Affairs*, 14:1 (1962).

Part 2

MEDICAL AND PSYCHOPHARMACOLOGIC PERSPECTIVES

Louis Lasagna | **4**

ADDICTING DRUGS AND MEDICAL PRACTICE: TOWARD THE ELABORATION OF REALISTIC GOALS AND THE ERADICATION OF MYTHS, MIRAGES, AND HALF-TRUTHS

IT HAS BEEN STATED, both by men with long experience in the field of addiction and by interested parties relatively new to the area, that discussions about drug addiction are often marred by inaccuracies. Dr. Lawrence Kolb, for many years a respected worker in addiction research, has referred to the popular "myths" about addiction, such as that relating narcotics usage to homicide rates, and "the false idea of the heroin maniac." President Kennedy, addressing the White House Conference on Narcotics and Drug Abuse, decried the "dearth of hard, factual data," and the Attorney General of the United States, at the same meeting, voiced "the depressing truth" that "we don't know very much about [narcotics]" and said that we need "to start building a reasonable and reliable body of information."[10]

My own experience in the practice of medicine and during some 10 years of research on narcotics and other drugs has led me to conclusions similar to those expressed by these distinguished men. This presentation will attempt to enumerate and

53

discuss briefly some facts—as I see them—about the use of these drugs. I hope that my remarks contain a minimum of the inaccuracies described above and that they may help in the rational formulation of our needs and goals.

The meaning of "addiction," "narcotics," "addicting drugs," and "dangerous drugs" is imprecise and ambiguous, and this semantic problem hampers the development of clear thinking in this field.

The terms just listed are so ill-defined, so different in their connotations for different individuals, as to have lost much of whatever utility they may once have had. Recently a World Health Organization Study Group tried to define a drug addict by focusing on the compulsive use of "any narcotic drug." Yet in various parts of the world there are extreme disparities in the concept of an addict. In Canada the definition includes the words "suffering from a disorder or disability of the mind," but in Finland the definition is linked to certain punishable offences, such as personal violence, driving under the influence of drugs, and neglect of dependents.

Nor do we have to travel abroad to find confusion. Within the United States one can find pharmacologists favoring one definition of addiction, psychiatrists another, sociologists another, and law enforcement officials still another. Even in trying to adhere to any one definition of addiction, the physician is puzzled by strange inconsistencies. Seeing the problem of alcoholism every day of the week, he is hard put to comprehend why a drug like alcohol, which so clearly fulfills all of the criteria in most definitions of an addicting agent, is not placed in the same category as morphine. Or, to take another example, if mescaline *fails* to qualify as a drug of addiction, why may "peyote addicts" theoretically be accepted for treatment at the U.S. Public Health Service Hospital at Lexington, Kentucky? Or again, how is one to explain to the physician who daily prescribes many drugs which can cause serious side effects, including death, why barbiturates and amphetamines should be singled out as "dangerous drugs"?

The physician may also be pardoned for a certain amount of

dismay over the lack of quantification in the definitions he encounters. Is the occasional user of "dangerous" or narcotic drugs an addict? Is the habitual user of heroin which is so "cut" as to be incapable of creating serious tolerance or physical dependence "addicted"? Is a person who has been off drugs for years and then takes one shot of heroin "in relapse"? Is the anxious patient who cannot visualize living without three or four phenobarbital or meprobamate tablets a day more—or less—of an addict than a "spree" user of heroin or cocaine?

Faced with the distressing inadequacies of such words as "addicting drugs" or "addict," the physician who wishes his words to be sharp and precise rather than mushy must either formulate his own definitions or discard these words in favor of others.

The appropriate, legitimate use of narcotic analgesics in medical practice poses no major problem so far as the induction of drug addiction is concerned.

The documentation for this statement is as follows:

1. Most people who receive morphine in therapeutic doses do not experience a true euphoria. This is true not only for volunteers who are not in pain, but for patients who are.[3] To be sure, gratitude and relief are experienced for the abolition of pain (Kolb's "negative pleasure"), but only rarely is there any impressive feeling of exhilaration, ecstasy, or fantasy (Kolb's "positive pleasure").[4]

2. Of the millions of patients who have received morphine or similar drugs for short-lived painful states, only a very small fraction will seek out narcotics extralegally after clinical exposure to these drugs.

3. Of those patients who require narcotic analgesics continuously for chronic pain, the majority can stop the drugs without difficulty if the cause of the pain can be eliminated.

The utility of narcotic analgesics in the practice of medicine is not fully exploited, because of the exaggerated fears of physicians and nurses regarding the addiction potential of these drugs.

It is not uncommon for a patient in severe pain after surgery to spend many hours in needless discomfort because of the inappropriate attitudes of medical personnel toward narcotic analgesics. Standard procedure calls for a fixed dose of narcotics to be prescribed "q. 3 h." (every 3 hr) or "q. 4 h." (every 4 hr), regardless of the patient's needs. The fact that the first dose of analgesic may not be sufficient to obtund pain significantly is usually apparent within an hour—certainly in less than 2 hr—so that one must ask, why the slavish devotion to the longer interval?

The answer is only in part related to the known pharmacology of morphine and similar drugs and to therapeutic reflex and custom. It is also related to the indoctrination of medical students and student nurses with the dangers of addicting innocent patients by excessive use of narcotics.

While it is usually good medical practice to use no more morphine than is required,[6] it is poor medical practice to permit pointless suffering when more flexible dosage regimens are both compassionate and safe. The unfortunate traditions of medication which are now so firmly established are reinforced by the absence of medical personnel from the bedside of the suffering patient. The only way that you can even begin to appreciate the discomfort of the patient in pain is to observe the patient closely for prolonged periods of time. The busy surgeon who spends the day in the operating room, and the overworked floor nurse with dozens of patients to attend to, are unlikely to achieve empathy for the miseries of the inadequately medicated patient.

It has been cynically said that better patient care will not result until one can substitute a drug which is as good an analgesic as morphine but is free of addiction liability, because it is too difficult to eradicate entrenched therapeutic habits. The statement may well be true. But I believe that we should realize that the fault here lies not so much in our drugs as in our own misconceptions.

The emphasis on finding nonaddicting analgesics has caused the neglect of medical goals which are more important for the majority of patients.

For decades now, many of us working on pain-relieving drugs have been preoccupied with the elimination of addiction liability, despite the facts, already mentioned, testifying to the minor importance of addiction in medical practice. Morphine is, of course, a useful drug; one would hate to practice medicine without it. But it does have drawbacks for some patients—it can produce nausea and vomiting as unpleasant as that due to any other cause; it can wreak havoc with the elimination problems of the bedridden; it can oversedate and depress respiration; it may produce dizziness and hypotension if one is walking about; it loses its efficacy on repeated administration to patients with persistent pain; and it is not as effective when taken by mouth as by injection.

Fortunately, these shortcomings are absent enough of the time so as not to counterbalance the enormous benefits of the drug, but the defects nevertheless exist and represent problems which deserve the investigator's attention at least as much as the overemphasized risk of causing addiction.

There is now considerable evidence that certain pharmacologic effects which have been considered to be inescapably linked can in fact be dissociated and that powerful analgesics exist which are free of some of the undesirable effects of morphine and older narcotic analgesics.

The data to support this statement are of several sorts:

1. In most cases, the pain relief seen with morphine does not seem contingent on the production of euphoria,[8] as already mentioned.

2. Although many normal individuals find the effects of amphetamine highly pleasant, the drug is generally thought to be either a weak analgesic agent or to be devoid of analgesic effect.[8]

3. Drugs have been developed which seem low or lacking in addiction liability but are excellent pain relievers. These include nalorphine,[5] methotrimeprazine,[7] and some benzomorphan derivatives.[1] Some of these agents differ from morphine, not only in regard to addictiveness, but also in the kinds of side effects produced.

There is thus hope that drugs can be introduced into medicine which can meet the needs both of those who are concerned primarily with addiction dangers and of those who seek drugs lacking some of the other disadvantages of morphine.

There is an undesirable entanglement of medical practice and law enforcement problems arising from the mistaken notion that legal strictures can be devised which will apply equally well to the legal and the extralegal use of narcotics.

Perhaps this point can best be made by discussing the heroin problem. It is an undisputed fact that in the United States the drug most commonly employed by narcotic addicts is heroin. It is not at all clear, however, that this represents anything more than the fact that dope peddlers sell heroin almost exclusively. This makes good business sense from their standpoint, since it only takes one-half to one-fourth as much heroin to produce a given effect as it takes of morphine,[11] so that any given amount of drug will provide two to four times as many "fixes" if the drug is heroin rather than morphine.

From these simple facts to the mythology and mystique of heroin, however, is a big leap. One looks in vain for documentation of claims as to the pernicious properties of this drug—that it more rapidly produces physical dependence and tolerance, that it rapidly leads to a deterioration of mental faculties, that addiction to it is more difficult to treat.

Some years ago,[8] we reported that volunteer students and "postaddicts" who did not know what they were receiving could not distinguish readily between the effects of heroin and morphine. Nothing in our data supported the accepted notion of a high euphorigenicity for heroin. Studies since then, by others, on nonaddicts [12] and postaddicts [9] have largely substantiated our earlier findings. In the words of some investigators from the U. S. Public Health Service Hospital at Lexington, Kentucky, the data do "not support the claim that addicts find heroin markedly superior to morphine," and "there was no indication that tolerance developed more rapidly to heroin than to morphine." Or, to quote from the conclusions of the report of the Ad Hoc Panel on Drug Abuse at the White House Conference: "There is a widespread misconception that heroin has effects significantly different from those of morphine. It does not, and this misconception should be dispelled permanently." [10]

Why, then, is the medical profession in this country prevented from prescribing heroin? Surely not because its former medical use turned most heroin-treated patients into addicts, since there is no evidence that this was the case. Is it because of a fear that the drug might be diverted from legitimate to illegitimate channels? It is hard to believe that this is a valid reason, since morphine itself can be easily acetylated to heroin. In any case, the medical profession and society should be able to weigh the advantages of having heroin available for therapy against the disadvantages of such availability.

There are some who still believe that heroin has unique therapeutic properties for relief of pain or cough. I am unaware of evidence supporting these beliefs, and I am inclined to doubt that the absence of heroin from the pharmacopeia is a serious loss. But the point I wish to make is that if it *were* a serious loss, it would be almost impossible today to reintroduce the drug into medical usage because of the real or imagined conflict of such usage with the goals of law enforcement officers whose eyes are focused on the eradication of the illegal use of heroin by addicts, and because of the horrible but ill-deserved reputation the drug has acquired over the years.

What makes this even more Alice-in-Wonderland-ish is the inconsistency of our prohibitions. Why is Dilaudid (dihydromorphinone) not under the same bans as heroin—the two drugs resemble each other pharmacologically at least as closely as do Dilaudid and morphine. And what of Demerol (meperidine)? Here is an analgesic which is admittedly the narcotic drug of choice among nurse and physician addicts. If excessive addiction liability is the criterion for removing a drug from the market, why not remove meperidine? I should like to emphasize that I do not favor such removal, but merely ask the question to indicate an inconsistency in legal sanctions.

Still another example of the failure of the law to jibe with known pharmacology is the preferential treatment accorded to a drug like Darvon (*d*-propoxyphene) as contrasted to codeine. The first drug is treated as nonaddicting, the second still carries narcotic restrictions. Neither is a really serious threat as an addicting agent, although both are known to cause addiction in an occasional patient.[2]

The physician is abrogating his responsibilities to mold compassionate and scientifically defensible cultural attitudes toward the use and abuse of drugs.

I do not believe that physicians are the fountainhead of all wisdom concerning the problems of addicting and other drugs and that there are no law enforcement problems regarding narcotics. Nor am I convinced that we would be better off if *all* the problems of addiction were suddenly dumped into the laps of the medical profession, as has been suggested by some.

What I *am* certain of is that the medical and allied professions have an expertise concerning drugs and disease which has not been brought adequately to bear on the thinking of nonmedical groups who are concerned with addiction. Let me briefly list a few items which give me concern as a physician, pharmacologist, and member of society:

1. The gross discrepancy between societal attitudes toward the sick alcoholic and the sick narcotic addict.

2. The contrasting attitudes of society toward such similar pharmacologic agents as caffeine and amphetamine. (Somehow it is perfectly respectable for a student or truck driver to drink gallons of coffee to stay awake, but unspeakable for the same people to use an amphetamine tablet for the purpose.)

3. The failure of society at large to admit that the use of any drug—including heroin—can have beneficial as well as harmful effects. (It is, for example, freely admitted that tranquilizers can be a blessing for the psychotic patient, but it is generally not granted that for many people alcohol and heroin may also normalize behavior, prevent conflict and violence, or even promote creative effort.)

4. The lack of appreciation, in our culture, of the principle of alternatives. One gets the impression, in most discussions about addicting and "dangerous" drugs, that the elimination of their illicit use will be an unalloyed blessing. In fact, there is reason to believe that the cessation of illicit heroin and amphetamine use might mean an increase in anything from psychopathology to truck accidents.

5. The failure of society to take cognizance of man's ancient proclivity for experimenting with everything from opium and gluesniffing to mountain climbing and Russian roulette. (Deneau has supplied evidence that man is not unique in this respect, since even one-third of a monkey population, given the opportunity, will prefer morphine solution to water, and some rodent species have long been known to prefer alcohol to water.) We have failed to come to grips with the *causes* of drug abuse; instead, we focus on the *symptoms* of such abuse. The successful treatment of drug abuse must depend eventually on an attack on the economic, social, and psychiatric factors which explain why people become addicted in the first place, just as the eradication of amphetamine abuse by truck drivers would be more rationally achieved by eliminating excessively long hauls than by trying to control amphetamine drugs.

6. The continuing lack of realization that the treatment of the drug addict is seriously hampered by the "criminal" aspects of addiction. There is, I believe, historical evidence that public stigma attached to tuberculosis, syphilis, cancer, and homosexuality has interfered with the detection and management of these conditions. One of the greatest boons of the tranquilizer era has been the change in public attitudes toward mental disease; the increased "respectability" of psychosis now that it can be treated by pills has been in no small measure responsible for the greater acceptance of psychotic patients by their families and the community. In addiction, the fact that a person has a record of arrests related to his disease complicates the future life of the addict in ways which must surely detract from the desire or ability of some such persons to stay off drugs, just as the fear of public and police reaction is a deterrent to the seeking of help by people who are addicts but are not known to be.

Let me now try to draw some conclusions from the above:

1. It would be intellectually desirable, and pragmatically useful, to remove from the consideration of drug abuse the elements of emotionality, hysteria, and exaggeration, so characteristic of the field. I do not believe it really helps, for example, to describe marihuana in the following terms:

> At the price of a few fleeting minutes of pseudocelestial miracles for a few, a hell of moral catastrophes arises for the community, for public health, and for the sane and laborious people. The individual himself is subjugated by this weed, messenger of a false happiness, panderer to a treacherous love, which can provide a superhuman enjoyment and misery, likewise superhuman, which makes him sick—morally more than physically—and changes thousands of persons into nothing more than human scum. It is this weed which sunders the bonds of inhibition that make it possible for men to live together in a society; weed of the brutal crime and of the burning hell; this weed which splits the personality, which invades the prison and the asylum, the hovel and the palace, which subjugates the savage and the cultured; this weed which attempts to convert paupers into kings, weaklings into champions, minutes into years, and evil into good; this weed which brings dreams, which sets free the spiritual and the bestial, and, with the ease that Baudelaire and Gautier pen famous pages, makes the rabble bespatter pages with blood. There you have the picture of this diabolical resin which approaches under the mask of pleasant friendship.[13]

Nor do I believe that we make much progress by distorted pictures of the effect of narcotics use on crime rates. At the White House Conference previously mentioned, one civic official found it "hard" to place the yearly figure for goods stolen by addicts in his city at less than half a billion dollars, and if one took his estimates at face value, the figure might be over $2 billion per year. Yet the Federal Bureau of Investigation in 1960 placed the property loss through robbery, burglary, larceny, and auto theft for the entire country [4] at only $570 million! One might conclude that there is needless puffery or gross error involved in such estimates as those quoted above; at the very least some reconciliation of the discrepant figures seems required.

Is it also necessary to overemphasize the deleterious effects of narcotics on body and mind? There are, admittedly, health dangers from the use of heroin and related drugs—septicemia, malaria, hepatitis, etc. But most of these are really due to lack of attention to sterile precautions in the illegal use of narcotics and represent harmful effects which could easily be eliminated if all addicts might somehow receive their total supply of drugs from medical facilities.

There is also evidence that creative people have functioned well despite—or perhaps as a result of—their use of drugs or alcohol. There are not only the famous addicts of other centuries such as De Quincy, Coleridge, and Wilberforce, but the alcoholic F. Scott Fitzgerald and the eminent Johns Hopkins surgeon and cocaine addict, Halsted, in our own century. Equally interesting are the data on addicts in the United States prior to and shortly after the passage of the Harrison Narcotic Act. According to a 1919 survey, 75 per cent of addicts were gainfully employed, and the number included "people of the highest qualities, morally and intellectually, and of great value to their communities." [4] I am aware that this high percentage no longer obtains, but I believe the older figures argue strongly against any automatic relationship between drug use and moral degradation. Many physicians have had the experience of knowing undetected addicts who functioned quite well despite daily use of narcotics or cocaine, and Kolb has reported on the increased work capacity of some addicts while on drugs.

2. Let us stop insisting on some sort of "heinousness ratings" for various kinds of drug abuse. It has been proposed that the barbiturates are more dangerous drugs than the opiates,[3] and the barbiturates certainly kill more people each year than do the narcotics. But why rank them on any single parameter? They are both useful classes of drugs, and both can cause trouble; why not focus on the specific problems posed by each?

And surely we ought to be civilized enough to stop considering the heroin addict as a lower species of humanity. [I confess to a certain bias in favor of the heroin addict who takes his drug to compensate for some serious psychiatric or socioeconomic deficiency as contrasted with the beatnik, psychology graduate student, novelist, or movie star who ingests LSD (lysergic acid diethylamide) or psilocybin at parties for kicks or "spiritual revelation."]

It is interesting to observe that those who beat the drums for one or another form of drug abuse as more "important" or more "awful" in terms of its consequences are unwilling to carry through their reasoning to its ultimate conclusion. If we were forced to create a priority for health hazards, we should have to stop spending so much time on narcotics and focus instead on cigarette smoking or alcoholism or even on automobile deaths.

3. Let us aim for a flexibility of approach to the problems of drug abuse. Drug addiction encompasses so many complex issues that we are sure to be inefficient in our solutions if we are unable to individualize our handling of persons afflicted with these problems. This is no field for mandatory sentences, blanket condemnations, and other black-and-white public postures. It is, rather, a field begging for the application of the most sophisticated pharmacologic, legal, sociologic, and other approaches.

An expert states: "Our approach so far has produced tragedy, disease, and crime." [4] Clearly some new techniques are worth trying, in experimental fashion, in the hope that greater success will crown our efforts. This would include the trial use of the narcotic "clinics," which have been both ardently advocated and extravagantly condemned. The potential usefulness of such clinics is an unknown quantity. They have neither demonstrated their value nor been shown by proper experimentation to be failures. Prejudging the efficacy of such clinics is an anti-intellectual exercise; an unbiased test, on the contrary, would be scientifically attractive and a venture which physicians would follow with interest.

Perhaps this notion has particular appeal for physicians, since there is nothing intrinsically repulsive to the medical profession about "maintenance therapy" for any chronic disease. Most serious ailments today are chronic ones, and physicians are no less proud of their ability to control chronic disease by continuous use of drugs than they are to cure pneumonia with a few days of penicillin therapy. The patient with hypothyroidism who must take thyroid extract for the rest of his life, the patient with pernicious anemia who will always require B_{12} injections, the diabetic who must forever take insulin, or the cardiac who requires daily digitalis may not represent, basically, a problem different from that of certain individuals who need narcotics to function. I do not pretend that the analogy is necessarily a good one or applicable to most addicts. But we should not rule out the possibility of similarity in any a priori fashion.

In any such experimental approaches, the medical profession must not be put in jeopardy of legal harassment. Despite *Linder v. United States* [268 U.S. 5 (1925)], physicians generally believe that they have almost no legal right to treat drug addicts. Unfortunately, they do run very real risks of various sorts in attempting to treat such people, and it seems essential to assure physicians that such attempts performed in good faith will not be rewarded by punitive retaliation on the part of Federal, state, or local authorities.

In summary:

1. The use of narcotic and "dangerous" drugs poses complicated problems.

2. Since our difficulties are multigenetic and their manifestations extraordinarily varied, the solutions must be varied and our approaches flexible.

3. To arrive at solutions which are equitable and workable will require open minds and a willingness to experiment.

4. The likelihood of coming up with such solutions will probably be inversely proportional to the distortions and lack of perspective in the picture we draw of the addict and of the addiction problem.

REFERENCES

1. Committee on Drug Addiction and Narcotics: Minutes of 24th Meeting, Jan. 29 and 30, 1962, p. 2819 and p. 2841.
2. Elson, A., and Domino, E. F.: Dextro Propoxyphene Addiction: Observations of a Case, *J. Am. Med. Assoc.*, 183:482 (1963).
3. Isbell, H., and Fraser, H. F.: Addiction to Analgesics and Barbiturates, *Pharmacol. Rev.*, 2:355 (1950).
4. Kolb, L.: "Drug Addiction: A Medical Problem," Charles C Thomas, Publisher, Springfield, Ill., 1962.
5. Lasagna, L., and Beecher, H. K.: The Analgesic Effectiveness of Nalorphine and Nalorphine-Morphine Combinations in Man, *J. Pharmacol. Exp. Therap.*, 112:356 (1954).

6. Lasagna, L., and Beecher, H. K.: The Optimal Dose of Morphine, *J. Am. Med. Assoc.*, 156:230 (1954).

7. Lasagna, L., and De Kornfeld, T. J.: Methotrimeprazine: A New Phenothiazine Derivative with Analgesic Properties, *J. Am. Med. Assoc.*, 178:887 (1961).

8. Lasagna, L., Von Felsinger, J. M., and Beecher, H. K.: Drug-induced Mood Changes in Man. 1. Observations on Healthy Subjects, Chronically Ill Patients, and "Postaddicts," *J. Am. Med. Assoc.*, 157:1006 (1955).

9. Martin, W. R., and Fraser, H. F.: A Comparative Study of Physiological and Subjective Effects of Heroin and Morphine Administered Intravenously in Postaddicts, *J. Pharmacol. Exp. Therap.*, 133:388 (1961).

10. *Proceedings, White House Conference on Narcotic and Drug Abuse*, Washington, Sept. 27–28, 1962.

11. Reichle, C. W., Smith, G. M., Gravenstein, J. S., Macris, S. G., and Beecher, H. K.: Comparative Analgesic Potency of Heroin and Morphine in Postoperative Patients, *J. Pharmacol. Exp. Therap.*, 136:43 (1962).

12. Smith, G. M., and Beecher, H. K.: Subjective Effects of Heroin and Morphine in Normal Subjects, *J. Pharmacol. Exp. Therap.*, 136:47 (1962).

13. Wolff, P. O.: "Marihuana in Latin America: The Threat It Constitutes," Linacre Press, Washington, D.C., 1949.

Nathan B. Eddy | **5**

CHEMOPHARMACOLOGIC APPROACH
TO THE ADDICTION PROBLEM

THE CHEMOPHARMACOLOGIC, PSYCHIATRIC, AND LEGAL APPROACHES are those having the greatest impact upon our understanding and, therefore, our handling of addiction and its problems. The first of these approaches has been the author's major interest for more than 30 years, particularly the attempt to dissociate the analgesic and physical-dependence-producing properties of morphinelike agents. The present report will outline the major steps in this attempt, as well as sum up the situation as it appears today.

Although morphine was discovered and named as the active principle of opium 150 years ago,[37] it had to await technological developments and the chemists' ingenuity in their application for the determination of its intimate structure and configuration. The accepted formula (Fig. 1) today is that of Gulland and Robinson,[20] confirmed eventually by total synthesis.[17] Early chemical manipulations of morphine were concerned mainly with its physical properties and tests for its identification. Even during the last half of the nineteenth century, when derivatives of morphine began to be described, there was much uncertainty about the nature and purity of the compounds and little evidence adduced on their pharmacologic action. The introduction of heroin in 1898

(Mering,[32] Dreser [6]) can be fairly pinpointed as the first of the claims for a nonaddictive potent analgesic, and, therefore, the first claim of significant dissociation by chemical modification of the good and bad features of the morphine pharmacologic picture. Not only did Dreser and others claim specific and unique effects of heroin on the respiratory mechanism and hence superiority as an antitussive, but also some of the early writers said that there was no danger of becoming dependent on the drug [5,31] and that, during the withdrawal treatment of addiction to morphine, heroin was a safe temporary substitute.[33]

The early impression and claim of relative safety for heroin and the change within a few years to a belief of high addictiveness came about, probably, through ignorance or disregard of facts now very familiar. A repetition of the errors regarding the addictive qualities of heroin, at least for the same reasons, should not now be possible with other compounds. No one was then aware of cross-tolerance, which prevents the appearance of abstinence phenomena and maintains physical dependence owing to the ability of one narcotic to substitute for another. The morphine-dependent individual showed no withdrawal distress when heroin was substituted. Symptomatic relief was achieved while the heroin was continued, and, therefore, there was no reason to discontinue it. Under these circumstances there was no opportunity for the physician to discover that his patient was in the same state of dependence as when morphine was being given. Also, heroin was introduced as an oral medicament, but before long its use hypodermically was begun. Unfortunately, relative effectiveness by the two routes of administration was not taken into account, and the subcutaneous doses, as large as those which had been taken by mouth, were two or three times as much as was optimal. It is now well established that amounts of narcotic beyond symptomatic need speed the development of physical dependence, and hence heroin's bad name was easily acquired.

The heroin experience was discouraging, but chemists nevertheless made other modifications of morphine during the next quarter of a century without notable improvement. The discovery by Pohl in 1914 [34] was an exception to which great attention should have been paid, but medicine was not ready to realize and build upon its significance.

In 1929 a really intensive effort was begun to determine the relationship between the components of the morphine structure, on the one hand, and its useful properties and disadvantages, on the other, by additions to and subtractions from the parent molecule. This was a cooperative chemical-pharmacologic-clinical program, which continued for 10 years under the direct supervision of the National Research Council. It is interesting, though it matters little now, that this program was based upon almost completely erroneous hypotheses. A great deal of cocaine abuse had existed in this country but had diminished and very largely disappeared following the synthesis and introduction of Novocain, a much simpler molecule with similar local anesthetic properties. Although cocaine was defined legally as addicting, its acute and chronic intoxications were not at all like those of morphine, and it produced no physical dependence. Also, although Novocain lacked the ability to produce some of the central effects of cocaine, the decrease in cocaine abuse stemmed much more from its decreased availability than from the production of a powerful local anesthetic with less central action. Nevertheless, it was said that since cocaine abuse had been ameliorated by the chemical success exemplified by Novocain, there was a possibility that the addiction liability and analgesic action of morphine might be separated by chemical modification.

Almost 150 modifications of the morphine molecule were prepared and studied in the Research Council's cooperative program. A great deal was learned about quantitative modification of morphinelike effects by chemical change (see Small et al., 1938), but throughout, almost complete parallelism between analgesic potency and addiction liability persisted. One approach to a partial success in the original objective was the discovery of a new type of chemical change, the introduction of a new substituent at a new position in the morphine molecule. The best example was metopon (methyldihydromorphinone, see Fig. 1). It was about three times more potent than morphine as an analgesic and though it was more potent orally and parenterally, its

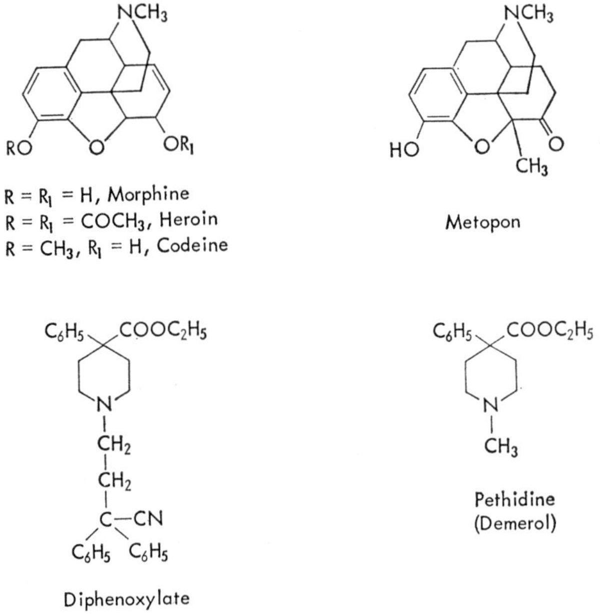

R = R₁ = H, Morphine
R = R₁ = COCH₃, Heroin
R = CH₃, R₁ = H, Codeine

Metopon

Diphenoxylate

Pethidine
(Demerol)

Fig. 1

relative superiority to morphine was most marked as an orally administered drug. A large series of clinical trials indicated a lower incidence of side effects,[7] but these trials were not controlled by crossover or even parallel observations with equally effective morphine doses, and the lower incidence of side effects was not confirmed in such controlled studies.[22] Tolerance and physical dependence developed less rapidly with metopon than with morphine, and tolerance was lost more rapidly, but at best the difference was not great.[29]

The Research Council's chemopharmacologic program not only modified morphine chemically but also synthesized nearly four hundred new compounds from simpler structures, mainly moieties of the morphine molecule, phenanthrene, benzofuran, etc. This work might have been considered steps toward complete synthesis of morphine, but this was not nearly attained. Evidence of analgesic and other properties of morphine emerged, but no compound of practical value in clinical medicine.

The next major step in the history of analgesics was an accidental discovery. German chemists were looking for a synthetic atropine and made a phenylpiperidine which was spasmolytic under some circumstances but strikingly morphinelike in many ways and effectively analgesic.[10] The compound, of course, was pethidine (meperidine, Demerol, Dolantin; it has many other names). It was put on the market and its popularity grew rapidly. Since it was a synthetic, it could be used at first without the restrictions applied to morphine and morphine-related analgesics. In many cases it would relieve pain as well as morphine if its dose was large enough, but unfortunately tests revealed that it would also produce morphinelike subjective effects, that it would substitute for morphine, though never quite completely, in an established morphine addiction, and that its continued administration would produce a primary physical dependence. In spite of this the producer was loathe to admit its addicting qualities until cases of addiction in clinical use began to be reported. The compound was brought under narcotics control quite promptly in Germany but only after several years in this country, and impressions of greater safety persist. Actually the compound, relative to its analgesic potency, is no safer than morphine.

Thousands of phenylpiperidines related to pethidine have been made with varying degrees of analgesic potency from none to thousands of times greater than that of morphine. Analysis and comparison of the members of this very large group is now underway and again will show the relation of analgesic potency to chemical modification, but, again, dissociation of analgesic action and disadvantageous properties is conspicuously lacking. One example of dissociation, in the wrong direction one might say, is worth noting, namely, the compound known as diphenoxylate (Fig. 1). It consists of the pethidine structure with a rather massive substituent attached to the nitrogen of the molecule. It has no analgesic action but possesses the ability of morphine to control intestinal activity and is being used as an antidiarrhoeic. It is extremely insoluble, but when it can be got into the organism, it can support more or less a morphine addiction. In other words analgesic effectiveness has been lost, but addiction liability and some other morphinelike properties have in some degree been retained.[13]

German chemists made another important discovery, which came to general attention in 1946.[36] This time they were carrying out a planned research program on potential analgesics, which resulted in the synthesis of methadon (Fig. 2) and its derivatives. This group of compounds was reviewed recently by Janssen of Belgium.[24] Methadon duplicated the effects of morphine in practically all respects qualitatively and in many respects quantitatively, but there were important time differences in its action in man. One difference which has been put to practical use was the

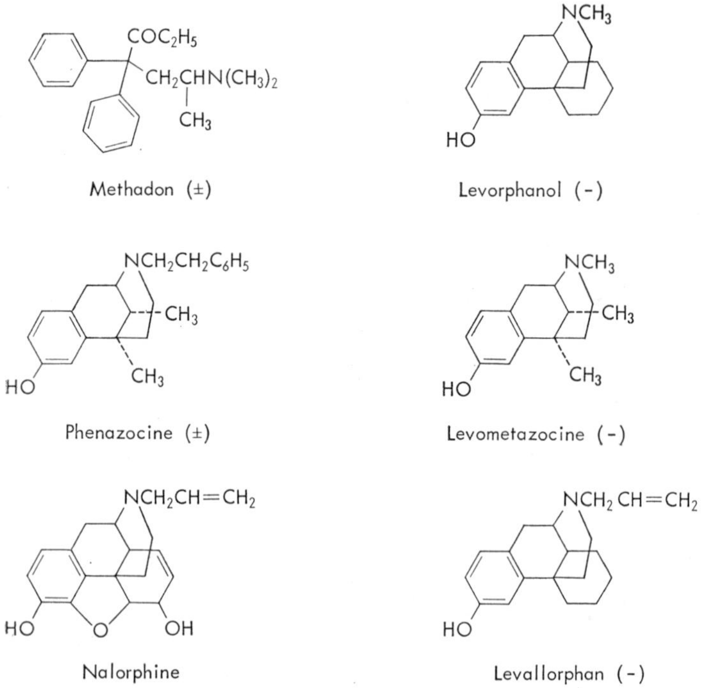

Methadon (±)

Levorphanol (−)

Phenazocine (±)

Levometazocine (−)

Nalorphine

Levallorphan (−)

Fig. 2

time course of the abstinence syndrome which followed abrupt withdrawal in an addicted individual and the effect of methadon on the course of the abstinence phenomena after substitution in individuals addicted to other narcotics. The methadon abstinence symptoms were not apparent until about forty-eight hours after the last dose of the drug, never reached more than low intensity, and were prolonged up to about two weeks. Similarly if methadon was substituted for another narcotic when physical dependence had developed, the subsequent withdrawal sequence was slow in onset, attenuated in intensity, and prolonged. This change could be attained by substitution of one or two 20-mg doses of methadon orally per day, and consequently such substitution constituted in most instances a very satisfactory treatment of the withdrawal phase of addiction.

The production of methadon, even more morphinelike in its effects than pethidine, was an added stimulus to the chemist to manipulate the molecule, since he was manipulating and continuing to modify pethidinelike structures. It stimulated also much speculation on structure-action relationships and the postulation of an essential molecular form to fit a receptor site for the production of morphinelike analgesia.[2] There followed an increased awareness of differences in analgesic activity, demonstrated when the racemic synthetic analgesic was resolved into its optical antipodes, such action occurring largely, often solely, with one isomer only. But again in the methadon as in the pethidine series the many chemical modifications did not result in useful dissociation of analgesic action and addiction liability.

The resolution and study of the isomers of active racemates had one interesting by-product, apparent dissociation of antitussive action. Heretofore analgesic and antitussive properties appeared to be closely related, but cough-suppressant action of useful degree was demonstrated in animals and man with the isomer which had no analgesic effect and no ability to substitute for morphine or to produce primary physical dependence. Dextromethorphan is a good example.[3,4,11]

Meanwhile another German chemist, working on the total synthesis of morphine, carried his work up to a morphinan structure,[18] and this in turn was developed into the clinically useful product, levorphanol, by Schnider and Grüssner. [35] 3-Hydroxy-*N*-methylmorphinan (levorphanol, Dromoran, Fig. 2) represented an incomplete morphine synthesis but demonstrated that some features of the morphine structure could be omitted without impairment of the characteristic morphine effects. Again the chemists went through the process of modifying the levorphanol molecule as had been done previously with the morphine molecule, and again essential parallelism between analgesic action and physical-dependence properties was demonstrated.[9] A development of major interest, however, shown first in the morphine series and repeated for morphinan derivatives, was the disproof of the long held belief that a methyl group on nitrogen was the optimal structure for analgesic action.[41,8] Of particular note were the observations that analgesic action in members of both series, which diminished when the group on nitrogen was changed from methyl to ethyl to propyl, was restored to or surpassed that of the parent *N*-methyl compound when the substituent was amyl or hexyl. Also the substitution of methyl by some aralkyl groups, particularly phenethyl, greatly enhanced analgesic effect.

Profiting by the demonstration that the complete morphine molecule was not necessary for morphinelike analgesic action, May began in 1952 the synthesis of a new series. He made, first, phenylmorphans and then benzomorphans, both only partial morphinelike structures. One of the phenylmorphans in its racemic form showed an analgesic effect in animal experiments almost as great as that of morphine, but greater interest developed in the benzomorphan series, and more than one hundred modifications have now been made.[3] A number of parallels between the effect of modifications in this series and the effect of similar modifications of morphine or morphinan derivatives have been established. For example, substitution of phenethyl for methyl on nitrogen again increased analgesic potency. The racemate, 2′-hydroxy-5,9-dimethyl-2-phenethyl-6,7-benzomorphan, phenazocine (Prinadol), has ten times the analgesic potency of morphine in laboratory animals and three to seven times its potency in man.

According to established practice, the more interesting benzomorphans were submitted to a monkey screening program at the University of Michigan for testing physical-dependence capacity, and some were tested in man. The monkey experiments test the ability of a compound to suppress the morphine abstinence syndrome and are considered to indicate qualitatively at least the ability of the compound to produce physical dependence. The predictiveness of the test had been good for many compounds of several chemical types. With the benzomorphans, however, even those with high analgesic potency, very low effectiveness was seen with regard to the suppression of the signs of morphine withdrawal. With phenazocine, for example, analgesic effectiveness was reported as ten times and abstinence suppressant potency as less than one-fifth that of morphine. This was encouraging and seemed to represent a major dissociation of analgesic and physical dependence properties, if the difference carried over to man or unless there was a much greater species difference in sensitiveness to the benzomorphans than had been seen in any other group of compounds.

The carry-over to man was not as good as hoped for, and consequently the difference just described was in part at least the result of species difference. Let us again take phenazocine as the example. As has been said, its analgesic potency in man is three to seven times that of morphine, depending upon the situation in which it is employed. Fraser and Isbell [12] reported that phenazocine was 3.2 times more potent than morphine in the production of morphinelike subjective effects in postaddicts and 8 times more potent than morphine in suppression of the abstinence syndrome during 24-hr substitution in morphine addicts. In direct addiction experiments the daily dose of phenazocine could not be increased as rapidly as was done commonly with morphine (slower rate of development of tolerance). Following abrupt withdrawal of phenazocine in such experiments, definite morphinelike abstinence phenomena appeared, which tended to be less severe than abstinence following withdrawal of equivalent amounts of morphine.

Another illustration of the effect of a benzomorphan in man was even more interesting. The morphine analog in the benzomorphan series, (-) 2'-hydroxy-2,5,9-trimethyl-6,7-benzomorphan (Fig. 2), had an analgesic potency in the morphine range in animals and man, perhaps slightly more effective in the former and slightly less effective in the latter. Its physical-dependence capacity in monkeys was very low, since it produced almost no suppression of the morphine abstinence syndrome at doses up to 10 to 15 times the suppressant dose of morphine, amounts which caused the appearance of signs of toxicity. In postaddicts this benzomorphan was the equivalent of morphine in the production of morphinelike subjective effects. In 24-hr substitution experiments, even an amount of the benzomorphan twice that of the dose of morphine on which the subjects were stabilized had little effect. It was estimated that in these experiments it was only one-eighth as effective as morphine. In direct addiction attempts the subjects (former opiate addicts) did not regard the drug as being as desirable as morphine, and on withdrawal the abstinence syndrome was definitely less intense than after withdrawal of morphine in other trials in the same subjects.

May one not conclude from the above observations that in the benzomorphan series some dissociation of morphinelike properties in the direction of less addictiveness is beginning to appear?

Let us go back now to a very early point in this discussion. Pohl's discovery in 1914 was mentioned as one to which we should have paid particular attention. Pohl succeeded in substituting an allyl group for methyl on the nitrogen, making *N*-allylnorcodeine, and he claimed that it antagonized the respiratory-depressant effect of morphine. Right there was the most important lead to dissociation of analgesia and addictiveness that we have even today. Almost thirty years later Merck chemists [40] made the morphine analog, *N*-allylnormorphine (nalorphine, Fig. 2), and it was shown that it could antagonize most of the morphinelike effects whether produced by morphine or another morphinelike analgesic.

Nalorphine on chronic administration did not produce physical dependence.[23] Given to an individual, animal or man, after the development of physical dependence on another opiate, nalorphine promptly precipitated a typical abstinence syndrome. This has been utilized to advantage in tests for the development of physical dependence under clinical conditions and is the basis of the Nalline test to detect the use of opiate drugs. Nalorphine did not show significant analgesic action in animal tests.

The structural relationship between morphine and morphinan led naturally to the preparation of the N-allylmorphinan analog (levallorphan, Fig. 2) which proved to have specific antagonistic properties several times greater than those of nalorphine. In both, series compounds with a wide variety of substituents on nitrogen have been prepared, and a wide range in antagonistic properties with these variations has been demonstrated. Generally, but not always, there has been no analgesic effect demonstrable in animals.

In 1952 Fromherz and Pellmont [16] reported that levallorphan in a ratio of 1:100 abolished the respiratory-depressant effect of morphine and morphinelike drugs (rabbit experiments), but that even when the ratio was 1:20, analgesic effect was not abolished. This suggested the possibility that a ratio of nalorphine (or levallorphan) to morphine might be found which could be administered as a mixture clinically, with a resulting decrease in respiratory and other side effects without interfering with the pain relief, and arrangements were made for clinical testing of this hypothesis. Lasagna and Beecher [28] conducted such a study in patients with postoperative pain employing mixtures of morphine-nalorphine, 5:1 and 3:1, and controlled their observation by administration of morphine alone and nalorphine alone. They found that 10 mg of morphine plus 2 mg of nalorphine produced analgesia and side effects indistinguishable from those achieved with 10 mg of morphine alone. Also the combination of 15 mg of morphine with 5 mg of nalorphine produced respiratory depression and subjective side effects similar to those with 15 mg of morphine. So, at these ratios at least, our objective was not attained, but another most surprising result was seen. Ten milligrams of nalorphine alone produced as much analgesia as 10 mg of morphine. These were crossover observations on the same patients, who received alternating doses of the two drugs on a double-blind randomized basis. Unfortunately side effects with nalorphine were as frequent as they were with morphine and often were most unpleasant to the patient. Later Keats and Telford [26] confirmed the analgesic effect of nalorphine in man as well as the incidence and unpleasantness of the side effects.

However, the work on modification of antagonistic potency by changing the nitrogen substituent had begun,[41] and in some instances the compounds which were poor antagonists showed some analgesic action in the laboratory. The work of Lasagna and Beecher and of Keats and Telford had shown that the results of testing opiate antagonists for analgesic action in animals could be false negatives, and it was possible there might be found among the opiate antagonists one with a combination of antagonistic and analgesic properties which would give adequate clinical analgesia without excessive and disturbing side effects. A search for such a compound with such a combination of properties has been underway now for a number of years. An added incentive was the observation already mentioned that nalorphine did not produce physical dependence, and the compound sought, hopefully, would retain sufficient antagonistic potency to be similarly unable to produce physical dependence. The search was carried out by Keats and his associates under the sponsorship of the Committee on Drug Addiction and Narcotics of the National Academy of Sciences–National Research Council.

Initially three compounds in the morphine series and three in the morphinan series were tested.[39] One of the latter, with the substituent on nitrogen, 3,3-dimethylallyl (Fig. 3), had very little antagonistic action, was as good an analgesic as morphine with a similar incidence of side effects, and, as might be expected from its low antagonistic action, produced morphinelike effects in post-addicts at the Addiction Research Center, at Lexington, Kentucky. The other five compounds were effective antagonists, varying in potency, and produced some degree of analgesia in man. The most effective compound, which had propargyl—the nitrogen substituent—was like levallorphan as an antagonist, like morphine as an analgesic, but like nalorphine with respect to side effects.

This was the situation when May developed his promising benzomorphan, phenazocine, which has already been described.

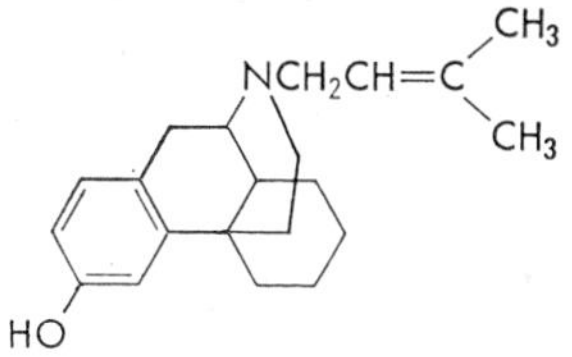

NIH 7446

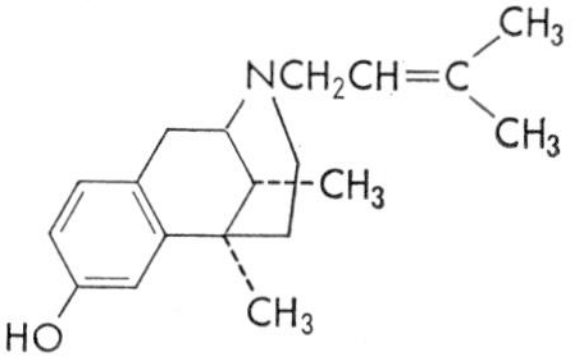

WIN 20,228

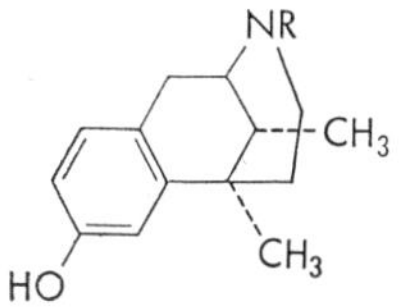

R = $CH_2CH=CH_2$, SKF 10,047
= Cyclopropylmethyl, WIN 20,740

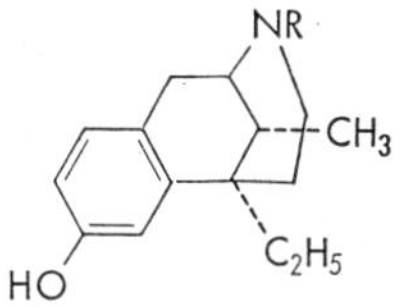

R = $CH_2CH=CH_2$, WIN 19,362

R = $CH_2CH=C\overset{CH_3}{\underset{CH_3}{}}$ WIN 20,264

Fig. 3

The suspicion or suggestion of some dissociation of morphinelike properties in the benzomorphan series, as well as structural relationships, excited the curiosity of chemists and stimulated them to make the N-allylbenzomorphan analog of nalorphine and levallorphan and later to make a series of compounds with different substituents on nitrogen. All these (some 25 compounds now) were assessed in the laboratory for antagonistic as well as analgesic properties, and examination of some has gone much further, now including rather extensive clinical testing.

The preparation of the N-allyl analog (Fig. 3) was described by Gordon, et al.[18] This proved to be like nalorphine in most respects. It showed no analgesic action in the laboratory, was not as good an analgesic as morphine or nalorphine in man (15 mg was less effective against postoperative pain than 10 mg of morphine), and it produced in some patients the disturbing psychic reactions which had been seen with nalorphine.

Four other members (Fig. 3) of this group are under study.

One of these corresponds in structure, so far as the antagonistic group is concerned, to the morphinan derivative mentioned which was almost completely morphinelike. The others represent variations of the *N*-substituent or minor variations in another part of the molecule or both. The antagonistic potency of these compounds varies from a tenth the potency of nalorphine to twice that of levallorphan. All of them are analgesics in man, again with a varying effectiveness. Two of them are specially interesting. Both are products of the Sterling-Winthrop Research Institute.

One may be identified conveniently as Win 20,228.[1,21,25,15] It has no analgesic effect in animals but is effective against postoperative pain in man at a dose of 20 to 40 mg as compared with 10 mg of morphine. It has not produced the bizarre psychic reactions which were troublesome with nalorphine. Side effects similar to those seen frequently after morphine were seen with the 40-mg dose. Win 20,264, similar to the previous compound, except for substitution of an ethyl for a methyl group at one position in the molecule, was quite similar to Win 20,228 in its action in man.

Win 20,228 has been studied at the Addiction Research Center. Its subjective effects in postaddicts were different from those of morphine. It had very little effect on the morphine abstinence syndrome, and subjects disliked it on chronic administration to the extent that seven of eight subjects voluntarily discontinued the medication. The conclusion of Fraser and Rosenberg[15] is that this compound has no significant degree of morphinelike addictiveness.

Win 20,740, the most potent as an antagonist of the compounds studied in this series, is noteworthy for its other effects. It is remarkably effective as an analgesic in man, the dose equivalent to 10 mg of morphine being only ¼ to ½ mg. At such doses its side effects are minor and not nalorphinelike. Unpleasant reactions may occur occasionally when the dose is increased to 2.0 mg, but one could not safely increase the relative dose of morphine as much in a nontolerant individual. The effects of Win 20,740 are not too different from those of Win 20,228 in postaddicts. This is the only really potent antagonist which has shown this sort of effect in man (strong analgesia, at least 20 times that of morphine, without nalorphinelike side effects at the effective analgesic dose). It was mentioned earlier that the nearest approach to Win 20,740 in potency, N-propargylmorphinan, was levallorphanlike in antagonistic action, morphinelike in analgesic potency, but nalorphinelike in subjective effects to such an extent as to make it quite impractical as a clinical analgesic.

These antagonists, in general, are not entirely devoid of respiratory-depressant effect, even though in suitable dose ratio they, the more potent at least, will antagonize the respiratory-depressant effect of morphine and other opiates. This defect in the clinical usefulness of morphinelike analgesics has not been corrected, but, for practical purposes, almost complete dissociation of analgesic and physical-dependence properties has been achieved. There are now available one or more opiate antagonists structurally based on the benzomorphan nucleus which can meet the needs for pain relief, in those fields where they have been tried, without unusual or bizarre side reactions and without the production of physical dependence. The question of tolerance to the analgesic effect of these compounds has not yet been explored.

The intensive study of the relationship of chemical structure to analgesic action and addiction liability began more than 30 years ago. It has been a long and frustrating search, and those engaged in it have been dedicated individuals. There are still many questions to be answered, but I think it is fair to say that at last there is progress.

However, assuming that one of the antagonists proves to be a sufficiently powerful analgesic without undue side effects and without physical-dependence properties, we will have reached the long-sought objective of many investigators which will be a boon to the clinician and his patient, but it will not solve the addiction problem, not overnight anyway. There will still be the opium-producing countries whose economic problems make difficult any effort to bring about cessation of poppy cultivation. There will still be the know-how and the established machinery for illicit production and distribution of heroin, which all the efforts toward narcotics control have not suppressed. There will still be all the individuals who seek a solution of their problems by resort to drugs. So the chemopharmacologic success which is postulated (anticipated, I am tempted to say) will help medicine, will furnish a sound basis for stepped-up control efforts looking to eventual banning of addicting morphinelike agents of natural or synthetic origin, and on both counts will contribute to, though it does not supply, a solution to the addiction problem.

REFERENCES

1. Archer, S., et al.: Narcotic Antagonists as Analgesics, *Science,* 137:541 (1962).
2. Beckett, A. H., and Casey, A. F.: Synthetic Analgesics: Stereochemical Considerations, *J. Pharm. Pharmacol.,* 6:986 (1954).
3. Benson, W. M., Stefko, P. L., and Randall, L. O.: Comparative Pharmacology of *d-, dl-,* and *l*-Dromoran and Related Ether Derivatives, *Federation Proc.,* 11:322 (1952).
4. Cass, L. J., and Frederik, W. S.: Evaluation of a New Antitussive Agent, *New Engl. J. Med.,* 249:132 (1953).
5. Daly, J. R. L.: A Clinical Study of Heroin, *Boston Med. Surg. J.,* 142:190 (1900).
6. Dreser, H.: Über die Wirkung einiger Derivate des Morphins auf die Athmung, *Arch. Ges. Physiol.,* 72:485 (1898).
7. Eddy, N. B.: Metapon Hydrochloride: An Experiment in Clinical Evaluation, *Public Health Rept., U.S.,* 64:93 (1949).
8. Eddy, N. B., Besendorf, H., and Pellmont, B.: Synthetic Analgesics: Aralkyl Substitution of Nitrogen of Morphinan, *Bull. Narcotics, U.N. Dep. Social Affairs,* 10 (4): 23 (1958).
9. Eddy, N. B., Halbach, H., and Braenden, O. J.: Synthetic Substances with Morphine-like Effect; Relationship between Analgesic Action and Addiction Liability, with a Discussion of the Chemical Structure of Addiction-producing Substances, *Bull. World Health Organ.,* 14:353 (1956).
10. Eisleb, O., and Schaumann, O.: Dolantin, a New Antispasmodic Agent, *Deut. Med. Wochschr.,* 65:967 (1939).
11. Fraser, H. F., and Isbell, H.: Effects and Addiction Liabilities of the Isomers of the 3-Methyl Ether of Dromoran, *J. Pharmacol. Exp. Therap.,* 106:397 (1952).
12. Fraser, H. F., and Isbell, H.: Human Pharmacology and Addiction Liabilities of Phenazocine and Levophenacylmorphan, *Bull. Narcotics,* 12 (2):15 (1960).

13. Fraser, H. F., and Isbell, H.: Human Pharmacology and Addictiveness of Ethyl 1-(3-Cyano-3,3-diphenylpropyl)-4-phenyl-4-piperidine Carboxylate Hydrochloride (R-1132, Diphenoxylate), *Bull. Narcotics, U.N. Dep. Social Affairs,* 13 (1):29 (1961).

14. Fraser, H. F., and Isbell, H.: Personal communication (1962).

15. Fraser, H. F., and Rosenberg, D. E.: Personal communication (1963).

16. Fromherz, K., and Pellmont, B.: Morphinan-antagonisten, *Experientia,* 8:394 (1952).

17. Gates, M., and Tschudi, G.: The Synthesis of Morphine, *J. Am. Chem. Soc.,* 74:1109 (1952).

18. Gordon, M., et al.: A New Potent Analgesic Antagonist, *Nature,* 192:1089 (1961).

19. Grewe, R.: Synthetic Drugs with Morphine Action, *Angew. Chem.,* 59:194 (1947).

20. Gulland, J. M., and Robinson, R.: The Constitution of Codeine and Thebaine, *Mem. Proc. Manchester Lit. Phil. Soc.,* 69:79 (1925).

21. Harris, H. F., and Pierson, A. K.: Further Studies with Antagonists in the Benzomorphan Series, *J. Pharmacol. Exp. Therap.* (1963), in press.

22. Houde, R. W.: Personal communication (1957).

23. Isbell, H.: Attempted Addiction to Nalorphine, *Federation Proc.* 15:422 (1956).

24. Janssen, P. A. J.: Synthetic Analgesics: Part 1. Diphenylpropylamines, in "International Series of Monographs on Organic Chemistry," vol. 3, Pergamon Press, London, 1960.

25. Keats, A. S.: Personal communication (1963).

26. Keats, A. S., and Telford, J.: Nalorphine: A Potent Analgesic in Man, *J. Pharmacol. Exp. Therap.,* 117:190 (1956).

27. Lasagna, L.: Personal communication (1963).

28. Lasagna, L., and Beecher, H. K.: The Analgesic Effectiveness of Nalorphine and Nalorphine-Morphine Combinations in Man, *J. Pharmacol. Exp. Therap.,* 112:356 (1945).

29. Lee, L. E., Jr.: Studies of Morphine, Codeine and Their Derivatives: XVI. Clinical Studies of Morphine, Methyldihydromorphinone (Metapon) and Dihydrodesoxy-morphine-D (Deso-morphine), *J. Pharmacol. Exp. Therap.,* 75:161 (1942).

30. May, E. L., and Eddy, N. B.: Synthetic Analgesics: Part II, B. 6,7-Benzomorphans, in "International Series of Monographs on Organic Chemistry," Pergamon Press, London, 1963, in press.

31. Medea, E.: L'impiego terapeutico dell'heroina, *Morgagni* 41 (part 1):381 (1899).

32. V. Mering, J.: Physiological and Therapeutical Investigations on the Action of Some Morphine Derivatives, *Merck's Jahresb.*, 1:5 (1898).

33. Morel-Levalée, A.: La Morphine remplacé par l'heroine pas d'euphorie, plus de toxicomanes traitement héroique de la morphinemanie, *Rev. Med.*, 20:872 (1900).

34. Pohl, J.: Über das N-Allylnorcodein, einen Antagonisten des Morphins, *Z exptl. Pathol. Therap.*, 17:370 (1914–15).

35. Schnider, O., and Grüssner, A.: Synthese von Oxy-morphinanen, *Helv. Chim. Acta*, 32:821 (1949).

36. Scott, C. C., and Chen, K. K.: The Action of 1,1-Diphenyl-1-(dimethylaminoisopropyl)-butanone-2, a Potent Analgesic Agent, *J. Pharmacol. Exp. Therap.*, 87:63 (1946).

37. Sertürner: De la morphine et de l'acide méconique, considérés comme parties essentielles de l'opium, Trommsdorff's *J. Pharmaz.*, 13:234 (1805); *Ann. Chim. Phys.*, 5:21 (1817).

38. Small, L. F., Eddy, N. B., Mosettig, E., and Himmelsbach, C. K.: Studies on Drug Addiction, with Special Reference to Chemical Structure of Opium Derivatives and Allied Synthetic Substances and Their Physiological Action, *Public Health Rept.*, U.S., Suppl. 138 (1938).

39. Telford, J., Papadopoulos, C. N., and Keats, A. S.: Studies of Analgesic Drugs: VII. Morphine Antagonists as Analgesics, *J. Pharmacol. Exp. Therap.*, 133:106 (1961).

40. Weijlard, J., and Erickson, A. E.: N-allynormorphine, *J. Am. Chem. Soc.*, 64:869 (1942).

41. Winter, C. A., Orahovats, P. D., and Lehman, E. G.: Analgesic Activity and Morphine Antagonism of Compounds Related to Nalorphine, *Arch. Intern. Pharmacodyn.*, 110:186 (1957).

Abraham Wikler | **6**

CONDITIONING FACTORS IN OPIATE ADDICTION AND RELAPSE

THEORETICAL CONSIDERATIONS

IN ACHIEVING an impressive degree of mastery over the world about us, the growth of the natural sciences has been characterized by an ever-increasing supplementation of "private operations" (sensing, feeling, inducing, deducing) with "public" ones (control and manipulation of measurable variables). As one result, even our "private" ways of perceiving the world have changed from those of our prescientific ancestors, so that at sunset, we no longer "see" the sun sinking into the sea, but "see" it disappearing beneath the horizon.

Such subtle but far-reaching changes have also occurred in our dealings with our hearts, livers, and kidneys, but in dealing with our own and other people's behaviors, most of us are still content with mentalistic explanations, the terms of which, "private" as they are, remain undefined though they may be quantified in the sense of counting the frequency of their occurrence in one or another situation. This mentalistic orientation has characterized most attempts to describe and explain drug (including opiate) addiction and relapse no less than other forms of

85

deviant human behavior. In consequence, the clinician has tended to accept his patient's mentalistic interpretation of his addiction and his frequent relapses to drugs as a valid one—for who else would know better what his feelings are than the patient himself? And does not one behave in accordance with one's feelings? To be sure, the psychoanalysts have often answered both questions in the negative, designating the patient's verbally expressed feelings as "conscious," and their own dissenting conscious feelings about the patient's feelings as "unconscious" ones of the patient. This certainly represents a commendable attempt to break out of the solipsistic straitjacket which, had it been allowed to restrain Columbus, would have left us convinced that the earth is flat because we "see" it that way. Unfortunately, however, the psychoanalyst's explanations of human behavior, including drug addiction and relapse, are also couched in mentalistic terms and hence cannot be tested for validity in the accepted manner of the natural sciences—i.e., by use of "public" operations, at least directly.

Possibly for these reasons, the clinician's interests in the problem of drug addiction and relapse have been focused on the occurrence of drug-induced "euphoria." It has been debated whether or not morphine, heroin, and other narcotic drugs (henceforth, morphine will be used as a prototype) produce euphoria in all persons or only in atypical or deviant ones,[16,21] but few have ventured to question the decisive importance of euphoria as the main determinant of the addict's behavior, both in his initial addiction and in his subsequent relapses—for this is also the addict's explanation. Likewise in agreement with the addict, clinicians have generally regarded morphine-induced physical dependence merely as an unpleasant complication, serving as a deterrent rather than as a motivating factor in relapse, for who but a masochist would see any virtue in those properties of a drug that produced "the agonies of the damned" when withheld after long-continued use?

The present writer would not deny that certain effects of single doses of morphine may be decisive in determining the initial *choice* of that drug from among many other "euphorogenic" agents for continued use by some persons. Indeed, in collaboration with several colleagues [9,10,15,11,7,8] he has presented data acquired by "public" operations indicating one class of effects of morphine on nontolerant postaddicts, which theoretically at least may play such a role—namely, reduction of the influence on behavior of motivating variables in general, and of nociceptive ones in particular, but whether or not such effects have anything to do with euphoria is indeterminable and, in this writer's opinion, quite irrelevant. Of more importance would be the development of methods for testing the hypothesis that other factors being equal, any drug possessing such effects, regardless of whether or not it also produces euphoria, would be chosen for repeated use by the same kind of person who uses morphine in this manner.

Be this as it may, however, the writer has stated reasons for doubting the prevailing opinion that the quest for euphoria and the fear of abstinence distress are responsible for self-maintenance of addiction to morphine.[25,27] Mainly, these are three: (1) tolerance to the euphoric effect of morphine develops quickly and is not achieved again in anything like the intensity of the initial effect despite progressive increase in dosage; (2) even with unlimited supplies of the drug and the privilege of self-injection in amounts and at intervals ad libitum, the addict, at least under experimental conditions, is a miserable creature, beset by remorse, guilt, and anxiety; and finally (3) there appears to be no adequate reason why experienced addicts cannot withdraw themselves in a relatively painless manner either by gradual reduction of dosage or substitution and subsequent withdrawal of methadon. In mentalistic terms, the conclusion drawn from these considerations and other subjective data gathered in a study of a patient during self-regulated readdiction to morphine [25] was that the motivations for self-maintenance of addiction in man are largely unconscious ones, above all the gratification by each dose of morphine of the need for the drug engendered by physical dependence. Furthermore, it was suggested [27] that "being hooked" furnishes the addict with a motivational basis for sustained activity ("hustling for drugs") directed to recurring but attainable goals, thereby preventing boredom and also securing approval from his peers, i.e., "addict society."

Likewise, the writer has doubted that the quest for euphoria constitutes the only, or even the major, motivation to relapse, in spite of the addict's conscious insistence thereon, for the acceptance of such an explanation would entail acceptance of the improbable assumption that the addict "remembers" only the euphoric effects of the first few doses of morphine and "forgets" the months or years of misery experienced during addiction. Rather, statements occasionally made by postaddicts to the effect that they have experienced symptoms resembling those of acute abstinence from morphine long after withdrawal of the drug[26] led the author to hypothesize that physical dependence may become conditioned to environmental situations specifically associated with availability of morphine, and hence "abstinence distress," or something very much like it, may be reactivated long after "cure" when the postaddict finds himself in a similar situation, thus providing an unconscious motivation to relapse and renewed self-maintenance of addiction as described above.[24]

Another way in which relapse might come about as a result of conditioning was suggested by Kolb[14] in the following terms:

> The addict, even if he has sufficient narcotics, becomes uncomfortable several times a day when the last dose wears down. If another dose is not available, he suffers acute distress in about 18 hours. Over a period of years, he relieves such discomfort or distress thousands of times by injection of morphine. During this same period he enjoys the drug in pleasurable association with friends and by taking it to get the effect that many of them describe by the statement, "It makes my troubles roll off my mind." By thus building up a strong association between pleasure and pain and the taking of a narcotic he becomes conditioned to taking one in response to most any situation that may arise.

Expressed for the most part in mentalistic terms, the validity of such speculations is difficult, if not impossible, to test directly, but to those who are familiar with behavioristic-conditionng theory, their similarity to certain concepts definable in terms of "public" operations should be apparent. Restating the writer's views in such terms,[28,29] relapse may be attributed at least in part to two factors operating during previous episodes of addiction: (1) classical conditioning of physical dependence through repeated temporal contiguities between a specific environment and the occurrence of morphine-abstinence phenomena; and (2) reinforcement of instrumental activity (morphine-acquisitory behavior) through repeated reduction by the drug of such abstinence phenomena as developed during intervals between doses. This "two-factor learning theory" of relapse could be expanded further by introduction of some additional concepts such as "secondary reinforcement," "drive (or stimulus) generalization," and "scheduling" of reinforcement for the purpose of redefining and testing other factors in the genesis of relapse already described in mentalistic terms, but only brief allusions to these concepts will be made in this paper because actual research to date has been confined to investigation of factors 1 and 2.

EXPERIMENTAL INVESTIGATIONS

Though some of the consequences of the two-factor learning theory of relapse may eventually be testable in man, both ethical and practical considerations require the use of animals for direct testing of the conditionability of physical dependence and the putatively reinforcing processes operating during addiction. With regard to the latter, similar hypotheses and data bearing upon them have been reported by Nichols et al.,[19] Nichols and Davis,[18] and Davis and Nichols,[2] who employed forced drinking of dilute (0.5 mg per ml) aqueous solutions of morphine under water-deprivation conditions for reinforcement of "choice" drinking of the same solution by morphine-abstinent rats; by Headlee et al.,[6] who reinforced head turning in a particular direction by making intraperitoneal injection of morphine contingent upon this operant in morphine-abstinent rats; by Beach,[1] who reinforced running of rats to one arm of a Y maze by establishing temporal contiguity between "residence" in that arm and presumed reduction of morphine-abstinence phenomena there by prior intraperitoneal injection of morphine; by Weeks [22] and Weeks and Collins,[23] who developed a technique for self-maintenance of addiction through intravenous (intracardiac) self-injection of morphine in rats; and by Yanagita et al.[32] and by Schuster and Thompson,[20] who utilized a similar method for reinforcing intravenous self-injection of morphine in monkeys.

In our own investigations (carried out exclusively in the rat so far) we circumvented difficulties encountered with forced drinking of morphine solutions or parenteral injections of morphine *for reinforcement* by use of a relatively new drug, etonitazene [1-(beta-diethylaminoethyl)-2-(*p*-ethoxybenzyl)-5-nitrobenzimidazole methane sulfonate] in very dilute aqueous solution for drinking. Though structurally unrelated to morphine [13] it has been shown to be 1,000 times as potent as morphine by parenteral injection for analgesia in the rat [5] and to have morphinelike effects not only in this species but also in monkey and man, in both of which it has been shown to suppress morphine-abstinence phenomena as well.[3,4] Preliminary studies [30] revealed that water-deprived rats would drink a 5 mcg per ml concentration of etonitazene in distilled water as avidly as tap water and that within 4 to 7 min after starting to drink, normal rats would show typical morphinelike effects (tail rigidity, exophthalmos, and stupor alternating with quick, jerky movements). This was also true for rats acutely (18 hr) abstinent from morphine, in which drinking of this solution also abolished an easily observable sign of abstinence, namely, increased frequency of "wet-dog" shakes (so-called because of their resemblance to those of a dog shaking water off its back). Later it was found that rats, morphine-addicted or not, will readily drink such dilute aqueous solutions of etonitazene even without any prior water deprivation, thus eliminating the necessity of introducing that condition as a complicating variable in the design of experiments on conditioning and reinforcement.

Because of these promising early results, more systematic investigations [17,31] were then undertaken to characterize as precisely as possible the phenomena of the morphine abstinence syndrome in the rat, and the effects thereon of drinking dilute aqueous solutions of etonitazene, without prior water deprivation. Those results bearing most directly on the conditioning and reinforcement studies to be described later may be summarized as follows:

1. Elevated wet-dog frequencies are reliable indicators of early morphine abstinence in the rat, roughly paralleling other signs of early abstinence such as increased activity, hypothermia, loss of body weight, and increased defecation, urination, and hostility

—all compared with observations made concurrently on normal control rats.

2. In rats maintained on single intraperitoneal injections of morphine at 8 A.M. daily (E's),* increased wet-dog frequencies, as well as other early abstinence phenomena, become manifest at least as early as 22 to 24 hr after the last previous injection of morphine.

3. When E's are permitted to drink a 10 mcg per ml aqueous solution of etonitazene instead of water over the preceding 17-hr period, no significant differences from normal rats receiving single intraperitoneal injections of saline at 8 A.M. daily (C's)* can be found on comparison 22 to 24 hours after the last previous injections.

4. Whereas E's drink very much larger volumes of 5 or 10 mcg per ml aqueous solutions of etonitazene than they do of water when only one or the other fluid is available from 3 P.M. to 8 A.M. next morning (during the latter part of which period E's are morphine-abstinent), the volumes of water or etonitazene consumed by C's during the same period under the same conditions are not significantly different (though one of a group of 4 C's died after drinking the 10 mcg per ml drug solution).

In light of this information, the studies on conditioning of physical dependence and reinforcement of drug-acquisitory behavior were designed in the following manner. Experimental conditions were arranged in such a way that over a 6-week "training" period, the occurrence of nocturnal morphine-abstinence phenomena in E's ($N = 7$) was repeatedly associated with "residence" in one (preferred) end of a three-compartment linear maze, where only distilled water was available for drinking, and relief from nocturnal morphine-abstinence phenomena was associated with "residence" in the other (nonpreferred) end, where only a 10 mcg per ml aqueous solution of etonitazene was available for drinking, the drug solution being also "tagged" with anise flavor to provide additional discriminative cues (food was available ad libitum in both ends at all times). Another group of E's ($N = 7$) was "trained" in exactly the same manner except that the drinking

* E, "experimental animals"; C, "control animals."

fluid in the nonpreferred end consisted only of anise-flavored water, and both training schedules were replicated concurrently for two groups of C's ($N = 7$ each) except that for the first of these two groups, the anise-flavored etonitazene solution contained 5 mcg per ml of that drug. For convenience, the four groups will be designated in the order described as ET, ENT, CT, and CNT.

Following the training period, all injections were terminated, and all rats were transferred to home cages (food and tap water ad libitum), where they remained thenceforth except on "relapse" and other test days conducted at intervals up to 155 days after termination of injections. On the morning of each relapse test day (9, 23, 44, 58, 72, 87, 94, and 142 days after termination of injections) wet-dog frequencies for each rat were measured immediately after removal from home cage, weighing, and returning to home cage, and also immediately after removal from home cage, weighing, and placing in the linear maze (preferred end), in alternate order from rat to rat; from 8 P.M. the same day to 8 A.M. next morning, each rat was afforded "free choice" between distilled water in the preferred and an anise-flavored, 5 mcg per ml aqueous solution of etonitazene in the nonpreferred end of its linear maze. Between the seventh (94th day of abstinence) and eighth (142d day) relapse tests, two successive extinction procedures were carried out. In the first free choice was permitted between distilled water in the preferred and anise-flavored water in the nonpreferred end, and in the second, between distilled water in both ends. In addition, six tests on forced drinking, without prior water deprivation, were made on all rats from 8 P.M. to 8 A.M. at intervals throughout the study—four on forced drinking of the anise-flavored 5 mcg per ml aqueous solution of etonitazene, one of the anise-flavored water, and one of the distilled water, each in the nonpreferred end. The purpose of these tests was to provide comparative data on how much each rat would drink of each of the fluids mentioned "by constraint" (forced-drinking tests) and "by choice" (relapse tests). Finally, a supplementary study was also carried out on four new E's and four new C's in which both groups were trained over a 9-day period in a manner similar to that already described for ENT and CNT, and then subjected, 9 and 23 days after termination of injections, to relapse tests conducted exactly as described above, except that the fluid in the nonpreferred end was only anise-flavored water, to determine whether or not previous addiction to morphine results in an increased affinity of rats for the anise flavor per se.

Considered in relation to the theory, the results were as follows:

1. **Classical Conditioning of Physical Dependence.** On every relapse test, wet-dog frequencies of E's (ET + ENT) were higher in the linear mazes than in the home cages, and although on some tests wet-dog frequencies of C's (CT + CNT) changed in the same direction, the magnitude of change was less. A mixed type of analysis of variance revealed that on the second relapse test (23 days abstinent from injections), F ratios for variances due to previous treatment (E's vs. C's), test conditions (linear maze vs. home cage), and "interactions" (E's vs. C's linear maze vs. home cage) were all significant. On the first relapse test (9 days) only one, but on the third (44 days), fourth (58 days), and fifth (72 days), two of the three F ratios were significant. All three F ratios were again significant when the analysis was made on means obtained for each rat on twelve tests (including the sixth, seventh, and eighth relapse tests as well as the single-day tests during the extinction procedures) from the 84th through the 155th days of abstinence.

Especially significant theoretically is that such presumptive evidence of "conditioned abstinence" was manifested by E's long after "cure"—i.e., after body weight, 24-hr tap-water consumption (home cage), and wet-dog frequencies *in the home cage* had returned to the levels of C's (from the 23d day of abstinence onward, although through the 72nd day, wet-dog frequencies of E's were generally slightly higher than in C's). As between ET and ENT, or between CT and CNT, no significant differences in wet-dog frequencies were found.

2. **Reinforcement of Instrumental Activity (Drug-acquisitory Behavior).** In each of the first four relapse tests (through the 58th day of abstinence) and again on the eighth (142d day) relapse test (after completion of the extinction procedures), the percentage of fluids consumed in the form of anise-flavored etonita-

zene solution (5 mcg per ml) by choice was significantly greater for E's (ET + ENT) than for C's (CT + CNT) by the Mann-Whitney "U" test. The ratios, volumes of the anise-flavored etanitazene solution consumed by constraint to those consumed by choice, were about 8:3 for E's and 5:1 for C's at 9 to 10 days, and about 2:1 for E's and approaching infinity (almost zero consumption of the drug solution) for C's at 142 to 155 days of abstinence. In the supplementary study, the percentage of fluids consumed in the form of anise-flavored water on the two relapse tests (9 and 23 days abstinent) was *less* for E's than for C's, though the difference was significant only on the first test. These results indicate that the greater intake of anise-flavored etanitazene solution by E's than by C's in the first four and in the eighth relapse tests cannot be explained merely as a reflection of "residual cross-tolerance" (between morphine and etonitazene) in E's or of a greater affinity of E's for anise flavor per se. Rather, the data suggest that relative to C's, etonitazene solution is less negatively (or more positively) reinforcing for E's, even long after cure. Not predicted by theory, however, were the findings that the etonitazene solution was reinforcing to equal degrees for ET and ENT on the first relapse test, and that whereas such reinforcement continued with little change for the ENT group, it fell progressively for the ET group over the next four relapse tests. These observations suggest that such "self-training" as the ENT rats may have undergone during the 12-hr (8 P.M. to 8 A.M.) free choice drinking period in the first relapse test could have been sufficient for maximal positive reinforcement; whereas the forced drinking of the anise-flavored drug solution which the ET group underwent in the programmed training period could have produced, in addition, some negative reinforcement based on pharmacologic properties of etonitazene other than morphine-abstinence reducing ones. Presumably, the negatively reinforcing properties of etonitazene were even more pronounced for the CT and CNT groups, since they were resistant to the extinction procedures, whereas the latter were effective for the ET and for the ENT group as well, which likewise exhibited evidence of negative reinforcement on the sixth and seventh relapse tests.

DISCUSSION

Though the data are consistent with the two-factor learning theory of relapse, this conclusion must be a tentative one at present, because the experiments described have not ruled out with assurance the possibility that the differences between E's and C's in the relapse tests were due to latent but long-enduring hyperirritability in the former as a result of previous addiction to morphine, rather than to the putative interactions between morphine abstinence and the specified stimulus arrangements in the linear mazes during training. While the low frequencies of wet dogs in the home cage on the relapse tests would seem to rule out such a possibility, they were somewhat higher in E's than in C's through the 72d day of abstinence as already noted, and in an earlier study [17] rats withdrawn from morphine at a final "stabilization" dose level of 360 mg/kg per day showed small but consistent differences from control rats for 4 to 6 months. Conceivably, therefore, the duration of time over which relapse tests in the present study were made may not have been sufficient to reveal the effects of conditioning and reinforcement during training as such.

These two interpretations (alternative or combined) of the data have a number of different consequences for further research and therapy in man. Thus, if the behavior of E's (compared with C's) in relapse tests was due only to residual hyperirritability, then the method of morphine withdrawal in the treatment of human addicts is not a crucial issue, provided it is sufficiently painless to ensure the addict's cooperation. Rather, the problem is to determine the exact physiological nature and the duration of such residual hyperirritability and to devise methods of treatment to shorten or control it by pharmacologic or other means. By use of the cold pressor test, Himmelsbach [12] was able to show that the autonomic reactivity of postaddicts is slightly greater than that of normal subjects for over 6 months after withdrawal of morphine. It is conceivable that with more refined techniques, differences of this sort would be revealed for even longer periods. If such proves to be the case, currently prevailing methods of treatment—withdrawal of morphine by substitution and subsequent withdrawal of methadon, supervised abstention from drugs of all kinds in a drug-free environment for as long a period of time as is practicable, combined with institutional and postinstitutional psychotherapy and social rehabilitative measures—would need to be modified only in details, not in principle.

If, on the other hand, the behavior of E's relative to C's in the relapse tests was due to the conditioning and reinforcing procedures employed during training, then the implications of the experimental results for the drug-withdrawal phase of treatment in man are quite far-reaching, for methods would have to be devised for extinguishing "conditioned abstinence" and reinforced drug-acquisitory behavior. This is not accomplished by *passive* withdrawal of, and prolonged abstention from, morphine in a "drug-free environment" with or without nonspecific psychotherapy, any more than satiating a rat with food and keeping it away from the Skinner box for a period of time will "cure" it of its lever-pressing "habit," previously reinforced by food rewards under conditions of food deprivation. Rather, true extinction of both processes would require an attack on each separately in reverse order under very different conditions. Thus, extinction of morphine-acquisitory behavior would require *maintenance* of the state of morphine deprivation, i.e., prolongation of the abstinence syndrome by some means passively, coupled with nonreinforcement of instrumental *activity* directed toward (unsuccessful) acquisition of the drug. Practical realization of such an extinction procedure would depend on the development of at least two new drugs, namely, one which if substituted for morphine would produce on abrupt withdrawal a prolonged, though not necessarily severe, abstinence syndrome, and another which, though not effective in suppressing abstinence phenomena produced by withdrawal of the first drug, would be sufficiently reinforcing on other grounds so that the addict would "work" for it on some schedule of reinforcement proven to be optimal by experiment. Of necessity, this phase of treatment would have to be carried out in an institution where, after its completion and withdrawal of the abstinence-maintaining drug, therapy could be directed toward elimination of the hypothetical residual hyper-irritability discussed above.

In addition, some elementary principles of reinforcement theory could be applied to what may be called "positive reconditioning" of the patient while he is still in the institution. This refers to scheduling of rewards for "work therapy." Monetary payment for socially useful work in crafts and industries within the institution would serve more effectively than verbal reinforcement for supplanting physical dependence on narcotic drugs as a motivational basis for "hustling," especially if such payment is made on a piecework (fixed ratio) schedule, and opportunities are provided for spending part of the wages for objects (other than drugs) that are immediately satisfying to the patient.

Ideally, however, extinction of conditioned physical dependence should be carried out in the addict's natural, "drug-available" environment, so that he could be exposed to that conditioned stimulus and the secondary reinforcers (addict society) repeatedly, provided that the hoped-for extinction of drug-acquisitory behavior previously carried out in the institution, coupled with close surveillance and, if necessary, appropriate nonnarcotic pharmacologic therapy and psychotherapy for suppression of conditioned abstinence and reduction of anxieties probably involving the same physiologic systems (stimulus or drive generalization) is sufficiently effective to ensure against reexposure to the unconditioned response, namely morphine-abstinence phenomena generated by readdiction.

These speculations have been presented not for the purpose of recommending immediate changes in our treatment programs for addicts but to illustrate how restatement of some mentalistic concepts about drug addiction and relapse in behavioristic terms may enable us to test their validity by experiment. Though, as stated, the role of conditioning factors in morphine addiction and relapse is not yet fully elucidated, the "public" operations by which they may be are quite readily discernible, and further research along the lines indicated may yet enable us to deal with these clinical problems more effectively than heretofore.

REFERENCES

1. Beach, H. D.: Morphine Addiction in Rats, *Can. J. Psychol.,* 11:104 (1957).
2. Davis, W. M., and Nichols, J. R.: Physical Dependence and Sustained Opiate-directed Behavior in the Rat: A Preliminary Report, *Psychopharmacologia,* 3:139 (1962).
3. Deneau, G. A., McCarthy, D. A., and Seevers, M. H.: Physical Dependence Liability Studies in the Monkey, Add. 1, Min. 20th Meeting, Committee on Drug Addiction and Narcotics, National Research Council, Washington, D.C., National Academy of Sciences, 10–11 January, 1959.
4. Fraser, H. F., Isbell, H., and Wolbach, A. B., Jr.: Addictiveness of New Synthetic Analgesics, Add. 2, Min. 21st Meeting, Committee on Drug Addiction and Narcotics, National Research Council, Washington, D.C., National Academy of Sciences, 11–12 January, 1960.
5. Gross, R., and Turrian, H.: Ueber Benzimidazolderivate mit starker analgetischer Wirkung, *Experientia,* 13:401 (1957).
6. Headlee, C. P., Coppock, H. W., and Nichols, J. R.: Apparatus and Technique Involved in a Laboratory Method of Detecting Addictiveness of Drugs, *J. Am. Pharm. Assoc., Sci. Ed.,* 44:229 (1955).
7. Hill, H. E., Belleville, R. E., and Wikler, A.: Studies on Anxiety Associated with Anticipation of Pain: II. Comparative Effects of Pentobarbital and Morphine, *A.M.A. Arch. Neurol. Psychiat.,* 73:602 (1955).
8. Hill, H. E., Belleville, R. E., and Wikler, A.: Motivational Determinants in Modification of Behavior by Morphine and Pentobarbital, *A.M.A. Arch. Neurol. Psychiat.,* 77:28 (1957).
9. Hill, H. E., Flanary, H. G., Kornetsky, C. H., and Wikler, A.: Relationship of Electrically Induced Pain to the Amperage and the Wattage of Shock Stimuli, *J. Clin. Invest.,* 31:464 (1952).
10. Hill, H. E., Kornetsky, C. H., Flanary, H. G., and Wikler, A.: Effects of Anxiety and Morphine on Discrimination of Intensities of Painful Stimuli, *J. Clin. Invest.,* 31:473 (1952).
11. Hill, H. E., Kornetsky, C. H., Flanary, H. G., and Wikler, A.: Studies on Anxiety Associated with Anticipation of Pain: I. Effects of Morphine, *A.M.A. Arch. Neurol. Psychiat.,* 67:612 (1952).
12. Himmelsbach, C. K.: Studies on the Relation of Drug Addiction

to the Autonomic Nervous System: Results of Cold Pressor Tests, *J. Pharmacol. Exp. Therap.*, 73:91 (1941).

13. Hunger, A. J., Kehrle, J., Rossi, A., and Hoffmann, K.: Synthese basisch substituirter, analgetisch wirksamer Benzimidazolderivate, *Experientia*, 13:401 (1957).

14. Kolb, L.: Drug Addiction As a Public Health Problem, *Sci. Monthly*, 48:391 (1939).

15. Kornetsky, C. H.: Effects of Anxiety and Morphine on the Anticipation and Perception of Painful Radiant Thermal Stimuli, *J. Comp. and Physiol. Psychol.*, 47:130 (1954).

16. Lasagna, L., Von Felsinger, J. M., and Beecher, H. K.: Drug Induced Changes in Man: 1. Observations on Healthy Subjects, Chronically Ill Patients and "Post-addicts," *J. Am. Med. Assoc.*, 157:1006 (1955).

17. Martin, W. R., Wikler, A., Eades, C. G., and Pescor, F. T.: Tolerance to and Physical Dependence on Morphine in Rats (abstract), *Pharmacologist*, 4:154 (1962).

18. Nichols, J. R., and Davis, W. M.: Drug Addiction: II. Variation of Addiction, *J. Am. Pharm. Assoc., Sci. Ed.*, 48:259 (1959).

19. Nichols, J. R., Headlee, C. P., and Coppock, H. W.: Drug Addiction: I. Addiction by Escape Training, *J. Am. Pharm. Assoc., Sci. Ed.*, 44:229 (1955).

20. Schuster, C. R., and Thompson, T.: A Technique for Studying Self-administration of opiates in Rhesus Monkeys, presented at 25th Meeting, Committee on Drug Addiction and Narcotics, National Academy of Sciences, National Research Council, Ann Arbor, Mich., 16 February, 1963.

21. Von Felsinger, J. M., Lasagna, L., and Beecher, H. K.: Drug Induced Changes in Man: 2. Personality and Reactions to Drugs, *J. Am. Med. Assoc.*, 157:1113 (1955).

22. Weeks, J. R.: Experimental Morphine Addiction: Method for Automatic Intravenous Injections in Unrestrained Rats, *Science*, 138:143 (1962).

23. Weeks, J. R., and Collins, R. J.: Some Factors Affecting Performance of Self-maintained Addict Rats, presented at 25th Meeting, Committee on Drug Addiction and Narcotics, National Research Council, National Academy of Sciences, Ann Arbor, Mich., 16 February, 1963.

24. Wikler, A.: Recent Progress in Research on the Neurophysiological Basis of Morphine Addiction, *Am. J. Psychiat.*, 105:329 (1948).

25. Wikler, A.: A Psychodynamic Study of a Patient during Self-regulated Readdiction to Morphine, *Psychiat. Quart.,* 26:270 (1952).

26. Wikler, A.: "Opiate Addiction: Psychological and Neurophysiological Aspects in Relation to Clinical Problems," Charles C Thomas, Publisher, Springfield, Ill., 1953.

27. Wikler, A.: Rationale of the Diagnosis and Treatment of Addiction, *Conn. State Med. J.,* 19:560 (1955).

28. Wikler, A.: Mechanisms of Action of Opiates and Opiate Antagonists, Public Health Monograph, no. 52, Government Printing Office, Washington, D.C., 1958.

29. Wikler, A.: On the Nature of Addiction and Habituation, *Brit. J. Addict.,* 57:73 (1961).

30. Wikler, A., Green, P. C., Smith, H. D., and Pescor, F. T.: Use of a Dilute Aqueous Solution (5 mcg/ml) of a Benzimidazole Derivative with Potent Morphine-like Actions Orally As a Presumptive Reinforcing Agent in Conditioning of Drug-seeking Behavior in Rats (abstract), *Federation Proc.,* 19:22 (1960).

31. Wikler, A., Martin, W. R., Pescor, F. T., and Eades, C. G.: Factors Regulating Oral Consumption of Etonitazene Solution by Morphine-addicted Rats (abstract), *Pharmacologist,* 4:154 (1962).

32. Yanagita, T., Deneau, G. A., and Seevers, M. H.: Physical Dependence to Opiates in the Monkey, with Demonstration, Presented at 25th Meeting, Committee on Drug Addiction and Narcotics, National Research Council, National Academy of Sciences, Ann Arbor, Mich., 16 February, 1963.

Part 3

SOCIAL-PSYCHOLOGIC PERSPECTIVES

Isidor Chein　|　**7**

THE USE OF NARCOTICS AS A
PERSONAL AND SOCIAL PROBLEM[1]

THERE ARE FOUR interrelated premises on which public policy
with respect to opiate addiction is based in the United States: (1)
that the number of addicts is so overwhelmingly large as to
gravely threaten the general social welfare; (2) that addiction is
an extremely contagious disease; (3) that by far the most important task that needs to be carried out in the treatment of addicts is to get them to stop taking drugs; and (4) that, given the
fact of addiction, all other factors that distinguish one addict from
another fade into insignificance. The last two of these premises
are generally not made explicit, but their tacit assumption is as
basic to American policy as are the first two.

I believe that these premises and the policy based upon them
are all wrong; that is, each of the premises is unsound and the
policy based upon them is indefensible. These are, of course, fighting words in the climate of our times. This paper undertakes to
support the challenge.

The first of the premises, that the number of addicts is so overwhelmingly large as to gravely threaten the general social welfare,
is set up on the basis of what can be described as a game of in-

flating numbers. Let me start with an anecdote that illustrates
the crudest version of this game. My colleagues and I were known
to be collecting data on drug use among juveniles in New York
City. Shortly before a major hearing by a legislative committee
on the narcotics problem in the city, we were visited by representatives of three agencies concerned with the problem. Each of
our visitors explained that he would be called upon to testify at
the hearing and would surely be asked about the number of juvenile addicts in the city. Each further explained that he did not
know the answer to this question and hoped we could tell him.
We gave them our figures and the nature of our data, viz., that we
were working on only three of the five boroughs, that we were
only dealing with detected cases, that we did not know the ratio
of detected to undetected cases (and, hence, did not know what
multiplier should be used to estimate the total number), and
that we did not know what proportion of our cases were already
addicted. Within a few days, we read newspaper accounts of the
testimony of each of our visitors. The distinction between a user
and an addict was not mentioned. The three witnesses testified
to widely varying number of juvenile addicts, presumably based
on arbitrarily chosen different multipliers, additions to include
the two missing boroughs, and possibly a few added cases lest
too rounded numbers might carry an aura of imprecision. None
of the witnesses mentioned the common source or indicated the
nature of the operations on the figures we had furnished. The
smallest of the testified-to numbers of juvenile addicts was, however, considerably larger than our total number of known drug-
involved cases.

The intention of these witnesses was doubtless benign. They
were concerned about increasing the resources available to cope
with a serious problem. Their position may well be expressed
by the district attorney who cautioned me to go easy in my criti-
cisms of existing statistics on addiction, lest I endanger the "considerable progress that has been made." [2]

The numbers game goes back a long time. In 1919, the Treasury
Department reported that there were 1 million addicts in the
United States, and other estimates were running as high as 5
million. Contrast these figures with the much more responsible

estimate by Kolb and Du Mez [3] of somewhat less than 215,000 at the beginning of the period 1915–1922 and of about 110,000 at the end of this period. I think that there is good reason to believe that even the Kolb and Du Mez estimates are grossly exaggerated if we were to take them to refer to seriously addicted individuals.[4] Bear in mind that the Harrison Act was passed in December, 1914, and that its enforcement as a repressive measure did not begin until 1919. Also bear in mind that prior to the Harrison Act opiates not only could be bought legally without prescription but were common ingredients of over-the-counter proprietary medications. Finally, bear in mind that there is no evidence of any extensive wave of violent reaction by the addicts to the withdrawal of their narcotic supplies. There does not seem to have been a wave of withdrawal sickness or any great upsurge in the number of robberies of pharmacies and physicians' offices as addicts attempted to replenish their supplies. Instead, the number of addicts was peacefully and quietly reduced to less than half of the original number. Even if we were to assume that, over the 7-year period, there was not a single new recruit to the ranks of the addicts, it seems clear that a large proportion of the original 215,000 could not have been very severely addicted.

Let us turn to more contemporary versions of the numbers game. In 1958, Inspector Joseph L. Coyle, then in charge of the Narcotics Squad of the New York City Police Department, wrote:[5] "From July 1, 1952 to February 28, 1958 . . . it shows that there are 22,909 drug addicts in the City of New York. . . ." The "it" refers to a list compiled from all sources that could be tapped in addition to the police department's own files. "From July 1, 1952 to February 28, 1958" is clearly a time span, but the list shows "that there *are* 22,909 addicts," i.e., in the immediate present. Despite this curious construction of the statement and despite internal evidence that suggests the inclusion of nonusing sellers, the absence of criteria of addiction, and the failure to provide any means of getting off the list, short of dying in New York City—despite these occasions for suspicion, 23,000 addicts became, for a while, the official statistic on the number of addicts in New York City.

Some perspective on New York City's purported 23,000 addicts as of 1958 comes from my next source, the Federal Bureau of Narcotics.[6] Beginning January 1, 1953, the Federal Narcotics Bureau began, on a national scale, to compile statistics on drug addiction. There were two improvements in the Federal procedure over that of the New York City Police Department: nonusers were not included, and a means was provided for getting off the list. Specifically, a person not reported as a user for 5 years is transferred from the active to the inactive file. There is a faulty aspect to this procedure: a person transferred to the inactive file is counted as an active addict for the entire 5 years that he has not been known to be using drugs.

Now, let us see what we can learn from the Bureau's statistics. In *1953 and 1954*, there were 16,725 "addicts" listed in the active file. As of the end of 1959, 6 to 7 years later, there were 10,804 of these, or 65 per cent of the original number, who had not again been reported. That is, as far as any one knows, 65 per cent of the 16,725 "addicts" reported in *1953–54* were cured, dead, or had left the country by December 31, 1959; at any rate, they were not known to have used drugs after getting on the list. *For 1955*, we do not know how many names were added to the list, but 7,234 of these cases were not heard from again as of the *end of 1959*. Even so, these 7,234 cases are included in the official count of 45,391 "active addicts" known to the Bureau as of the end of 1959. Even more interesting is the fact that more than one-third of these 7,234 cases had no known history of drug use prior to 1955; in other words, 2,473 cases were not known to be drug users either before or after 1955, but they are nevertheless counted as active addicts as of the end of 1959.

One final comment on Bureau statistics: *On September 19, 1962*, the Acting Commissioner of Narcotics was quoted in the press as having asserted that there are 46,798 addicts in the United States. When you compare this with the 45,391 of December 31, 1959, you note an increase of only 1,407 cases in the almost 3 years that have elapsed, and you may be inclined to breathe a sigh of relief at the declining rate. If so, that merely shows that you have not yet caught on to this particular numbers game. To get from 45,391 to 46,798, you must first subtract from 45,391 the 7,234 nonrecurring cases from the 1955 additions and also the nonrecurring cases from the 1956 and 1957 additions to the active file. To the remainder (which consists of the repeaters from prior to September, 1957, and both the repeaters and nonrepeaters of the last 3 or 4 months of 1957 and the repeaters and nonrepeaters of 1958 and 1959) you add the entire group (including, of course, those who will be transferred to the inactive file in 1966 and 1967) of 1961 and 1962 cases up to September, 1962.

It will perhaps now be clear why the count of 46,798 addicts as of September, 1962, cannot be relied on, unless one is willing to define as *active* addicts a group whose members *no longer use drugs* but are included in the total of 46,798. Of the latter number, the number of repeaters seems likely to come to considerably less than 20,000 if the 1953–54 experience is at all dependable, i.e., less for the entire country than the official statistic I mentioned before for New York City alone. The 1955 data suggest that the proportion of nonrepeaters is, if anything, increasing: if we were to assume that the total number of names added in 1955 equaled the average of the numbers added in 1953 and 1954, the percentage of nonrecurrence would exceed 85 per cent as compared with 65 per cent for 1953–54; and there is reason to believe that the numbers added to the list would diminish from year to year during the early years of building the file, since the early years would have the advantage of listing cases already known from previous years. Even among the 7,234 nonrepeaters of the 1955 listing, 9 per cent give a history of drug use of 10 to 51 years.

The reader should note that the question has not yet been raised whether being reported more than once in the course of several years as a "regular user" of narcotics is a sufficient basis for the diagnosis of addiction, to say nothing of the absence of criteria that form the basis of the designation "regular use."

Lest one discount the effectiveness of the Federal Narcotics Bureau, and of all the agencies cooperating with it, in discovering cases of narcotics addiction, it should be pointed out that, while there are doubtless many instances of drug use that do not come to be known by any agency, the nature of the statistical bias is entirely in the direction of weeding out the least seriously involved drug users. It is exceedingly difficult, if not impossible, for a seriously involved drug user to escape attention for very long, since every addict must be repeatedly involved in lawbreaking, usually in association with other lawbreakers. In its list-building activity, the Bureau is assisted not only by its own agents but also by its state and local counterparts, to say nothing of the public and private medical and social agencies cooperating in this enterprise. A case missed by one source is very likely to be detected by one or more of the many others who are on the lookout for it. The very nature of the statistics I have just cited indicates that the net is so tightly woven as to catch very small fish indeed; to argue that there may be large numbers of seriously involved drug users who go undetected is virtually to argue that the more seriously involved the drug user is, the less is the likelihood of detection.

The conclusion is inevitable: not that there is no addiction to speak of, but that the number of addicts, in any serious sense of the latter term, must be far less than the official statistics would seem to indicate. There is a serious problem of addiction, but it is not nearly of the magnitude we have come to take for granted.

Let us turn now to the second premise underlying public policy, the contagiousness of addiction. It is, of course, true that many a drug user was first initiated into drug use by an addict and that there are addict-pushers who do try to recruit customers from the ranks of nonusers. If this is to be interpreted as contagion, however, we must add that a basic condition of such contagiousness is the fact that the addict has no legitimate access to narcotics, to say nothing of legitimate access at a reasonable cost. The simple fact of the matter is that the spread of addiction is self-limiting. As shown by the Kolb and Du Mez figures on the prevalence of addiction prior to the enforcement of the Harrison Act, that is, under the conditions of a completely open market, of the loading of proprietary medications with narcotics, and of far less caution in the prescription of narcotics by physicians than prevails today, there were far fewer than one-quarter of a million addicts in the country—and even this figure is achieved only by the inclusion of relatively minor degrees of involvement and the inclusion of drug users who could only have been addicted in the sense of having developed some degree of physical dependence.

We are in a position today to comprehend some of the reasons for the self-limiting spread. To begin with, normal people do not find the psychic effects of narcotics attractive.[7] The obverse of the last statement is the admittedly not too-compelling fact that when addicts come to psychiatric attention, they seem to be, without exception, suffering from one or another of a variety of mental disturbances, apart from their addiction.

The author and his colleagues, as well as other investigators, have found that the spread of drug use is associated with conditions of human misery. Drug use is, of course, a necessary condition of addiction, so that the epidemiologic vectors of drug use may also be taken as relevant epidemiologic vectors of addiction.[8]

A map of Manhattan, the Bronx, and Brooklyn was used to mark off every census tract that had three or more cases of 16-through 19-year-old boys who were known to have been involved with narcotics in the period 1949–1952. Similarly, every tract with one or two cases was marked off if it was adjacent to a tract that had at least three cases. The result was a set of sizable "islands," which were referred to as the epidemic areas. These epidemic areas, which collectively included 83 per cent of the drug-involved late-teen-aged male youth, were composed of only 15 per cent of the census tracts in the three boroughs studied and included less than two-fifths of the late-teen-aged male youth.

When the epidemic and nonepidemic areas were compared with respect to virtually every undesirable characteristic we could think of and on which census tract data could be obtained, the epidemic areas were found to be worse in 20 out of 24 indices. Taking only the tracts in the epidemic areas and the immediately adjacent drug-free tracts,[9] we calculated correlation coefficients between the various indices and the drug-involvement rates. The multiple correlation was found to be .86 for Manhattan, .83 for the Bronx, and .63 for Brooklyn. The lower correlation in Brooklyn may be due to (is a function of) the lower variability in drug rates. Poverty alone (indexed by the percentage of income units earning $2,000 or less) yielded correlations of .65, .66, and .43.

As one approach to the investigation of the impact of such deprived environments on the youth, we administered a questionnaire touching on a wide variety of issues to all eighth-grade boys in three lower-class, high-delinquency neighborhoods that differed with respect to the rates of drug involvement of the youth. The responses were analyzed by a statistical technique that could identify attitudes that tended to occur (or cluster) together. One such cluster we identified as reflecting a *delinquent* orientation to life—a mood of pessimism, unhappiness, and futility, on the one hand, and of mistrust, negativism, and defiance on the other. In the low- and medium-drug-rate areas certain attitudes favorable to drug use tended to go along with the delinquent orientation. This also happened in the high-drug-rate area, but in a much more complex fashion. In this neighborhood, which ranked highest of the three in terms of our indices of deprivation, the delinquent orientation became differentiated into two related but nonetheless distinguishable strands; one emphasized the mood of pessimism, unhappiness, and futility, and the other the mood of mistrust, negativism, and defiance. Both these strands were associated with attitudes favorable to drug use, but there were important differences consistent with the emphasized mood. For instance, along with the version of the delinquent orientation that emphasized pessimism, unhappiness, and futility, there was a wholesale rejection of reasons for not taking heroin. There was no such tie-in with the other version of the delinquent orientation.

Similarly, in our study of drug use in delinquent street gangs, it appeared that the threshold of maturity was a critical point. The more normal youth became more and more occupied with relatively adult concerns, steady girl friends, and jobs, while, as the cohesiveness of the gangs was threatened, the already-defeated youth turned to narcotics. And, in a study of penitentiary inmates, one of the authors' students, Stanley Schiff, obtained the following interesting results. He compared five groups of inmates on an elaborate measure of self-esteem—an addict group still in their teens, a nonusing group of teenagers, an adult addict group that started drug use while in their teens, an adult addict group that started drug use after they had passed their teens, and an adult nonusing group. The two teen-aged groups could not be distinguished from each other with regard to level of self-esteem, but both had levels *higher* than those of the late-starting adult addicts and the nonusing adults. Thus, it appears that, in this population, self-esteem declines with age; it is a population that is becoming more and more defeated. But what of the early-starting adult addict group? Their level of self-esteem was just like that of the teen-agers. It seems that they could preserve their self-esteem by taking to narcotics as an alibi for failure.

Obviously, not all the youth in the deprived areas turn to narcotics. By far the worst record in any census tract was a 10 per cent rate of involvement with narcotics among the late-teen-aged youth. What keeps the others away? One clue is provided by our study of attitudes of eighth-grade boys. The delinquent orientation and related attitudes are strongest in that segment of this population which already has the longest record of failure, those assigned to the "adjustment" classes in schools in the high-drug-use area. A second clue comes from our study of four groups of boys coming from similar neighborhoods; delinquents with no history of drug use, drug users with a prior history of delinquency, drug users with no prior history of delinquency, and boys who stayed clear of both narcotics and delinquency. The most important differences were between this last group and the others. These boys came from more cohesive families and were much more likely to have a father, a teacher, or a priest to whom they could talk about personal problems. They also gave many signs of being able to perceive a meaningful and productive future and of working toward the attainment of that future. Lastly, these boys seemed to be actively resisting the pull of their neighborhood environment.

One would also expect that a major difference between those who give in to their degrading environment and those who resist it is to be found in the life-history patterns that establish the personality organization. Psychiatric and clinical psychologic studies [10] have indicated the existence of severe personality disturbances among addicts. Certain characteristics seem to be most common: They are not capable of enduring intimate relations with others; they have difficulty in assuming their appropriate sex roles; they are frequently overcome by a sense of futility, expectation of failure, and general depression; they are easily frustrated and made anxious and find frustration and anxiety intolerable, and, in psychoanalytic terms, they suffer from weak egos and inadequate functioning superegos. It is not necessary, and indeed it would be false, to assume that such personality characteristics are unique to addicts. Note, however, how these personality characteristics fit in with the environmental and personal-history vectors toward drug use that have already been described. In other words, if we look upon addiction as a form of behavior, addiction is no exception to the general rule that behavior is a function of personality and environment.

There is, however, a chicken-and-egg problem in connection with the studies of personalities of addicts. To what extent is the observed personality pattern a cause and to what extent is it an effect of the addiction? To illuminate this issue, we proceeded as follows: We drew up a hypothetical picture of the kind of family life that would be expected to produce the personality pattern described. We then set out to find whether this kind of family life is more characteristic of addicts than of nondelinquent, non-drug-using controls. In a word, *it is!* Much more important, however, is that we had expected to find negative cases—addicts with a more normal family life and controls with the kind of family life we had hypothesized. We wanted to study these negative cases intensively. However, there were no negative cases. Such trivial overlap between the two groups as there was—and it was trivial—melted away when we turned from our indices to the case protocols.

I have only touched upon the evidence that supports my proposition that drug use is a product of human misery. It should be clear, however, that any talk of addiction as contagious is profoundly misleading. The addict is a person with serious problems, and the spread of addiction reflects unsolved problems that are focused on limited segments of our society.

This brings us to the third premise, which states that by far the most important task that needs to be carried out in the treatment of addicts is to get them to stop taking drugs. In the light of the preceding discussion, we can see that this premise focuses on the wrong issue. The important task is to help addicts solve their problems, and that they take narcotics is, per se, the least of these. Also bear in mind that narcotics addiction does, in many cases, have an adaptive function just as do the symptoms of psychoneurosis, and that eliminating recourse to such symptoms without producing any more fundamental change leaves the patient in dire peril indeed. Consider, too, that addicts have been known to lead useful and relatively productive lives despite their addiction. Finally, realize that the worst consequences, by far, of addiction are entirely a result of our public policy with regard to addiction. With no access to quality-controlled drugs, the addict literally risks his life every time he takes a shot. He is compelled to move in criminal circles, giving up any normal associations he may have had. The jobs for which he is equipped cannot provide for the black-market prices. And so he is forced into a never-ending rat race with no time or energy or resources for the simplest of health measures, an adequate diet, and so on.

Defining addiction legally as a disease, as has recently happened in New York State, is no solution because, as I have already suggested, this definition turns out to be a euphemism for the term crime, since the addict is locked up, albeit in a hospital rather than in a jail, without any regard to the question of whether he can benefit from such treatment. Alternatively, since the hospitals cannot cope with the most seriously involved drug users, they tend, in practice, to define as sick only the least seriously involved drug users and leave the rest to continue as criminals.

I believe that if we can do nothing better for the addict, the least we can do for him is to provide him with quality-controlled drugs at inexpensive prices—all that he needs to give him an illusion of contentment, not merely all that he needs to stave off the symptoms of withdrawal. However, I am not advocating simply abandoning individuals to narcotics without even trying to give them something better. I would hope that this would be a recourse of last resort, but this recourse should be available until we can do something better. Obviously it should be a medical matter of individual diagnosis and experience with the individual patient whether to provide drugs in the course of a program of rehabilitation. No legislature, judge, district attorney, or police officer has the competence to prescribe a line of treatment for a given patient—to say nothing of indiscriminately prescribing a line of treatment for all patients.

Hence, to the final premise—that, given the fact of addiction, all other factors which distinguish one addict from another fade into insignificance. There are many facts, which time will not permit me to review, that point to the existence of different kinds of addicts. The etiologies of these different varieties of addiction are probably different, and the therapeutic considerations are undoubtedly different. One would also expect to find some personality differences between them. I have, for instance, not mentioned passive-dependent personalities as a common feature of addiction-personality organization, but that is because I think that dependency takes rather different forms in the various types of addiction.

Apart from familiar diagnostic differences among addicts (e.g., schizoid vs. psychopathic personalities), sex differences, socioeconomic differences, and various demographic differences—all of which are relevant—the evidence seems to point to four major varieties of narcotic addiction. But, before outlining these varieties, we must refer to certain concepts which help to differentiate them.

There is the fact of *craving*, that is, needing the drug for its direct psychopharmacologic effects in the experience of the "high" and the relief of anxiety, tension, and pain. Craving is basically independent of the state of physiologic dependence. It is related to psychic tension. Many a hospitalized patient, for instance, long since detoxified, experiences no craving in the ordered routines of hospital life but experiences intense craving upon release.

There is the fact of personal *involvement* in the activities of procuring drugs, in the personal relationships, in the rituals of taking narcotics, etc. My notion of involvement is obviously related to Wikler's notion of hustling as a secondary reinforcer and to Lindesmith's notion of personal identification with the addict subculture, but there are also differences. I think of the role of personal involvement in connection with narcotics as an effort to fill a void, to find a place for oneself in the world, and to find something to which one can experience some sense of commitment.

Finally, I want to point to the fact that, under existing conditions, taking narcotics offers another form of being delinquent, of thumbing one's nose at the respectable elements of society.

Here are the four types of addicts:

1. There are addicts strongly influenced by craving but with relatively little personal involvement. That is, their addiction is rooted in the direct psychopharmacologic effects of the drug.

2. There are addicts strongly influenced by personal involvement but with relatively little craving. That is, they have no strong need for the direct psychopharmacologic effects of the drug and are, for instance, little affected by the tolerance that they develop.

3. There are addicts with both strong craving and personal involvement.

4. There are, finally, addicts with neither strong craving nor personal involvement—individuals with frequently repeated histories of personal dependency. This group includes individuals who are simply unable to resist the pressures of their immediate environment, perhaps because they must prove to themselves that they are not "chicken" or because they must win the approval of the only other persons who will accept them; but, in the main, I think it is made up of those who thumb their noses at society. It is noteworthy, perhaps, that my colleagues and I could not find male delinquents, aged 16 through 19, in the highest-drug-use neighborhoods who did not also have a history of drug use.

And, of course, there are the nonaddict users, from those who take an occasional fling to the weekend party users who rarely, if ever, develop any high degree of physiologic dependency. The simple fact of occasional dependency, with long intervals between occasions, does not seem to be sufficient to define an addict. In fact, I believe that only the first and third types should be thought of as *true addicts;* that is, *craving* must be an essential characteristic of *true addiction*. To this, one must add that available evidence indicates that the majority of users are not true addicts but are of the second and fourth types.

From the foregoing it can be questioned whether the law can define a treatment policy for all addicts. The inescapable conclusion is that the law should get out of the business of treating addiction and that those who are competent to do so be allowed and given the necessary resources to get to work in the diagnosis and treatment of addicts, without hindrances, qualifications, and restrictions other than those contained in existing codes of professional ethics.

REFERENCES

1. The data described in this paper are presented and discussed in detail, as is much of the argument, in Chein, I., Gerard, D. L., Lee, R. S., and Rosenfeld, E., with the collaboration of Daniel M. Wilner: "The Road to H: Narcotics, Delinquency, and Social Policy," Basic Books, Inc., Publishers, New York, 1964.

2. This "progress" presumably refers to the redefinition of addiction as a disease and the increasing interest in civil, rather than criminal, commitment. Not only can the attitudes underlying such progress be seriously questioned, but also I do not believe that gross exaggeration of the magnitude of the problem before us offers an effective means of mobilizing support for remedial measures. All that the gross exaggeration accomplishes is to make the problem look insurmountable and to misdirect attention from the kinds of remedial measures that are needed.

3. Kolb, L., and Du Mez, A. G.: The Prevalence and Trend of Drug Addiction in the United States and Factors Influencing It, *Public Health Rept., U.S.*, 39: 1179 (1924).

4. The major basis on which Kolb and Du Mez arrived at their estimate was to divide the total amount of available opium by an estimated average daily intake by an addict, and *without any allowance for the opium used in medical practice or for export*. Moreover, the average daily intake was set at only 40 per cent of the consumption of an *average* addict if the latter were "allowed to fully satisfy his appetite." The latter, in turn, would be consuming only about three-eighths as much as an addict like De Quincy. To get to the Kolb and Du Mez daily dose of 6 grains of

rphine or heroin (admitted by them to be "an amount considerably smaller than that shown by the clinics"), one of their "average" addicts fully satisfying his appetite would have to be counterbalanced by, say, three addicts averaging only 3 grains; and one De Quincy would have to be counterbalanced by more than 11 three-grainers. In other words, even if the Kolb and Du Mez "addicts" were the only users of opiates in the country, the great majority of them must have been at very low intake levels, indeed.

5. Coyle, Joseph L.: The Illicit Narcotics Problem, *N. Y. Med.*, 14: 526 (1958).

6. U. S. Treasury Department, Bureau of Narcotics: Prevention and Control of Narcotic Addiction, 1960; Winick, C.: Maturing Out of Narcotic Addiction, *Bull. Narcotics, U.N. Dep. Social Affairs*, 14:1 (1962); Winick, C.: The 35 to 40 Age Dropoff, in *Proceedings, White House Conference on Narcotic and Drug Abuse*, Washington, 1962, p. 153.

7. See, for instance, Lasagna, L., Von Felsinger, J. M., and Beecher, H. K.: Drug Induced Mood Changes in Man, *J. Am. Med. Assoc.*, 157:1006, 1113 (1955).

8. What follows is a brief description of several studies in which I have participated and which are described in Chein, Gerard, Lee, and Rosenfeld: *op. cit.*

9. This procedure leads to an underestimation of the correlation that would have been obtained if we had used all of the tracts in the three boroughs.

10. See especially, Gerard, D. L., and Kornetsky, C.: Adolescent Opiate Addiction: A Study of Control and Addict Subjects, *Psychiat. Quart.*, 24:457 (1955).

Alfred R. Lindesmith | **8**

PROBLEMS IN THE SOCIAL
PSYCHOLOGY OF ADDICTION

I SHALL BE CONCERNED in this paper with problems that arise in
the search for a general theory concerning addiction to opiate-
type drugs. There are, of course, phenomena of different sorts
involved in addiction, and they are appropriately dealt with by
various specialties. Since much dispute and misunderstanding in
this area stems from the multidisciplinary nature of the total problem and a diversity of methodological assumptions, I shall try to
state explicitly those assumptions which will be basic in the subsequent discussion. It should be noted that because I will be concerned only with matters that seem relevant to the development
of a general theory at the level of social psychology, and because
of limitations of space and time, many aspects of addiction will
necessarily be slighted or omitted entirely. This in no way implies
that these aspects are regarded as of no importance or that they
may not be of central importance to someone asking other kinds
of questions.

One could, I think, frequently predict in advance what kind
of theory of addiction will be proposed by a given investigator
from knowledge of his training and intellectual background, for
each tends to find in the phenomena confirmation of the general

theories of human behavior which he brings with him to the study. Insofar as this is true, it implies that theories of addiction are based upon something other than the facts of addiction. If the data serve only to confirm diverse preexisting convictions, the resulting controversy is likely to be a noisy and futile interdisciplinary squabble not conducive to the convergence of professional opinion, which is essential to scientific progress.

On the assumption that such controversy would be more productive if disputing theorists explicitly stated what their basic methodological assumptions are, I shall state four which are basic to the remarks on the addiction problem made here: (1) Addiction must first of all be defined so that we know what we are talking about and, ideally, so that we can sort all persons into two contrasting categories, addicts and nonaddicts, with a small additional number who are in a state of transition from one category to the other. (2) A definition of addiction as a behavioral phenomenon is not an arbitrary matter which each investigator can make to suit his own tastes, but should rather be the result of an investigative process which specifies what the essential or common aspects of the behavior in fact are. (3) A general theory of addiction must be applicable to all the cases covered by the definition, not merely to some or most of them or, what is worse, merely to those that a given researcher happens to be interested in. (4) An acceptable general theory should be falsifiable; i.e., it should suggest or imply the nature and possible source of the empirical evidence which will definitely discredit or disprove it if it is false.

Of course, it is one thing to affirm these principles and another to apply them in the study of complex human behavior. Nevertheless, when a theorist makes his assumptions explicit, the critic is in a position of knowing whether he should discuss the evidence or concern himself with the theorist's conceptions of scientific method and logic.

DEFINITION OF ADDICTION

There is actually considerable confusion about the definition of addiction. There are, for example, some who equate it with physical dependence and tolerance. Although this condition is indispensable in the origin of addiction and although it is highly important that it be investigated and explained, addiction as a behavioral phenomenon cannot be defined in terms of it alone if one accepts the previously stated methodological principles. If physical dependence is equated with addiction, no specific unitary form of behavior has been identified; for the definition would extend to lower animals, to infants born of drug-using mothers, and to unconscious patients receiving drugs without their knowledge, and it would not cover addicts who are forced to abstain from using drugs solely because of incarceration or who do so voluntarily.

I recall a discussion with an investigator who held the common view that addiction arises from defects of personality but also insisted that lower animals, even decorticate dogs, that are given morphine become addicts. To maintain both of these views, one would also be logically required to attribute the addiction of the dogs to personality defects. Other writers have concluded, also inappropriately, that, because lower animals and newborn infants can be addicts (as defined by them), addiction has nothing whatever to do with personality, motivations, beliefs, and so on, and is purely a biological matter.

Additional problems are indicated by the various terms applied to persons who have been addicted but are not currently using drugs, either because they are locked up or because they are voluntarily abstaining. The former are ordinarily called addicts, but sometimes they are not. Those who are voluntarily abstaining may be called "former addicts," "nonaddicts," "postaddicts," or simply "addicts who are not using drugs." If a person is declared to be an addict even though he is not using drugs, an adequate behavioral definition must cover the situation and be equally applicable to addicts who are using drugs and to those who are not.

A further problem is that of defining a "cured addict." The World Health Organization has proposed a definition, often cited, which includes the following: "Drug addiction is a state of periodic or chronic intoxication, detrimental to the individual and to so-

ciety, produced by the repeated consumption of a drug. . . ." Apart
from the question of whether it is correct to say that a heroin
addict is in a state of intoxication, this definition suggests that if
the regular use of an opiate has effects which are not demonstra-
bly detrimental to the individual or the society, such a person
would not be an addict. There are many studies which have made
the point that there are addicts in whom detrimental effects appear to be absent or minimal and that there are some in whom the
effects appear to be beneficial.[6,7,17,18,29,30] Addicts of the latter
sort might be former alcoholics, persons with certain types of
mental disease, certain sex offenders and violent criminals, and
addicted persons receiving drugs medically for the alleviation of
pain. It is inappropriate that a scientific definition include a mor-
alistic judgment such as that implied by the word "detrimental."

My inclination is to regard that behavior designated as the
"craving" for drugs as the central and defining feature of addiction
and to think of the tendency to relapse and of other commonly
emphasized features as corollary aspects. From this standpoint a
person does not need to be using drugs to be an addict and he
might be physically dependent upon them without being addicted.
Those who have experimented with the lower animals generally
assert that the characteristic craving for drugs in human addicts
cannot be induced in lower species.[9]

The most difficult problem posed by this kind of definition is to
identify the craving for drugs in the nonusing addict who is voluntarily abstaining or locked up in an institution where drugs are
not available. Abstaining addicts frequently assert with evident
sincerity their intention never to use drugs again, and they may
also deny that they feel a desire to use them. Nevertheless, such
persons do relapse. It is commonly believed that, given the appropriate circumstances and temptations, almost anyone who has
been "hooked" will resume his habit. This suggests that the im-
pulse to relapse exists in a latent or unconscious form, which the
person himself often does not recognize. Another possibility is
that the craving of the nonusing addict is partly based upon cognitive factors, i.e., upon knowledge gained from experiencing the
drug's effects. The person who has been "hooked" might be com-

pared with one who has had his first sex experience; both have learned things which it will be exceedingly difficult for them ever to forget, even if they do not repeat the experience.

In characterizing the behavior of addicts for the purposes of developing a general theory, it is necessary to avoid taking any particular limited historical aspect as representative of the total picture. For example, during the long history of opium use it was first used orally for thousands of years; later it began to be smoked. Also opium has been used in all social classes and in an extremely wide range of contexts. Morphine addiction dates only from the beginning, and hypodermic addiction from about the middle, of the nineteenth century. Intravenous injection of heroin is exclusively a twentieth-century phenomenon. Allowance must be made for all of these variations. If this is not done, theories are likely to be based on passing contemporary fads. We need to remember that, although hipsters and adolescent delinquents are frequently addicted in our contemporary society, they were not during most of the previous century [12] and are not in most other Western nations. The emphasis on addiction in the underworld needs to be balanced by a consideration of the fact that the most persistent ecological feature of addiction rates in the Western world has been the high prevalence of addiction in the medical profession and its ancillary professions.

THE EFFECTS OF OPIATES

For one who wishes to learn of the effects of an opiate-type drug as perceived by the user, there are only two primary sources of data: One must either talk with and observe someone who uses it, or one must oneself use the drug. The former method is generally preferred, and the latter carefully avoided, even by those who hold to theories which imply that they would not become addicted. Considering that this leaves the addict as the main source of information, there is an astonishing disregard and even lack of interest in what he has to say. The addict is said to be unreliable, a pathologic liar, and prone to rationalize, and it is therefore assumed permissible for a given writer to attribute effects to the drug which the users deny experiencing.

The assessment of the drug's psychologic and other effects is a matter of central importance to theory, for every theory rests upon some sort of assumption of what the essential effects are. The matter is confused by a number of factors which are peculiar to opiate-type drugs but which are not operative in the case of alcohol or marihuana, or at least not to the same extent. In the first place, the "hopped-up dope fiend" in the throes of uncanny psychologic experiences is a popular stereotype, which, by frequent repetition, has acquired a certain authority. Then, too, the effects of regular doses over a period of time change so that the effects upon the addict are not comparable with those upon the beginner. Effects also vary from person to person; they vary according to social context; and they differ with different methods of administration. Finally, distinctions must be made between impact effects immediately following an injection and subsequent effects, and one must discriminate between those which may be regarded as part of the pharmacology of the situation and those which are psychogenic in origin in the sense that they arise from such factors as the addict's craving, his knowledge of what he is taking, and other similar influences.

Perhaps one of the most interesting features of the effects of drugs is the marked differences at all stages of drug use between the reports of addicts and those of nonaddicts or persons who do not know what they are receiving. It has been observed, for example, that when nonaddicts were given small injections of heroin or placebos without knowing which, those who received the placebos reported somewhat greater pleasurable effects than those who took heroin.[3] Isbell has observed that effects generally perceived as unpleasant by the uninitiated, when the drug is first used, are valued positively by the addict who has learned to regard them as evidence of the potency of the shot.[16] The hospital patient receiving regular morphine injections without being addicted makes reports on the drug's effects which bear little resemblance to those that addicts make and shows, in contrast to the latter, relatively little need for increased doses after a certain minimal level is reached.

In general, one may say that many of the perceived or reported effects of drugs upon addicts are not so much effects of the drug as they are of the user's craving for drugs. Although it is true that the addict craves drugs because he likes the effects, there is also truth in the statement that he likes the effects because he craves the drug. Future research with the use of placebo techniques may well unravel some of these matters which presently seem paradoxical. There is reasonably reliable evidence at hand to indicate, for example, that addicts can be deceived into believing that they are under the influence of drugs when in fact they are not and that they are not under the influence of drugs when in fact they are.[7,25] This assertion does not apply to intravenous injection or to the addict suffering acute withdrawal distress. However, it appears that if the method of intake is changed, say, from intravenous to oral use, and control of the dose is taken away from the user, he is likely to complain that he cannot feel the effects and under certain conditions may reach the conclusion that he is not receiving drugs, and he may then even exhibit withdrawal symptoms.

Shortly after the Second World War it was thought for a time that a new form of heroin addiction which did not involve withdrawal distress had been discovered. What had actually happened was that the drugs were being so heavily diluted that some addicts, without their knowing it, had been virtually taken off drugs by the peddlers and were using primarily sugar of milk flavored with a little quinine. Mr. Harry J. Anslinger has provided an interesting account of a prominent lady of Washington society, a personal friend of his, who was addicted to Demerol and who was successfully taken off drugs by means of a gradual ambulatory withdrawal without her realizing it.[1]

Chopra has reported from India on a device employed by him which involved administering opiates to addicts, who failed to recognize the effects.[7] The device was used to distinguish patients with genuine medical complaints from addicts who came to the hospital faking symptoms in order to be given opiates. Chopra prepared a tonic, called "tonic X," which had opium, disguised in taste and smell, as its essential ingredient. Persons who complained of symptoms for which opiates were customarily given were provided with this tonic, and it was found that the malingering addicts invariably betrayed themselves by denying that they felt any relief.

Some of the difficulties involved in accepting the popular conception that addicts use drugs to obtain an ecstatic sense of euphoria may be illustrated in the statement of an addict published in December, 1917, in *American Medicine*. The author, whose identity was known to the editor and whose good faith was vouched for by him, was a prominent member of the New York Bar. After relating that he had been given morphine for nearly a year by his physician to relieve attacks of gallstones and gallbladder inflammation, the author described his inability to get along without drugs and commented as follows:

> I have since then kept my daily amount of morphine medication at a minimum which permitted me to work and maintain good health and bodily function. The idea which I have heard so often expressed, that addicts tend to increase their daily intake of narcotic, is certainly untrue in my case, and there seems to me no reason nor temptation to do so. . . . As I have never experienced the slightest pleasurable or sensually enjoyable sensations from the administration of morphine, there seems to me no foundation for this prevalent idea of tendency to increase. It may be true of the degenerate who has become addicted, but it certainly is untrue in my case, and must be untrue of the thousands like me. . . ." [4,11,22]

Reports of this sort are not uncommon from persons who do not use the drug intravenously, who are not members of the underworld subculture of users, and who become addicted through therapeutic use. If one also considers that the addicted individual commonly reports upon a great many unpleasant effects associated with addiction, such as those of anxiety, fear, remorse, and guilt, as well as various painful physical effects, the pleasure theory seems wholly inadequate. [24,29]

An additional inconsistency of the pleasure theory is indicated by the fact that marihuana seems greatly superior to opium as a pleasure-producing agent; its pleasures do not fade as do those of opium with continued use; its psychologic effects are described with enthusiasm and hyperbole; its pleasurable effects are not counterbalanced by the extensive evil social and physical consequences which ordinarily bedevil heroin addicts. If pleasure is the key, marihuana should be the prime drug of addiction, far ahead of either opium or alcohol.

It appears that perhaps the only generalization about the effects of an opiate upon addicts that one can make with relatively complete assurance is that this drug, regardless of any other circumstances, does relieve the pains of withdrawal.

If addicts are readily available as subjects, various types of experiments suggest themselves which might help to discriminate between various aspects and phases of the psychologic effects of opiates. For example, drugs and placebos might be administered by oral route, by subcutaneous injection, by intravenous injection, and perhaps by means of suppositories,[28] to groups of addicts under circumstances which would indicate what the possibilities of deceiving the addict are and how his perceptions of effects are altered by knowledge of what he is getting. We might thus be enabled to distinguish more sharply between the essential effects of the drug and those that are peculiar to a specific mode of use. Systematic observations on the perceived effects by nonaddicted hospital patients who receive the drug regularly would also be of great value for comparative purposes.

THE MOTIVES OF ADDICTS

The motives for using opiate-type drugs which addicts report or which are attributed to them by others are legion, and it is probably impossible to make any simple kind of generalization about them or to find any particular motive or set of motives that can be ascribed to all addicts. The situation is complicated by the fact that the motives for first use characteristically differ from those for continued use to the point of physical dependence, that motives for use after dependence is established are not the same as those at earlier stages, and that motives for relapse have their own characteristics. Writers in this field commonly fail to distinguish between the various stages and often seize upon a single type of motive common at some point in the process among addicts of a particular group or type, project it into all phases, and hail it as the essential motive of all addicts.

The social psychologist, who is committed to the idea that an explanation of the behavior of addicts must be sought in motives, has to contend with the fact that many persons have become addicted without ever themselves taking drugs voluntarily. This still occurs now and then in the course of medical practice, and during the nineteenth century it happened more frequently than now. Few, if any, substances have been used for more purposes in medicine than has opium, which was a prime therapeutic agent for more than 2,000 years. During these centuries there were undoubtedly millions of persons who became addicted as a simple consequence of following the instructions of a physician and many others who became addicted by having the drug administered to them without being consulted or instructed in the matter. It has been suggested that addicts of this sort should, in all fairness to them, not be called addicts (Ref. 2, p. 40), and of course it would be a great advantage to a psychologic theory of addiction if convincing rationalizations could be found for ignoring these cases.

The initial trial of opiates among those who use drugs voluntarily commonly occurs in our society as a result of such motives as the desire to have thrills, to satisfy curiosity, and to do what others are doing; sometimes, no doubt, using opiates is also a gesture of defiance, rebellion, protest, or despair. In other cultures, depending upon the popular beliefs and fads of the time, opium has been used for religious purposes, as an aphrodisiac to prolong sexual pleasure by delaying the orgasm, to restore fertility or cure impotence, to relieve fatigue or the tedium of old age, as a popular remedy for countless diseases, and simply as a matter of social custom. Opium smoking appeared as a passing fad in a relatively elite section of the American underworld during the late nineteenth and early twentieth centuries. Preoccupation with drugs, including heroin, emerged as a fad during this century among persons variously designated as "hipsters," "cool cats," "beats," and so on.[12] Drug-using fads have also appeared in the upper classes, for example, among intellectuals and literati.

Whatever the motives for initial use may be, they tend to change with continued use because the effects of the drug change, but initial motives may also persist until addiction is established. Sometimes, persons who have begun to use drugs will abandon their use before they become addicted. After physical dependence is established, new motives commonly appear; the most important of these are avoidance, postponement, or alleviation of the pain of withdrawal. But again, not all of those who become physically dependent upon drugs become addicts.

The motives attributed to addicts are often thought to be linked with the effects of the drug, although this is not necessarily the case; for the drug may be used to the point of addiction for the sake of an effect which it does not in fact produce as, for example, when it is used to restore fertility or sexual potency. In most theories it is assumed that the motivations of the user are based upon the euphoric effect. Since this effect tends to be greatly reduced or eliminated when physical dependence is established, and is, moreover, heavily counteracted by many dysphoric or unpleasant effects, it is difficult to see how this position can be maintained.

If one considers the variety of social contexts in which opiates have been and are being used, it seems necessary to admit that there are many paths that lead to addiction and that there is no motive or set of motives which can be said to be characteristic of all addicts. Certainly no general motivational theory can be based on a particular group of addicts using drugs in a certain way and in a specific social context without taking into account the multitudinous other patterns that are known.

A new and popular idea in sociologic circles has been developed in recent years from the study of young, urban, delinquent male addicts in this country. It is that addiction and other forms of deviance arise from what is called "anomie." This term is taken to refer to the discrepancy between such culturally indoctrinated goals as that of achieving success and status and the perceived or available means of reaching such goals. The inner conflict or frustration that results is thought to exert pressure upon the individual to resort to some sort of adaptive device to relieve tension. Addiction is conceived of as one such device by which the person escapes his problem by renouncing society's goals as well as the established norms for attaining them. The addict, in short, is said to be a "retreatist," who solves his problems by withdrawing from them into a quasi-private world dominated by the self-contained "kick" of the heroin fix. Cloward and Ohlin have elaborated on this view by suggesting that the persons who are double failures, that is, in both the legitimate and the criminal worlds, are those who tend to become addicts.[8]

Although it is not clear whether Cloward and Ohlin regarded their hypothesis merely as a special theory for some adolescent drug-using gang members in contemporary America or as a general theory of addiction, there is clearly some disposition to regard it as the latter. As such, it is inapplicable to addiction in the medical profession, to the opium smokers of the nineteenth century, and to addiction arising from the popular or medical-therapeutic use of opiates. It also is inapplicable to addicts who are successful criminals, whatever that may mean. It is well known that most addicted thieves in this country, like most nonaddicted thieves, are of the petty variety, who might be called failures. However, there are also numerous exceptional addicted shoplifters, pickpockets, con men, and others who have extraordinary criminal competence. Some of these, it is thought, may owe some of their success to the fact of their addiction, which provides them with extraordinary motivation to practice their skills. In the legitimate world also, highly successful and even eminent persons become addicted, and some of these retain their eminence, their occupations, and their social positions while they are addicts. Although there are admittedly few such cases, their theoretical significance is not diminished by their limited numbers.

The conception of the addict as a "retreatist" is also inaccurate, for the newly addicted individual quickly discovers that the demands of his habit, especially the economic ones, force him to attach more, rather than less, significance to monetary success and put him into an extraordinarily active and abrasive contact with society. De Quincey stated the matter as follows:

> The opium-eater loses none of his moral sensibilities or aspirations; he wishes and longs as earnestly as ever to realize what he believes possible, and feels to be exacted by duty; but his intellectual apprehen-

sion of what is possible infinitely outruns his power, not of execution only, but even of power to attempt.[10]

This statement contradicts the anomie theory of addiction, for it affirms as a consequence of addiction what the theory takes as a cause or antecedent.

The fact of illegality is a matter of the greatest importance in determining the nature of the drug problem, the ecology of addiction, and the motives for which drugs are used. The consequences that follow from legal definitions and practices need to be examined in greater depth than has thus far been done. One obvious consequence is to create a synthetic association between addiction and criminality. Another is to create a pattern of availability of drugs which not only makes them accessible to, but almost literally thrusts them upon the attention of, the underworld. The correspondence between addiction in the medical profession and the slums is not to be found in the area of motivation and personality but rather in the availability of narcotics.

THE ADDICTION-PRONE PERSONALITY

The way in which personality types said to be predisposed to addiction are characterized appears to depend strongly on the nature of the investigator's specific experiences with addicts and upon his intellectual training and orientation. In this respect there has been little material change since 1928, when Terry and Pellens made the following observations:

> The evidence submitted in support of such statements, in practically every instance coming under our notice, has been secured *after* the development of the addiction and was not based on knowledge of the individual's condition *prior* to addiction. . . . It may be said with equal truth, considering the claims of those who state that certain types of individuals comprise the bulk of chronic opium users, that for one reason or another in the writings of many, "types" as generally understood are not considered as such until extraneous circumstances, possibly even the use of the drug itself, have altered the individual or group in question. . . . Wherever the truth may lie, the evidence submitted in support of the statements appearing in this chapter dealing with type predisposition and with the effects of opium on mental and ethical characteristics is, in our opinion, insufficient to warrant the

opinions expressed. . . . In general, however, it would appear from the data submitted that this condition is not restricted to any social, economic, mental or other group; that there is no type which may be called the habitual user of opium, but that all types are acually or potentially users (Ref. 27, pp. 514–16).

The direct and indirect consequences of addiction have still not been sorted out, and there is much confusion between the antecedents and consequences of addiction. The legal-system process by which the addict is exposed, arrested, and processed itself has tremendous effects upon personality and motivation and tends to make all addicts look somewhat alike. Investigators are strongly disposed to project the apparent postaddiction similarities of addicts upon the person prior to addiction and have long engaged in what may well be a futile search for the addiction-prone personality type.

In addition to considering the effects of institutionalization upon addicts, one must also consider its effects upon investigators. The institutionalized researcher or observer who is accustomed to handling inmates in an authoritarian setting tends to assign certain types of traits to those over whom he exercises power. He is in a unique position to note the recalcitrance of inmates who do not respond as it is thought they should to the benevolent and well-intentioned programs imposed upon them. By long familiarity with institutional life he sometimes comes to attach little significance to the loss of liberty by others, and he may have difficulty in understanding why addicts seem not to understand or appreciate that they are being locked up for their own good.

There is substantial political and sociologic literature on the effects of power both upon those who govern and those who are governed. A particularly relevant portion of this literature analyzes "total institutions," of which the prison is an example.

Goffman has observed that the staff of such an establishment ". . . tends to evolve what may be thought of as a *theory of human nature*. As an implicit part of institutional perspective, this theory rationalizes the scene, provides a subtle means of maintaining social distance from inmates and a stereotyped view of them, and gives sanction to the treatment accorded them." [14] Staff stereotypes of the inmates are consensually validated in private conversation between staff members and by feedback from indoctrinated inmates and sycophants who have learned the staff vocabulary. There is no better illustration of this point than Marie Nyswander's candid description of the changes in her attitudes toward addicts which occurred when she left Lexington and began dealing with them in private medical practice.[23]

The prison inmate, Goffman observes, feels mortified, humiliated, and threatened by the impersonal routine and petty requirements of institutional life. He is stripped of his autonomy and his possessions, his privacy and identity are violated, and he feels reduced to almost childlike dependence on his captors. As Sykes has remarked, "In a very fundamental sense, a man perpetually locked up in a cage is no longer a man at all; rather, he is a semi-human organism with a number. The identity of the individual, both to himself and to others, is largely compounded of the web of symbolic communications by which he is linked to the external world." [26]

An astonishing variety of terms have been employed in the attempt to characterize the addict, particular types of addicts, and the addiction-prone personality, usually with the assumption that the attribute named has some etiologic significance. From a small segment of the literature the following examples have been gleaned: "aliented," "frustrated," "passive psychopath," "aggressive psychopath," "emotionally unstable," "nomadic," "inebriate," "narcissistic," "dependent," "sociopath," "hedonistic," "childlike," "paranoid," "rebellious," "hostile," "infantile," "neurotic," "over-attached to the mother," "retreatist," "cyclothymic," "constitutionally immoral," "hysterical," "neurasthenic," "hereditarily neuropathic," "weak character and will," "lack of moral sense," "self-indulgent," "introspective," "extroverted," "self-conscious," "motivational immaturity," "pseudo-psychopathic delinquent," and, finally, "essentially normal." [2,27]

It is of interest to observe that in this list opposite traits are sometimes mentioned; that most of the same terms are applied to other groups, such as alcoholics, prisoners, tramps, sex offenders, and thieves; that almost all these descriptions are based on observations of addicts in captivity or on secondhand reports of such observations; that many of the alleged attributes are clearly effects or integral aspects of addiction, rather than antecedents, and that all of them are poorly defined concepts, frequently used simply as expressions of disapproval. The very multiplicity of these characterizations is scientifically embarrassing, and their number is increasing.

The process of evaluating the addict's personality is usually one that involves interaction or a series of transactions between two parties, each of whom inevitably evaluates the other. Just as there tends to be a staff stereotype of inmates, so also are there inmate stereotypes of the staff, and both of these, and the situation which gives rise to them, ought to be known if one wishes to give an objective evaluation. Like inmates, investigators also have personality needs, peculiarities, emotional problems, and other personal attributes which are likely to influence the judgments they make of incarcerated deviants as heavily stigmatized as drug addicts are. That psychodynamic and cultural factors influence evaluations of addicts' personalities is strongly suggested by the persistence with which even tough-minded investigators use appellations which lack any semblance of objective or operational definition. Whenever general intuitive evaluations are replaced by specific objective tests accompanied by the use of adequate control populations, the alleged special attributes of addicts either disappear entirely or are found both among addicts and nonaddicts, with a somewhat greater frequency in one group than in the other.[13]

A GENERAL THEORY OF ADDICTION

Instead of asking "What are the motives for using drugs?" I have approached the matter in another way by, in effect, rephrasing the question to read, "What is the experience in which the craving for drugs is produced?" The latter question does not inquire into motives and cannot be answered in terms of them. The suggestion which I made in 1947 as an answer to this question was that the characteristic craving of the opiate addict is generated in the repetition of the experience of using drugs to relieve withdrawal distress, provided that this distress is properly understood by the user.[20,21] The essential idea involved was not original with me but may be found in the literature, although without elaboration (Ref. 27, pp. 601–2).

I feel that the strength of this position has increased. The attempt to account for addiction in terms of an addiction-prone personality type or in terms of the euphoric effects of drugs seems more inadequate and confused than ever now that more investigators have entered the field. It seems especially remarkable to me that Wikler, from a very different background and basic orientation, has recently suggested a theory which seems to be very similar in many essential respects to mine.[24] In the study of alcoholism there are also some signs of a significant convergence of interest on withdrawal symptoms as a matter of critical significance.

The position that I have proposed has been misinterpreted in a number of ways. For example, some have interpreted it to mean that a person becomes an addict when he defines himself as such; others, that addiction arises from and consists of the motive of avoiding or alleviating withdrawal distress; and still others, that an individual becomes an addict in the instant of time when he first experiences and understands withdrawal distress. Actually I did not intend to say any of these things.

The argument was that when the experience of withdrawal distress is assimilated and grasped conceptually, the individual thereafter learns to crave the drug and acquires the behavior and attitudes of the addict from the repetition of the experience. No one can be a full-fledged nonaddict in one moment of time and a full-fledged addict in the next. From the repetition of the experience, in what may be called a cognitive-conditioning process, the individual's responses to and attitudes toward the drug are established as a conceptually controlled pattern. The withdrawal distress is indispensable only in the origin of this pattern, not in its continuance. The person does not become an addict because he defines himself as one, but defines himself as an addict because he realizes that he is one. An addict does not relapse because of withdrawal distress but because of the previously established craving, which may be thought of as something like the results of conditioning in the lower animals except that it is conceptually elaborated. It is, I think, of considerable relevance to the position that abstaining addicts when placed in a position that tempts them to relapse, sometimes experience, along with a desire for drugs, some of the actual symptoms of withdrawal, indicating a basic, psychologically primitive linkage between the two phenomena. It is also pertinent to observe that the addict's anticipatory anxiety about having his drugs cut off greatly intensifies his reaction to incipient withdrawal symptoms and by the same token enhances the perceived effects of a shot.

This position has some pronounced theoretical and practical virtues. For example, it offers a ready explanation of the relatively low or absent addictive potential of a number of substances that produce considerable euphoria, such as marihuana and cocaine. By linking addiction with linguistic and conceptual processes found only in socialized human beings, it harmonizes with the fact that most of those who have administered opiate-type drugs to lower animals take the view of Dr. Maurice H. Seevers: "In any [lower] animal that we have ever studied there is no such thing as development of actual desire for continuous repetition of the drug experience." [9] The origin of addiction is attributed not to influences which are present in some instances and absent in others, but to experiences which all addicts undoubtedly have.

From the point of view of verifiability, or falsifiability, as stated at the beginning of this paper, the proposed hypothesis implies that if a randomly selected group of ordinary adults were to receive regular shots of morphine or heroin over a prolonged period of time in accordance with the other conditions specified, all of them would become addicted regardless of personality traits, character, social class, or motives.

The contrary view could conceivably be tested by a similar experiment with a previously identified group composed 50 per cent of psychopaths (or addiction-prone types) and 50 per cent of nonpsychopaths. In this view, the prediction would then presumably be that the psychopaths would become addicted and that the others would not. It is, of course, interesting to note that persons who hold to the addiction-prone-personality theory are generally very careful not to test it on themselves even when they are certain that they do not qualify as the addiction-prone type.

The view proposed by the author emphasizes the wisdom of this sort of caution and may shed some light on famous last words of persons before being addicted, to the effect that they will not become addicts because they are not the type. From this standpoint, addiction is based, not upon the initial effects of opiates, which are experienced by many persons who never become addicted and which diminish or vanish about the time physical dependence is well established, but rather upon effects which appear only after physical dependence is established. If we can agree that simple hedonistic theories which seek to account for human behavior in terms of rational assessment of pain and pleasure are unacceptable today, this also is a point in favor of the theory. The addict's craving, it is implied, is not a rational assessment or choice of any sort, but basically an irrational compulsion arising from the repetition of a sequence of experiences in a process like that which leads to a conditioned response. It is assumed that the principal difference between the consequences of the conditioning process in human beings and lower animals lies in the fact that human beings are capable of conceptual thought and language behavior, and therefore the craving is symbolically elaborated, and responses arising from it are directed or controlled by conceptual processes.

The psychologist D. O. Hebb has suggested that the human hunger for food is comparable with the hunger for opium and that both come to be controlled by conceptual processes. He observes, concerning the hunger for food: "Finally, the development of conceptual processes controlling eating makes possible an association of eating with other conceptual processes." [15]

Following this cue, it may be said that the observed effects of addiction upon personality and character follow from the indirect conceptually mediated effects which addiction has upon the person's conceptions of himself and his status in society. They assuredly cannot be attributed directly to the drug, for in that case the same effects would be found in hospital patients who receive drugs without their knowledge and in persons dying of cancer.

There is a measure of agreement here with the psychoanalytically oriented approach, which also rejects the hedonistic calculus and conceives of the craving as a basically irrational and unconscious compulsion which gets to be symbolically elaborated in very complex ways in the motivations and rationalizations of addicts.[5] There are also, of course, many points of disagreement and dissimilarity, which I will not attempt to discuss.

Finally, it should be remembered that if any given general theory of the origin of the craving for drugs could be conclusively proved, this would by no means answer all questions. Indeed, if one may judge from experience in other fields, the problems would multiply rather than diminish. There are, moreover, many important problems with respect to addiction which, although related, are analytically separate and distinct from those which have been considered here. For example, it is of the greatest importance that we know more than we do about the individual motives and the social environments conducive to the abuse of drugs; a relatively unexplored problem is that of tracing the effects of availability of drugs upon addiction rates and exploring the relationships between control policies, legal definitions, availability, and patterns of use; an area of theoretical interest is the comparison of various forms of addiction; the determination of how addicts are selected in a statistical sense from exposed populations is an important matter. And it would be of the greatest interest to examine and attempt to account for the various public attitudes toward addicts and the narcotics problem, including such matters as changing images of the addict projected by the mass media, the addict as a scapegoat, vested interests in the narcotics problem, and many other similar matters.

REFERENCES

1. Anslinger, H. J., and Oursler, Will: "The Murderers: The Shocking Story of the Narcotics Gangs," p. 175, Farrar, Straus & Cudahy, Inc., New York, 1961.
2. Ausubel, D. P.: "Drug Addiction: Physiological, Psychological, and Sociological Aspects," Random House, Inc., New York, 1958.

3. Beecher, Henry K.: "Measurement of Subjective Responses," p. 321, Oxford University Press, Fair Lawn, N.J., 1959.
4. Bishop, Ernest S.: "The Narcotic Drug Problem," p. 137, The Macmillan Company, New York, 1921.
5. Chessick, R. D., The "Pharmacogenic Orgasm" in the Drug Addict, _Arch. Gen. Psychiat._, 3:545 (1960).
6. Chopra, R. N.: The Present Position of the Opium Habit in India, _Indian J. Med. Res._, 16:389 (1928).
7. Chopra, R. N. and Bose, J. P.: Psychological Aspects of Opium Addiction, _Indian Med. Gaz._, 66:663 (1931).
8. Cloward, R. A., and Ohlin, L. E.: "Delinquency and Opportunity: A Theory of Delinquent Gangs," p. 179, The Free Press of Glencoe, New York, 1960.
9. N.Y. Academy of Medicine, Committee on Public Health Relations: "Conferences on Drug Addiction among Adolescents," p. 123, McGraw-Hill Book Company, New York, 1953.
10. De Quincey, Thomas: "Confessions of an English Opium-eater," p. 163, Mershon, New York (undated).
11. Emmerich, Otto: "Die Heilung des chronischen Morphinismus," p. 123, Berlin, 1894.
12. Finestone, H.: Cats, Kicks and Color, _Social Problems_, 5:2 (1957).
13. Gerard, D. L., and Kornetsky, C.: Adolescent Opiate Addiction: A Study of Control and Addict Subject, _Psychiat. Quart._, 24: 457–486 (1955).
14. Goffman, Erving: "On the Characteristics of Total Institutions: Staff-Inmate Relations," in D. Cressey (ed.), "The Prison," p. 78, Holt, Rinehart and Winston, Inc., New York, 1961.
15. Hebb, D. O.: "The Organization of Behavior," p. 199, John Wiley & Sons, Inc., New York, 1949.
16. Isbell, H., and White, W. M.: Clinical Characteristics of Addictions, _Am. J. Med._, 14:558 (May, 1953).
17. Kolb, Lawrence: Pleasure and Deterioration from Narcotic Addiction, _Mental Health_, 9:699 (1925).
18. Kolb, Lawrence: Drug Addiction—A Study of Some Medical Cases, _A.M.A. Arch. Neurol. Psychiat._, 16:389 (1928).
19. Kolb, Lawrence: Drug Addiction in Its Relation to Crime, _Mental Hyg._, 9:74 (1925).
20. Lindesmith, Alfred R.: "Opiate Addiction," Principia Press of Trinity University, San Antonio, Tex., 1947.
21. Lindesmith, Alfred R.: Problems and Implications of Drug Addic-

tion and Related Behavior, in "Emerging Problems in Social Psychology," The University of Oklahoma Lectures in Social Psychology, Series III, p. 249, Institute of Group Relations, University of Oklahoma, Norman, Okla., 1956.

22. Meyers, Fritz: Ueber einge seltener vorkommende Formen von Rauschgiftsucht, *Munchen. Med. Wochschr.*, 80:732 (1933).

23. Nyswander, Marie: "The Drug Addict as a Patient," p. ix, Grune and Stratton, Inc., New York, 1956.

24. *Proceedings, White House Conference on Narcotic and Drug Abuse*, Washington, Sept. 27–28, 1962, p. 150.

25. Report of the Mayor's Committee on Drug Addiction to the Honorable Richard O. Patterson, Jr., Commissioner of Correction, New York City, *Am. J. Psychiat.*, 10:433 (1930).

26. Sykes, G. M.: "The Society of Captives: A Study of a Maximum Security Prison," p. 6, Princeton University Press, Princeton, N.J., 1958.

27. Terry, C. E., and Pellens, Mildred: "The Opium Problem," The Committee on Drug Addiction with the Bureau of Social Hygiene, Inc., New York, 1928.

28. Vaille, C., and Stern, G.: Drug Addiction: Medical and Social Aspects in France, *Bull. Narcotics, U.N. Dep. Social Affairs*, 6(2):10 (1954).

29. Wikler, A.: "Opiate Addiction: Psychological and Neurophysiological Aspects in Relation to Clinical Problems," Charles C Thomas, Springfield, Ill., 1953.

30. Wolff, P.: Alcohol and Drug Addiction in Germany, *Brit. J. Inebriety*, 31(4):141 (1933).

Leslie T. Wilkins

9

SOME SOCIOLOGIC FACTORS IN DRUG-ADDICTION CONTROL

THE PURPOSE OF THIS PAPER is to attempt some explanation of differences in the present patterns of drug addiction which appear both within the United States and between the United States and the United Kingdom. I do not want to suggest that there is necessarily anything in the British system which the United States might copy. I do not claim that we in England have been particularly clever in dealing with drug addiction. Indeed, I think it is possible that the situation might change and that we in England might find ourselves with a considerable problem of drug addiction in the future. The types of "drugs" available will change as medical science develops, but this factor is not considered here.

I would like to suggest some hypotheses which, if sustained, could be helpful in a general way. If we in England have been successful in controlling drug addiction, we should seek to know what particular elements have given rise to this success, since with this knowledge we shall be able to preserve it.

The majority of students of the problem of drug addiction and its control in the United States have, at different times, expressed an interest in the claim that in England there is no real problem

140

in this area. There are some writers who have doubted this claim, and it has been suggested that the official figures do not reveal the true position.

Schur,[11] who studied the problem of drug control over a period of 2 years in England, states that there are about five hundred registered addicts. I have no reason to doubt this figure, nor to doubt the other data which he derived from various sources and has reported in his works. His descriptions of the facts as he found them do not differ from my personal experience. I have no reason to believe that the standard official publications dealing with the British system of control and our criminal statistics are biased or incorrect in any detail.

BRITISH CONTROL SYSTEMS

Drug addiction in Britain is regarded as a medical problem. Moreover, the medical profession has complete freedom to use treatment that may be considered desirable for the welfare of the patient. Very nearly the whole population is covered by, and takes advantage of, the National Health Insurance Scheme. Of course, the National Health Insurance Scheme cannot claim the credit for the control of drug traffic and addiction, because there were very few addicts before the scheme became fully operational. It is, however, possible that the future control of addiction may be assisted by the controls which now form part of the insurance system. For example, the Ministry of Health maintains a check on "excessive prescribing" by medical practitioners and sends experts to advise any really unusual cases which are observed. I may mention that this system of control covers the cost of drugs and treatments as well as other factors of medical importance.[8]

The British register of drug addicts is not based on any statutory requirement of registration. The voluntary nature of the register may be taken by some persons to suggest that it is hopelessly incomplete, but I do not think this is so. In England a number of voluntary systems are in operation and seem to work better, perhaps even in terms of completeness, than compulsory schemes.

The British police force is not a national force. Local police

forces, with the exception of the Metropolitan Police, which covers the London area, are operated by the local authorities. There
is a Conference of Chief Constables which serves as an integrating
reference for the hundred or so separate forces. The Metropolitan
Police (which is known for its location in New Scotland Yard) is,
unlike other police forces throughout the country, responsible to
the Secretary of State for Home Affairs.

The Conference of Chief Constables and other like systems of
administration may, perhaps, be termed loosely "self-regulating
systems." If officials can be persuaded that a particular policy or
operation is in the national interest, they will normally accept this
as a controlling factor in their own behavior. Enforcement by
statute is then unnecessary. The acceptance of the concept of
national interest as a regulator of official and professional behavior is used in the administration in many sectors.

It may be fair to summarize what has been called "the British
system" as a *lack of system*, one, however, that provides a powerful control. Whether it will continue to operate in that way it is
difficult to say. I think that it is a good "lack of system" to stay
with so long as it continues to work!

THE PUBLIC "IMAGE"

Although I have given a personal view of the British administrative system (or lack of system), I do not suggest that this
system is the explanation of the absence of an addiction problem
in Britain. Indeed it is my thesis that those who have been comparing different systems of drug addiction control in order to find
an explanation of the differences in addiction patterns are giving
primary importance to what may be a secondary variable. I do
not think that a simple cause-and-effect type of explanation is
adequate to discuss the problem of addiction. It is possible, even
probable, that our lack of success in scientific explanation of human behavior may lie in the fact that we have looked to simple
cause-and-effect models to provide explanations.[12]

Models based on deviation-amplifying systems have become
necessary to explain economic behavior, and it is perhaps no great
degree of originality to propose similar models to explain other

forms of satisfaction-seeking human behavior. I think that more sophisticated models are necessary, and the following postulates are an attempt to provide certain models of human behavior which in turn can help to structure our thinking about the problem of drug addiction. There are a number of postulates apparently unrelated, which are basic to the development of the argument I wish to submit. I will present these postulates singly and attempt to integrate them at the end.

My first postulate is:

People tend to behave with respect to situations and things as they perceive them to be rather than as they "actually are."
This statement is based upon the theory of perceptual processes. Since most of my subsequent arguments are based upon it, I will attempt a brief summary of this theory.

No knowledge is obtained directly. The signals we receive through our senses are "codes" which we "decode" into our experience in different ways. Perception is the process of observing, recording, and organizing the experience we have from the world around us—people and things. We do not behave with respect to things as "they are" but to things as we perceive them to be. Indeed it is doubtful that there is any meaning in discussing things "as they are." There will be measures of consensus between observers, which may conveniently be regarded as "truth," but it is safer to propose degrees of subjectivity rather than a dichotomy between subjectivity and objectivity. If, for example, you have a contemporary coffee table in your lounge, and it is perceived by a visitor to your home to be a chair or a stool (a mistake one can make with some furniture), he may well be expected to sit upon it! Differences between systems may be unimportant, even non-existent, and may be irrelevant to behavior if the important factor is the *perception of the system* and the variables with which the system is concerned.

Brill and Larimore,[1] after a visit to the United Kingdom, wrote that they were "unable to find any indication that there exists anywhere in that country the practice of medically maintaining indefinitely otherwise healthy persons on continued doses of opiates under medical supervision. . . ." It might be that the perception of the "otherwise healthy person" differs between observers. Each medical practitioner has his own views on medical matters, and these views are respected both by the administration and by the law. It is my personal view that the concept of a person being at the same time "healthy" and an "addict" would not fit very well with the British perception of "health" and "addiction." Addiction is *by definition an illness* and tends to be *perceived as such,* not only by the authorities, but also by the general population. For example, in a sample survey of 147 twenty-one-year-old persons in one London borough, the question was asked, "What should be done with drug addicts? Should they be sent to prison, put in hospital or merely left alone?" Ninety-three per cent said that they should be put into hospital, two per cent said that they should be left alone, and five per cent responded "don't know." Not a single person suggested that addicts should be put into prison. This is particularly important when it is noted that the same sample revealed half with the opinion that "prison is too good for sex criminals, they should be publicly whipped or worse." The sample may not be representative of the whole British population, but the London area would be the area where addiction would be most probable if the pattern were similar to other countries.

Brill and Larimore stated in their report: ". . . it was clear that the British practice with respect to addicts was not fundamentally different from our own, nor does the British medical view of addicts differ from our own. . . ." I assume that this lack of difference relates only to medical factors, since certainly penal treatments differ and so also does public opinion. Perhaps the *perceptual* differences explain more than the *procedural* differences. Furthermore, *public opinion* may be more important as a controlling factor than *public policy.*

For a number of years advertisers of consumer goods have realized the importance of the "public image" of their products. Even where two products are identical, the sales may differ by enormous amounts only because of the nature of the image of the product. The difference in image may seem rather unsubstantial, but perhaps the image of drug addiction in Britain explains more of the situation than the control system, although the control system may itself play a very important part in determining the nature of the image.

DRUGS AND ALCOHOL

Freeman [6] suggests that the perception of the function of alcoholic liquors differs markedly between those who subsequently become alcoholics and those who do not. One wonders what the perception of the function of drugs is when *for the first time* an addict decides to take a shot. It seems very unlikely that he would perceive himself as one taking on a most expensive habit which will have the consequences it in fact does. The reasons for initial drug use may be quite different from the reasons for continuance, and the perceived function of drugs may differ from their actual function. Explanations in terms of the actual function may be totally unsatisfactory to explain behavior which is determined by perceptual processes.

Cloward and Ohlin [2] suggest that it is the "two-time losers," those who have failed to make a success either of criminal or legitimate activities, who turn to drugs as an *escape*. But are drugs actually perceived as a means of providing an escape by the *would-be* users? The most useful question is not what function drugs fulfill, but what function they are perceived as fulfilling. Unfortunately, with a problem like addiction, it may be impossible to find out in retrospect what the initial perception of the drug user was. None the less, perceptual-process theory models may tell us a good deal.

Brill and Larimore suggest that the differences in addiction rates between Britain and the United States "may be part of a broader question in comparative psychiatry, which, for example, also indicates that rates for alcoholism and alcoholic psychosis are lower in the United Kingdom than in the United States. . . ." It is certain that the rates for alcoholism are much lower in England; how much lower it is difficult to estimate with any precision. Estimates can be derived in different ways and afford different types of comparisons. In New York State in 1959, admissions to mental hospitals for alcoholic psychosis are reported to have been 1,929, while Great Britain had only 531 with a population 2½ times that of New York State. If this is a reasonable indicator, it seems that the rate for alcoholism in Britain is about one-tenth of the rate in the United States.

The Jellinek formula, which in most countries provides a reasonable estimate of alcoholism from various other indices, has been shown not to provide good estimates for the United Kingdom. Thus it appears that the usual correlates of alcoholism do not apply in Great Britain. If alcoholism and drug addiction have anything in common, and if, as Freeman has demonstrated, the perception of alcohol differs between alcoholics and others, it also seems highly probable that the nature of the concept or image and the basis of perceptual process may afford some sort of explanation of both types of difference between Great Britain and the United States.

Merely to say that the image difference explains the differences affords no explanation at all. Merely to move the explanation from an unknown to a mirror image of an unknown does not make anything more known. It is necessary to explore further.

The second postulate is:

> *Where the* balance *between legitimate and illegitimate opportunities remains constant, the amount of crime will tend to remain proportional to the* total *opportunities.*

That is to say, the more cars in a community, the more stealing of and from cars; the more transfers of money by legitimate means (the affluent society), the more transfers of money by illegitimate means. The *balance* between legitimate and illegitimate means will be the factor determining the proportion of criminal activity.

The third postulate is related to the theory of strategy and states:

> *People do not play "expected values." (An expected value is that derived from the product of the probability and the sum involved.)*

In the cultures from which drug addicts tend to come, there will be observed other forms of behavior which indicate a poor appreciation of the "utilities" arising from any strategy, due to the distortions of the expected values.

The fourth postulate, which I shall use, states:

Definitions of deviance are made by cultures, and cultures vary in their perceptions of forms of behavior, and some definitions are vestigial traces of earlier cultural systems.

I will later give details of this summary statement.

The fifth postulate is:

Since perceptions influence behavior, the definitions (perceptions) of the culture have an influence upon the members of the culture and the subcultures as perceived and defined by the culture itself.

Finally, I wish to draw upon the well-known fact that there are self-regulating and equilibrating systems in which the simple one directional cause-to-effect relation does not provide an explanation of what is taking place. Consider the thermostat: does the temperature change cause the thermostat to move, or does the movement of the thermostat cause the temperature to change? Although the majority of feedback systems are deviation-counteracting, there are also deviation-amplifying mutual causal processes.[9] A negative feedback tends to move the system toward stability with a damping of the distorting effects, however generated, while a positive feedback tends to force the system toward instability and an increase in the distorting forces.

Postulate 2 can be supported from criminal statistical data. The criminal statistics for England and Wales for the years 1938–1961 show an almost complete correlation between the number of cars registered and the number of thefts from cars. When the number of vehicles on the roads dropped, the number of thefts dropped similarly and rose when the number of vehicles rose. It is proposed, therefore, that the balance between legitimate and illegitimate opportunities is a factor in criminal behavior. It certainly cannot be held that our moral values deteriorate and improve in strict proportion to the increases and decreases in the number of motor cars. It must be noted particularly that it is the relationship between opportunities which is stressed and not the absolute number of thefts or cars.

Postulate 3 states that people do not play expected values, and this also has the support of experimental evidence. It is a characteristic of human behavior in many fields. People have difficulty in assessing rational actions in which the probabilities of gain and loss are very small (e.g., football pool betting). Prestige gets committed, and there are all kinds of public humiliation, which tend to pressure individuals into a distorted strategy in determination of their behavior. Moreover, it is not the actual expected values which may be the determining factor, but the perception of the expected values. The risk of becoming an addict may be regarded as small, the risk of being caught may be perceived as less than it in fact is, and the tendency to fail to play even expected values may hold for distorted estimates in an amplified form.

Postulate 4 states that definitions are made by cultures, and cultures vary in their perceptions of forms of behavior. Clearly if all persons behaved in exactly the same way in *any sort* of society, then no matter what form that behavior took, none of the behavior could be defined as criminal, even though by some external standard all the behavior was criminal. A nomadic society has no difficulty within a culture which accepts the nomadic way of life, but this way of life becomes quite unacceptable to a society in which land is defined as belonging to people or organizations.

Distinctions between what is perceived as legitimate and illegitimate are made culturally and legally, and legal definitions tend to follow the cultural definitions. In general a religious society will define deviance from the religious norms as heresy, and if the deviance is perceived as sufficiently bad, some form of punishment will be prescribed. A communist society will define deviance with respect to its theoretical concept of collectivism, whereas a capitalist society will define certain other forms of economic behavior as sufficiently deviant to need the isolation of the offender from the remainder of society. All people have some idea of what they regard as deviant or "rare" events, but no one has any prior knowledge of normality. Each person has only the sum of his own experience against which to assess the unusual or deviant events and to serve as a basis for differential classification. *It is as though the human mind has a storage system linked with some classificatory and integrating device, which is used for purposes of subjective prediction of behavior in accordance with levels of expectation.*

Human actions do not divide into classifications "bad" and "good," black and white, or crime and no crime. It is possible to suppose a distribution of human actions forming a continuous function from very saintly to very sinful. There will be very few acts which will be defined as very saintly or very sinful. The majority of actions will be "normal" and within the limits tolerated by the culture. A distribution very similar to that used to describe the distribution of intelligence might suffice quite well as a model of the distribution of the ethical content of human actions.

Crimes will, at least in the main, be represented by actions at the "bad" end of the distribution. It will be obvious that the proportion of incidents which are defined as "crimes" will depend upon the point at which the tail of the distribution is truncated. There will be no doubt about the classification of actions which are extremely deviant (say, 5σ or more), but these unusual acts form a rather small proportion of the total distribution. It is possible that as societies improve, more incidents will be defined as "criminal" because more rigorous standards of conformity will be required.

It would appear that societies have, in general, been more aware of the *degree* of deviance than the *direction* of deviance. A very large proportion of the deviants perceived by the society of the time as sinners have subsequently been canonized. The deviant saint and the deviant sinner are likely to suffer a similar fate, depending upon the degree of their deviance rather than upon its nature.

Postulate 5 states that because perceptions influence behavior, the definitions made by a culture have an influence upon the behavior of members of that culture and its subcultures. In other words a feedback mechanism is proposed. Perhaps an example will make this proposition clear.

It is well recognized that the village culture, as a culture, is able to deal with and integrate members of the community who deviate widely from the norm. For example, both the village idiot and the village squire are acceptable members of the village community. If, however, the village idiot were to move into an urban environment, he would be rejected by that culture. It may be proposed, therefore, that the total range of human behavior which the village, as a system, can accommodate is greater than the range of human behavior which can be accommodated within an urban system. But although the range of behavior accommodated by the village system may be wider than that of the urban culture, each individual member of the village has a very closely specified role. It may, for example, be perceived as appropriate for the village plumber to blow the village church organ on Sunday, but quite beyond his status to aspire to play it. In the urban culture the plumber would have wider room for maneuver outside of his hours of business. Any member of the village community who, for any reason, deviates from the narrowly defined role finds his behavior interpreted and controlled by social pressures within the community.

Dentler [4] studied deviance and social controls in small Quaker work camps. The members of these groups were in close and continuous face-to-face communication. The level of communication was very much higher than that to be expected in the village culture, and, not unexpectedly, the level of integration of the members of the groups was also higher. Dentler's findings confirm the general hypothesis suggested by this theory; that is, small groups can perceive specific roles for each member, whereas large groups tend toward the perception of individuals in terms of stereotypes. Also, at one extreme, the small group actively resists any trend toward alienation of members whose behavior is deviant, whereas the larger society tends to find it necessary to reject deviants.

It will be noted that each member of a village receives some training in the sociology of the village by observation and informal "village pump politics." A form of apprenticeship in group management and social communication and control is available to all. The training may be primitive and based on folklore and a sociology at the level of anecdote interleaved with prejudice, but information about the working of the system is fed into the system, and information covers the whole system, and this information is perceived as relevant. By contrast the information available to the urban dweller as part of his experience is much restricted. The information available within the small work group, and to a lesser extent to the village culture, enables the members of these groups to make predictions of behavior over a wider range of events than does the information available to the urban resident.

Thus there are *systems* which can accommodate wider ranges of behavior than other systems. In terms of the probability calculus the value of x in $x\sigma$ differs with respect to individuals and systems. In the village x is small for individuals but larger for the system, whereas within the urban culture x is larger for individuals and smaller for the system.

FROM STATIC TO DYNAMIC MODELS

It has been noted that definitions of deviance relate to information and cultural experiences of individuals and to types of systems. It is necessary now to consider a dynamic model in which the definitions made by the culture (i.e., "power groups" or bureaucratic systems [13]) may influence the behavior of members of the culture. It is suggested that when sanctions applied by a society to its deviants are perceived by them to be extreme, the persons defined as deviants become alienated from their parent society. The rejection of an $x\sigma$ deviant, if the value of x is not large, may act as an information set modifying his own individual tolerance $x\sigma$ through his own "store," that is, his experience of the culture.

It would appear that when a society truncates its normal distribution of values at any point having a relatively small $x\sigma$ value, that act of definition will reduce the cohesiveness of the social order. Or, simply, lack of "tolerance" (in the statistical and quality-control meaning of that term) by a society for behavior which is not completely intolerable may defeat society's ends by inducing a self-definition of deviance where such a definition is not justified in terms of the social dysfunction of the behavior. There is experimental evidence for this type of positive-feedback process—a deviation-amplifying system.

Mannheim and Wilkins [7] showed that, in general, "open" borstal institutions appeared to have a lower rate of recidivism than "closed" (secure) institutions, after making full allowance for the fact that "open" institutions received lower-risk groups. It was at first thought that the difference was due to better "treatment," but later data made this interpretation improbable. Croft and Grygier,[3] using sociometric analysis in schools, found that in most classes delinquent boys were rejected by others (had more enemies), that truants were isolated (had fewer friends), and that boys rated by the teachers as behavior problems were disliked by other boys. In most cases they found that the choices on their sociometric scales tended to follow the values of the teachers; but in the classes reserved for children who were defined as "backward," the situation was different. In those classes, conforming behavior was unrelated to sociometric status. Both truants and delinquents were more popular in the "backward" classes.

Moreno and Jennings had earlier reported that in prisons and reformatories the most popular individuals tended to have had an outstanding record of antisocial activity.

Follow-up studies of children placed in different "streams" in English schools revealed a marked relative drop in the IQ scores of children placed in lower streams and a relative increase in the scores of those who at separation had the same scores but who were placed in the higher streams. The defining act provided a possibility of self-definition and had the effect of changing the "information set," or experience, of the defined groups in accordance with the nature of the definitions.

It would appear that a group which has been defined to be, or defines itself to be, cut off from the general norms develops its own norms, which tend to reveal some deviation-amplifying qualities—a centrifugal force driving away from the distribution of values from which they have themselves been rejected. This is a similar phenomenon to that noted on the stock exchange; even a rumor of bad trading leads to worse trading conditions.

It is realized that the supporting data for the postulates upon which our model is based may seem inadequate. Nonetheless the following dynamic system is proposed.

1. Certain types of information in relation to certain systems lead to more acts being defined as deviant to the extent that the

individuals so defined are "cut off" from the values of the parent system.

2. The defining act leads to more action being taken against those perceived as deviant, and the individuals so defined begin to perceive themselves as deviant. (Perhaps the main way in which one gets to know what sort of person he is, is through feedback from other people.)

3. The self-perception and the action taken by society at large leads to the isolation and alienation of the persons defined as deviant.

4. The deviant groups tend to develop their own values which may run counter to the values of the parent system which has defined them as "outlaws" (or, in terms of the probability calculus, "outliers").

5. Deviation-amplifying (centrifugal) forces thus develop within the deviant group and lead to more deviant behavior.

6. The increased deviance demonstrated by the deviant groups (resulting from a deviation-amplifying feedback system) results in more forceful action by the conforming groups against the nonconformists.

7. Thus information about the behavior of the nonconformists [6] received by the conforming groups leads to more acts being defined as deviant—and back to the first step and around and around again.

This type of model has few unfamiliar features. Indeed, it would be surprising if people who were excluded by a system were to continue to regard themselves as part of it. If this is a fair model of the system, certain deductions can then be made.

The lower classes may create defenses against middle-class value systems in which they cannot excel by setting up other value systems. Those defined as deviant will insulate themselves from value systems excluding them and establish systems which determine for them some needed structure.

If a model of this kind applies, it is not necessary to show that the individual parts have a very large effect on any detail of the system. The important feature of this type of model is that it represents an *unstable system*. Small initial differences, perhaps even due to chance variations, in the network can build up into very large forces. A number of mutual causal processes can be identified in economic behavior where the initial stimulus was extremely small and possibly randomly generated, but where the results were of very considerable importance.

AN APPLICATION TO THE DRUG-ADDICTION PROBLEM

Applying the theoretical structure proposed above to the problem of explaining the difference between drug addiction in Great Britain and in the United States, I want to propose the following:

1. The image of the use of drugs in Great Britain is different from that in the United States.

2. The image of the addict is different.

3. The image of the police is different.

4. Small differences in the control system or even the *perception* of the control system could generate large differences in the image of addiction, and this could amplify the effects of the official controls.

5. Fewer actions are defined as "crimes" in Great Britain, and as a result fewer people are in general defined as "criminal," whether in respect of social or economic deviance.

6. Certainly for drugs, the balance between legitimate and illegitimate means for obtaining them differs.

7. The "information set" (or folklore—it does not have to be true) modifies behavior.

I think that points 1, 2, and 3 will be agreed to be demonstrated as true without further support. Point 4 follows from, and is indeed the center point of, the theory. Point 5 is evident from any of the forms of criminal statistics. Point 6 may require some further explanation. It seems fairly clear that the *opportunities* for obtaining by *legitimate* means certain quantities of drugs are greater in Great Britain, whereas in the United States the *illegitimate opportunities* for obtaining drugs are greater, especially for the vulnerable social groups. It is not necessary to consider the legitimate and illegitimate opportunities in absolute terms, but only the balance between them. I think it may be said with reasonable certainty that the balance between legitimate and illegitimate opportunities differs between our two countries. If one could express the illegitimate opportunities as a percentage of all opportunities, the United States would show a higher ratio. It is at this point that I think the deviation-amplifying system may find purchase. Certainly if the balance is correctly assessed, the perception or image of drugs will be related to the image of illegitimacy in one case and the legitimacy in the other.

With regard to point 7, it may be true, as Brill suggests, that there are no procedural differences between the control system in Britain and in this country, but the existence of a different *set of beliefs* is quite sufficient to change behavior. In fact, objective differences which were *not* perceived would be unlikely to make any difference.

It is possible that the success of Britain in limiting the use of drugs to a very small percentage of the population is built upon some very slender foundations. At least, these foundations would look very slender or nonexistent from the viewpoint of a cause-to-effect model. I cannot say, however, that I am myself convinced that perceptual processes and the concept of image provide slender foundations. Advertising agents know quite well how difficult it is to change the image that the public may have formed of their products. Perhaps the difference between the problem of drug addiction in this country and in Britain is based on a phenomenon similar to that which determines what type of gas you buy for your car, or what brand of cigarettes you smoke. Perhaps these determinants are slender, but they can make extremely large differences in behavior. Some businesses prosper and some go bankrupt on less substantial differences.

Perhaps a society can effectively control only those who perceive themselves to be members of that society. And perhaps the major point of distinction between a criminal and a sick person is that the sick person can still be identified and still identify himself as within the social system, whereas by definition a criminal cannot.

REFERENCES

1. Brill, H., and Larimore, G.: Great Britain's Treatment of Drug Addiction, White House Conference Paper, Washington, D.C., 1963.
2. Cloward, R. S., and Ohlin, L. E.: Illegitimate Means and Delin-

quent Sub-cultures, "Delinquency and Opportunity," The Free Press of Glencoe, New York, 1961.

3. Croft, I. F., and Grygier, T.: Social Relationships of Truants and Juvenile Delinquents, *Human Relations,* 9:439 (1956).

4. Dentler, R. A., and Erikson, K. T.: The Function of Deviance in Groups, *Social Problems,* 7:98 (1960–61).

5. "Departmental Committee on Morphine and Heroin Addiction," H. M. Stationery Office, London, 1926.

6. Freeman, H.: Paper in preparation—private communication.

7. Mannheim, H., and Wilkins, L. T.: "Prediction Methods in Relation to Borstal Training," H. M. Stationery Office, London, 1955.

8. Martin, J. P.: "Social Aspects of Prescribing," William Heinemann, Ltd., London, 1957.

9. Maruyama, M.: The Second Cybernetics, Memo, 1962.

10. Ministry of Health: "Interdepartmental Committee on Drug Addiction," H. M. Stationery Office, London, 1961.

11. Schur, E. M.: "Narcotic Addiction in Britain and America," Indiana University Press, Bloomington, Ind., 1962.

12. After I completed this paper, my attention was drawn to a mimeographed article by Maruyama,[9] which makes this point most clearly. Referring to deviation-amplifying systems, he says, "Similar conditions may result in dissimilar products." This, as he also points out, is not in keeping with the "sacred laws of causality in the classical philosophy [which] stated that similar conditions produce similar effects." The law of causality may now be revised to state: "A small initial deviation, which is within the range of high probability, may develop into a deviation of very low probability [or more precisely, into a deviation which is very improbably within the framework of probabilistic unidirectional causality]."

13. For an explanation of this aspect of control systems see the following: Merton, R. K.: "Social Structure and Social Theory," The Free Press of Glencoe, New York, 1957.

Part 4

TREATMENT AND RELAPSE

James F. Maddux | **10**

HOSPITAL MANAGEMENT OF
THE NARCOTIC ADDICT

I N 1935 the Public Health Service Hospital at Lexington, Kentucky, was opened for treatment of persons addicted to narcotic drugs. Three years later, in 1938, the Public Health Service Hospital at Fort Worth, Texas, was opened for the same purpose. These two hospitals have been the largest centers in the world established primarily for study and treatment of narcotic addiction. Since 1935 there have been over seventy thousand admissions of addict-patients to the two hospitals.

Staff members of the Addiction Research Center, located at Lexington, and of the two hospitals have contributed substantially to the literature on narcotic addiction. The contributions include reports of clinical characteristics of addict patients,[18,21,7] classification of abstinence signs,[12] the methadon substitution method of withdrawal,[15] the discovery that morphine analgesia arises substantially from reduction of anxiety associated with pain,[10] and the abstinence-precipitating effects of N-allylnormorphine.[16] Reviews by Wikler [28,26] in 1953 and 1958 summarized the physiologic and psychologic mechanisms of action of opiates.

A paper by Lowry [20] in 1956 gave a comprehensive description of the treatment program for addicts at the Lexington hospital. Most of his remarks about program content remain generally true in 1963 not only for the Lexington program but also for the Fort Worth program. The primary change has been the development of milieu therapy. During the last decade other papers by Fraser and Grider,[8] Rayport,[24] Rasor,[23] Lewis and Osberg,[19] Blachly and others,[2] and Berliner [1] have dealt comprehensively or partially with the treatment programs at Lexington or Fort Worth.

PROCESS OF NARCOTIC ADDICTION

The clinical symptoms and physiology of addiction, and the abstinence illness, have been fully described in the literature. Wikler,[26] Wikler and Rasor,[29] Isbell,[15] and others have discussed the etiology of the addiction process. Although their formulations and emphases vary somewhat, they generally assume that addiction begins, persists, and recurs after treatment as an outcome of interacting features and events attributed to the individual, the drug, and the social and physical environment.

Drug use by individuals appears to be a response to physical pain or psychologic distress. The sources of pain or distress vary widely. Drug use may be initiated to reduce the pain associated with cardiovascular disease, rheumatoid arthritis, gallbladder disease, or other chronic physical illness. However, at the present time we see few patients who have become addicted in connection with chronic physical illness. Nearly all of them have begun using drugs to alleviate psychologic distress. These patients report anxiety, depression, and tension, occasionally accompanied by somatic equivalents of anxiety. Tension frequently seems to arise from the effort to control inner rage.

Some patients explain their drug use on the basis of positive pleasure. They report that the drug makes them feel "good" or that their goal is to experience the "kick" which occurs with intravenous injection. This led Kolb [17] in 1925 to identify a "positive euphoria," sought from morphine by psychopathic thrill seekers. The concept of positive euphoria may serve to mislead. In my observation, the addict who states that he seeks positive pleasure from narcotics suffers rather from a chronic dysphoria. This may not be conveyed to an observer on casual contact. Because tension or depression has been with him most of his life, the patient may accept affective distress as "natural." For example, a young heroin addict told me that he took the drug because it made him feel good.

I asked, "How do you mean that?"

"I liked the feeling it gave."

"Tell me about the feeling."

"It relaxed me."

"How did it relax you?"

"It relieved my worries."

"What worries?"

The patient then described long-standing feelings of insecurity, inadequacy, and helplessness. He attributed these feelings primarily to financial insecurity occurring in his broken parental family. Another patient told me that heroin stimulated him. While using the drug he felt energetic and active, and worked better. He then went on to explain that when not using drugs he felt bored, dull, and apathetic.

With the development of physical dependence, an additional source of distress, the abstinence illness, appears to cause continued drug use. The cycle of recurrent abstinence discomfort regularly relieved by the drug, together with other observations, prompted Wikler [27] to formulate a conditioning hypothesis to explain the addiction process and relapse after cure. An antisocial attitude facilitates use of the socially disapproved narcotic-drug method of reducing pain or distress. Hill [11] has recently emphasized the significance of social deviance in the etiology of addiction.

Opiates have a number of complicated effects on humans, but addicted persons seem to be seeking mainly the analgesic and so-called euphoric effects. Apparently the euphoric effect arises from reduction of anxiety, depression, and tension.

An obvious requirement for the occurrence of addiction is the availability of drugs. It is the fact of high availability which, at least in part, accounts for the great prevalence of addiction in slum areas of large cities. Prevalence of narcotic-drug use appears to be higher among physicians than among the general population. Physicians have greater access to drugs than the general population. During 1962, 1.5 per cent of admissions to the two Federal hospitals were physicians. This is about ten times the proportion of physicians in the United States population.[22]

CONTEXT OF THE PUBLIC HEALTH SERVICE HOSPITALS

The treatment programs of the two Federal hospitals are shaped by the legal, regulatory, financial, and geographical context in which they exist.

The hospitals were established primarily to treat and rehabilitate Federal prisoners addicted to narcotic drugs. They may accept voluntary patients to the extent that facilities remain available after Federal prisoners are admitted. Only persons addicted to opiates and other specified drugs are eligible for admission; persons addicted to barbiturates or alcohol cannot be admitted unless they are also addicted to a narcotic drug.

The hospitals are not supervised by the Federal Bureau of Prisons, but they operate consistently with laws and regulations governing care of Federal prisoners. Prisoners who are considered dangerous or high escape risks are not sent to the hospitals.

The hospitals are supervised by the Division of Hospitals, a part of the Bureau of Medical Services, which is one of the three operating Bureaus of the Public Health Service. The Addiction Research Center, a laboratory of the National Institute of Mental Health, is located at the Lexington hospital.

For several years, it is felt, the hospitals have been understaffed and underfinanced.

The Lexington hospital serves patients from states east of the Mississippi River, and patients from states west of the Mississippi are admitted to the Fort Worth hospital. The Fort Worth hospital does not have a unit for women addicts, who are sent to the Lexington hospital. Most of our patients, therefore, are hospitalized hundreds of miles from their families and communities, thus limiting interaction of the patient with his family and community. Although treating patients far from their home communities is contrary to contemporary concepts of psychiatric practice, I believe this provides an advantage in treatment of some patients. Many of our patients come from disorganized multiproblem families, both parental and marital, in which their emotional disorders have been developed and perpetuated. Some patients need a temporary sanctuary or refuge from provocation by disturbed family members.

The geographical distance separating our patients from their communities and the large number of communities from which our patients come have created some handicap in developing an integrated continuum of service with community agencies. Geographical distance, however, has not created the major rehabilitation problem. We have been able to obtain the willingness of community agencies to provide service for our patients. The main obstacle has been presented by the patients themselves. Most of them do not have sufficient motivation and stability to use the service of a community agency. Many need an active reaching-out service, and others need involuntary supervision. The latter is provided for prisoner patients who leave the hospital on parole, but, unfortunately, increasing numbers of our prisoner patients do not have eligibility for parole.

On June 30, 1962, the Lexington and Fort Worth hospitals had a combined total of 788 prisoner addict-patients. Of these, 301, or 38 per cent, had sentences of 5 years or longer and were not eligible for parole.

Both hospitals are located adjacent to urban communities. Staff members of the hospitals serve in many local professional and civic organizations, and both hospitals have affiliations with university medical centers. The treatment programs of the hospitals, however, require only minimal contact with local agencies.

CHARACTERISTICS OF THE ADDICT-PATIENTS

Tables 10-1 through 10-8 give the distribution of selected characteristics of addict-patients admitted to the Fort Worth and Lexington hospitals during 1962. Although 84.5 per cent (Table 10-1) of the patients admitted came voluntarily, involuntary prisoner and probationer patients make up over half of the hospital census. This occurs because the prisoner patients stay longer than the voluntary patients. Table 10-2 shows that men outnumber women about five to one. The proportions of Negroes (Table 10-3), and persons of Puerto Rican or Mexican background (Table 10-4), appear substantially higher in our admissions than in the United States population. Nearly 74 per cent or about three-fourths of our admissions were in the young-adult age range, age 20 to 39 (Table 10-5). About one-fourth of the United States population falls into this age group.[9]

At the time of admission each patient is asked to state his principal occupation during the 6 months prior to hospitalization. As shown by Table 10-6, 48.6 per cent reported themselves as unemployed, and 11.4 per cent reported their principal occu-

Table 10-1   **HOSPITAL STATUS, 1962 ADDICT ADMISSIONS**

| | | | Total | |
Status	Ft. Worth	Lexington	No.	Per cent
Voluntary	390	2,481	2,871	84.5
Prisoner and probationer.	138	390	528	15.5
Total	528	2,871	3,399	100.0

Table 10-2   **SEX, 1962 ADDICT ADMISSIONS**

| | | | Total | |
Sex	Ft. Worth	Lexington	No.	Per cent
Male	528	2,304	2,832	83.4
Female	—	563	563	16.6
Total	528	2,867 *	3,395 *	100.0

* Unknown = 4.

Table 10-3   **RACE, 1962 ADDICT ADMISSIONS**

| | | | Total | |
Race	Ft. Worth	Lexington	No.	Per cent
White	491	1,679	2,170	63.9
Negro	36	1,174	1,210	35.6
Oriental	1	12	13	0.4
American Indian.	—	2	2	0.1
Total	528	2,867 *	3,395 *	100.0

* Unknown = 4.

pation as illegal. In Table 10-7 it can be seen that 66.5 per cent, or about two-thirds, had not completed high school. Social position of patients was determined by using Hollingshead's Two-Factor Index of Social Position.[13] Table 10-8 shows that 94.3 per

Table 10-4 CULTURE GROUP, 1962 ADDICT ADMISSIONS

Culture	Ft. Worth	Lexington	Total No.	Per cent
Puerto Rican................	32	321	353	10.4
Mexican	142	17	159	4.7
Other	354	2,531	2,885	84.9
Total	528	2,869 *	3,397 *	100.0

* Unknown = 2.

Table 10-5 AGE, 1962 ADDICT ADMISSIONS

Age group	Ft. Worth	Lexington	Total No.	Per cent
Under 20	17	75	92	2.7
20–39	354	2,146	2,500	73.6
40–59	124	547	671	19.7
60 and over	33	103	136	4.0
Total	528	2,871	3,399	100.0

Table 10-6 OCCUPATION, 1962 ADDICT ADMISSIONS

Occupation	Ft. Worth	Lexington	Total No.	Per cent
Unemployed	146	1,505	1,651	48.6
Illegal	3	384	387	11.4
Legal (except physicians)......	368	943	1,311	38.6
Physicians	11	39	50	1.5
Total	528	2,871	3,399	100.0

Table 10-7 EDUCATION, 1962 ADDICT ADMISSIONS

Education	Ft. Worth	Lexington	Total No.	Per cent
High school graduate.........	177	959	1,136	33.4
Non-high school graduate.....	351	1,911	2,262	66.5
Total	528	2,870 *	3,398 *	100.0

* Unknown = 1.

Table 10-8   SOCIAL CLASS, 1962 ADDICT ADMISSIONS

Social class	Ft. Worth	Lexington	Total No.	Total Per cent
I	15	36	51	1.5
II	8	25	33	1.0
III	32	76	108	3.2
IV	178	489	667	19.6
V	295	2,245	2,540	74.7
Total	528	2,871	3,399	100.0

cent of our patients fell into classes IV and V, the lowest social positions.

The histories of most of our patients reveal that they come from unstable or grossly disorganized families, deprived socially, economically, and educationally. In childhood they seem to have been exposed to inconsistent mixtures of seduction and rejection, indulgence and deprivation, and overprotection and neglect. They tended to drop out of school, and minor delinquency often began in adolescence. Their employment records are generally poor. Their first drug use generally occurred about the age of 20.

Diagnostic study of the addict-patient nearly always leads to diagnosis of mental disorder. Although the categorical diagnoses range through most of the nomenclature, about 90 per cent fall into the personality-disorder category.

Passive-aggressive personality and sociopathic personality disturbance occur with great frequency in our categorical diagnoses. Lewis and Osberg [19] distinguished three overlapping groups among the addict-patients at the Fort Worth hospital. These were a primarily passive group, a primarily aggressive group, and a narcissistic group. They found evidence, as have others, of oral fixation, arising primarily from deprivation. Cutler,[4] on the other hand, felt that the orality observed among addict-patients usually represented a regression.

The concepts of ego psychology as applied to character disorders are used in our staff discussions. Diagnostic formulations will characterize one patient as having a weak ego, unable to control impulses, another as having a strong ego with a corrupted or weak superego, another as having superego lacunae, another as responding to a hostile superego introject and complicating things further by projecting the hostile introject.

Lewis and Osberg described three interpersonal defense mechanisms among the addict-patients. These were manipulation, corruption, and wedging. Manipulation involves perception and action by which an emotional response in another person is evoked leading to gain for the manipulator. Corruption consists of the attempt to precipitate dishonest or immoral behavior in another. Wedging involves the attempt to provoke disagreement among others. Another interpersonal mechanism, which could be called infuriation, has been observed. Some patients seem to feel gratified when they have managed to provoke overt anger in another person.

COMPONENTS OF THE TREATMENT PROGRAM

The Lexington hospital has a constructed capacity of 1,042 beds; the Fort Worth hospital has a constructed capacity of 777 beds. The Lexington hospital is always full, and the average patient census is about the same as the constructed capacity. The Fort Worth hospital has been overcrowded, operating at about 111 per cent of its constructed capacity. Both hospitals have units for care of nonaddict mentally ill persons who are beneficiaries of the Public Health Service. Both hospitals have insufficient space for rehabilitation activities, and building modernization has become a pressing need.

The Fort Worth hospital has a total staff of about 480. Eighteen are physicians, and, of these, six are psychiatrists. Other staff includes 4 dentists, 36 nurses, 160 nursing assistants, 7 social workers, 2 psychologists, 12 occupational and recreational therapists, 10 vocational and educational staff members, and 43 security staff members. The Lexington hospital has a staff similar in composition, but somewhat larger.

Treatment begins on admission when the patient is asked to surrender any narcotic drugs in his possession and a search of his clothing and personal effects for concealed drugs is carried out. The medical history is obtained, the physical examination is carried out, and the patient is then sent to the withdrawal unit.

Withdrawal is usually accomplished within a week, using the methadon substitution method, by which the patient experiences only moderate discomfort. Withdrawal is accompanied by difficulty only on occasions when the patient has a simultaneous addiction to a barbiturate or other drugs, or when the patient has a complicating serious illness. After withdrawal, the patient receives an orientation to the hospital organization and activities. A psychiatric evaluation is carried out, together with vocational and educational evaluations. Following this, a wide range of services and activities is available to the patient. To some of these he is assigned, in others he is encouraged to participate, and in still others he participates voluntarily. The ward physician generally guides the activities of each patient, in collaboration with other units of the hospital. At the Fort Worth hospital about 140 addict-patients receive individual or group psychotherapy at any one time. Every patient who is physically able to work is assigned to vocational therapy or training. Formal apprentice trade training is available for patients who have sufficient stability and motivation to engage in it. At the Forth Worth hospital during 1962, 38 patients received certificates for satisfactory completion of apprentice training. In addition, trade courses are offered in typewriting, welding, television and radio repair, watch repair, accounting, and drafting. These are provided mainly in the evening.

Neither hospital operates an accredited school, but emphasis is placed on elementary and high school courses. At Fort Worth, patients who have less than a fifth-grade educational achievement are required to go to school. During 1962, 58 patients having this severe educational handicap were brought to the fifth-grade level of scholastic achievement, thus acquiring basic minimum skills in reading, writing, and arithmetic. High school equivalency certificates were earned by 71 patients during 1962.

In addition to their vocational and educational handicaps, many of our patients have limited leisure-time skills. Large libraries and supervised reading clubs are provided at both hospitals. Team and individual athletic activities include most major indoor and outdoor sports. Contract-bridge clubs and chess clubs are recurrently active, depending upon interests of patients. Ward parties and other social group activities are encouraged. Television, motion pictures, and stage shows, provided by patients or visiting groups, are presented for passive entertainment, and many patients participate both actively and passively in music programs. There is also an occupational therapy program for creative hobby work.

Religious programs for the three major faiths include services, individual counseling, and group instruction and discussion.

The Fort Worth hospital has an active athletic-association group of over one hundred members. This group is affiliated with local AA groups in the community. Also at Fort Worth, volunteers participate in the program for addict-patients. During 1962, about eighty volunteers assisted in educational and recreational activities.

Discharge planning is begun shortly after admission of the patient, and to this end the social-work staff provides casework services on personal, family, and other problems, assists the prisoner patient in parole planning, and maintains liaison with probation officers.

DEVELOPMENT OF MILIEU THERAPY

Both Hippocratic medicine and the mental hospitals of the early nineteenth century recognized the influence on the patient of his social-psychologic environment. In the middle of the twentieth century the social milieu of the hospitalized patient seems to have been rediscovered, and the psychiatric literature now contains many descriptions, prescriptions, and theoretical discussions of milieu therapy. Concepts of milieu therapy vary. As milieu therapy is discussed here, it includes the full 24 hr-day living experience of the patient.

During the 1950s, the staffs of the Lexington and Fort Worth hospitals began to pay more concentrated attention to the hospital milieu. Although some aspects of the milieu experience of patients have remained fairly stable for years, others are evolving, and a current description of them soon becomes out of date.

The milieu program does not occur by prescription. It evolves from experience, from staff discussions, and from sequences of decisions, actions, and evaluations. It is determined only partly by staff. Outside influences constantly affect it, and patients contribute substantially to creation of the milieu.

As implied earlier, management of addict-patients in the hospital has become primarily management of character-disorder patients. They represent a troublesome group of people to take care of. Most of the staff of the two hospitals share the general notion that the hospital milieu attempts to provide a corrective-living experience for the patient. Since our patients are conceived as having malformed or maldeveloped egos, the treatment is operated with the goal of facilitating effective ego growth. The milieu program does not directly attempt resolution of internal conflict, but rather deals with conflict between ego and environment. Therefore, many activities are directly aimed not at modifying symptomatic behavior, but rather toward increasing basic educational and vocational skills for living in modern society.

We attempt to make the social milieu stable, firm, consistent, orderly, and giving. By giving I do not mean indulging; I mean responding with attentive interest and concern to the patient's feelings and behavior.

Every employee having contact with patients is therefore conceived of as having a therapeutic role. This concept seems fairly well accepted by most employees of both hospitals. Historically, however, it is a new idea. About ten years ago therapy meant mainly psychotherapy. In addition to the participation of most employees in maintaining a stable social milieu, formal programs of individual and group counseling by nonmedical personnel have developed. These are directly supervised by a psychiatrist. Nurses, dietitians, vocational supervisors, security staff, and others serve as counselors. At the Fort Worth hospital, 145 patients are in the counseling program at the present time.

Every employee in contact with patients sooner or later becomes the object of attempted manipulation, wedging, corrupting, or infuriation by patients. A patient will perform a special favor for an employee or give him an article he has made. The employee then finds it difficult to correct idleness at work or minor violations of rules, or he may find himself requested to smuggle out a letter for the patient. Or, without doing any specific favor for the employee, the patient may manage to make the employee feel so sorry for him that the employee feels prompted to provide some special concrete gratification. Controversy among staff sometimes results from these events. Some employees avoid these problems by withdrawing from any psychologic contact with patients and by limiting themselves to mechanical enforcement of the rules.

Wedging by patients requires prompt communication among staff members concerned. This and other forms of disruptive symptomatic behavior result in flexible formation of *ad hoc* treatment teams composed of staff members directly concerned. Such a team may form quickly, confer by telephone or in conference, reach agreement, and then dissolve, all in one day. Others exist for longer periods in the form of regularly scheduled staff conferences or as committees. The flexible formation, dissolution, and re-formation of teams often requires crossing of formal organizational lines.

Because the patient's psychologic disorder is expressed mainly in symptomatic action, we control and limit behavior of patients. They have regularly scheduled periods for working, eating, sleeping, and playing. Patient traffic is limited to certain areas of the hospital. Patients are required to keep their living quarters in a reasonably sanitary and orderly condition. Swindling, stealing, fighting, conniving, and refusing to work are met with prompt discipline, usually consisting of deprivation of privileges and reduced autonomy.

The regulated living, the limit setting, and the discipline result in blocking of symptomatic behavior and consequent increase of anxiety or anger. At this point the patient may become accessible to psychologic contact. His anger and tension become expressed verbally to the nearest available staff member, to his ward physician, in ward meetings, or in group counseling or psychotherapy. Staff members are encouraged to acknowledge the distressed feeling, to maintain the limits, and when possible, to discuss the patient's behavior in relation to expectations and reactions of the hospital community and outside society. This may be similar to what Redl [25] has called "reality rub-in." Presumably by use of the projection mechanism, our patients often seem to misinterpret the intent and meaning of actions of persons around them. We might say that if insight occurs with psychotherapy, then "outsight" occurs with milieu therapy.

A significant aspect of milieu therapy for our patients may consist of the enforced experience of anxiety or tension without action and without drugs. The patients seem to experience anxiety or other affective distress as a dreadful, intolerable crisis, and the hospital milieu permits the patient to learn that anxiety does not mean catastrophe. In this connection, our addict-patients do not generally seem to have the relative freedom from anxiety which Cleckley [3] observes in psychopathic states. Our patients have plenty of anxiety; the problem is that they are unable to endure it.

Although both hospitals provide opportunities for training in trade skills, many patients have a problem of learning how to work regularly and satisfactorily on any kind of job. Work therapy, rather than trade-skill training seems a more basic need.

From time to time staff members express alarm and regret because of the controls and discipline we impose on patients. We restrict their freedom of movement, we deprive them of drugs, we schedule much of their activity, and we require that they work. We subject them to what most persons would feel as indignity and mortification. Occasions do occur when a staff member exhausts his reserve of patience, and discipline may become more retaliatory than corrective. Most staff members seem to work through their anxiety or guilt feelings in this area. I think they do it partly by examining again the repetitive self-defeating patterns of behavior which made our patients socially helpless and brought them to our hospital. They also perceive that the person without effective inner controls needs external controls.

The hospital provides graduated degrees of autonomy for patients as they demonstrate that they can use it effectively. About 80 per cent of the addict patients at Fort Worth have ground privileges. Well-behaved patients may move to self-care or "honor" units, where no nursing personnel are assigned. Patients govern most of their own ward living on these units.

The milieu probably reaches the aggressive patient more effectively than it does the passive, conforming patient. Vocational supervisors and others often call a passive, obedient patient the "good" patient. He tends to do time quietly and to slip out of psychologic sight of the psychiatry staff. Only sporadic efforts are made to reach this patient, partly because of shortage of staff, but also because a balance has to be struck between how much anxiety can be mobilized among the patient population and how much patient unrest the hospital can contain.

I stated earlier that the hospital milieu is designed to facilitate ego growth, and we can now surmise how this occurs. In brief, the milieu imposes a social regression which tends to induce a psychologic regression in the patient. This is accompanied by anxiety, some loosening of response patterns, and vulnerability to change, so that new identifications and new responses can be developed.

RESULTS OF HOSPITAL TREATMENT

A dismal attitude about effectiveness of treatment of addiction seems to prevail among professional and nonprofessional groups. This presumably arises from the reports of high relapse rates. I would like to comment briefly on follow-up studies of treated addicts.

The follow-up study by Hunt and Odoroff [14] indicated that about 90 per cent of 1,881 former addicts discharged to New York City from the Lexington hospital became readdicted within 1 to 4½ years. Patients were not contacted after the initial judgment that readdiction had occurred, and it was not learned how many readdicted patients became abstinent during the study period. It would be possible to identify a sample of 1,881 addicted persons and follow them until they became abstinent. By dropping them from study at this point, we could probably demonstrate that over 90 per cent of addicts become abstinent.

Duvall, Locke, and Brill [6] have recently reported a 5-year follow-up study of a sample of 453 Lexington patients discharged to New York City. Although over 97 per cent of this group became readdicted during the 5 years after discharge from Lexington, by the fifth year after discharge, 25 per cent were voluntarily abstinent. The age groups over 30 had a higher rate of voluntary abstinence, 35.6 per cent.

Other follow-up studies have indicated that former addicts on parole have higher rates of abstinence than patients without such supervision. The report of Diskind[5] indicated that 42 per cent of addict-parolees did not relapse while on parole during a 6-month to 3-year period.

Frequency of relapse does not measure effectiveness of hospital treatment. A rigorous evaluation study would require a matched control group of addicts who had the same life experiences as the treated group except for the event of hospitalization.

I believe that nearly all patients receive some benefit from hospitalization at Lexington or Fort Worth. Most recover from physical dependence on the drug and show a general improvement in physical condition. As noted above, some patients improve their educational and vocational skills. A degree of characterologic change seems to occur in some patients, but this may require a period of several years with repeated admissions. Staff members who have worked at one of the hospitals for more than a couple of years begin to accumulate names of successfully recovered patients. These patients achieve indefinitely prolonged periods of abstinence, some over 20 years. Some stay in contact with the staff member by correspondence or visits and attribute their start on prolonged abstinence to interpersonal experience at the hospital.

REFERENCES

1. Berliner, Arthur K.: The Helping Process in a Hospital for Narcotic Addicts, *Federal Probation*, September, 1962.
2. Blachly, Paul H., Pepper, Bertram, Scott, Winfield, and Baganz, Paul: Group Therapy and Hospitalization of Narcotic Addicts, *Arch. Gen. Psychiat.*, 5:393 (1961).
3. Cleckley, H. M.: Psychopathic States, in Sylvano Arieti (ed.), "American Handbook of Psychiatry," Basic Books, Inc., Publishers, New York, 1959.
4. Cutler, Robert P.: Discussion of Lewis and Osberg.[19]
5. Diskind, Meyer H.: New Horizons in the Treatment of Narcotic Addiction, *Federal Probation*, December, 1960.
6. Duvall, H. J., Locke, B. Z., and Brill, Leon: Follow-up Study of Narcotic Drug Addicts Five Years after Hospitalization, *Public Health Rept., U.S.*, 78:185 (1963).

7. Felix, R. H.: An Appraisal of the Personality Type of Addict, *Am. J. Psychiat.*, 100:462 (1944).

8. Fraser, H. F., and Grider, James A., Jr.: Treatment of Drug Addiction, *Am. J. Med.*, 14:571 (1953).

9. U.S. Department of Health, Education, and Welfare: *Health, Education, and Welfare Indicators*, March, 1963.

10. Hill, H. E., Kornetsky, C. H., Flanary, H. G., and Wikler, A.: Effects of Anxiety and Morphine on Discrimination of Intensities of Painful Stimuli, *J. Clin. Invest.*, 31:473 (1952).

11. Hill, H. E.: The Social Deviant and Initial Addiction to Narcotics and Alcohol, *Quart. J. Alc.*, 23:562 (1962).

12. Himmelsbach, C. K., and Small, L. F.: Clinical Studies of Drug Addiction, *Public Health Rept. U.S.*, Suppl., 125:1 (1937).

13. Hollingshead, A. B.: *Two-Factor Index of Social Position*, Multilithed, 1957.

14. Hunt, G. H., and Odoroff, M. E.: Follow-up Study of Narcotic Drug Addicts after Hospitalization, *Public Health Rept., U.S.*, 77:41 (1962).

15. Isbell, Harris: Medical Aspects of Opiate Addiction, *Bull. N.Y. Acad. Med.*, 31:886 (1955).

16. Isbell, Harris: Nalline: A Specific Narcotic Antagonist, *Merck Rept.*, 62:23 (1953).

17. Kolb, L.: Pleasure and Deterioration from Narcotic Addiction, *Mental Hyg.*, 9:699 (1925).

18. Kolb, L. and Ossenfort, W. F.: The Treatment of Drug Addicts at the Lexington Hospital, *Southern Med. J.*, 31: 914 (1938).

19. Lewis, J. M., and Osberg, James W.: Observations on Institutional Treatment of Character Disorders, *Am. J. Orthopsychiat.*, 28:730 (1958).

20. Lowry, James V.: Hospital Treatment of the Narcotic Addict, *Federal Probation Quart.*, 20:9 (1956).

21. Pescor, M. J.: A Statistical Analysis of the Clinical Records of Hospitalized Drug Addicts, *Public Health Rept., U.S.*, Suppl. no. 143 (1943).

22. Peterson, Paul Q., and Pennell, M. Y.: Physician Population Projections 1961–1975: Their Causes and Implications, *Am. J. Public Health*, 53:163 (1963).

23. Rasor, Robert W.: Narcotic Addicts: Personality Characteristics and Hospital Treatment, in P. H. Koch and J. Zubin (eds.), "Prob-

lems of Addiction and Habituation," Grune & Stratton, Inc., New York, 1958.

24. Rayport, Mark: Experience in the Management of Patients Medically Addicted to Narcotics, *J. Am. Med. Assoc.*, 156:684 (1954).

25. Redl, Fritz: Strategy and Techniques of the Life Space Interview, *Am. J. Orthopsychiat.*, 29:1 (1959).

26. Wikler, A.: Mechanisms of Action of Opiates and Opiate Antagonists. Public Health Monograph no. 52, *Public Health Rept., U.S.*, 73:4 (1958).

27. Wikler, A.: On the Nature of Addiction and Habituation, *Brit. J. Addict.*, 57:73 (1961).

28. Wikler, A.: "Opiate Addiction," Charles C Thomas, Publisher, Springfield, Ill., 1953.

29. Wikler, A., and Rasor, R. W.: Psychiatric Aspects of Addiction, *Am. J. Med.*, 14:566 (1953).

Alfred M. Freedman | **11**

STUDYING AND TREATING THE ADDICT
IN AND OUT OF A CITY HOSPITAL

THE RECORD OF FRUSTRATION AND FAILURE that has attended the treatment of narcotic addicts for so long a period of time can be seen, on examination, to stem from a number of causes. The complexity of addiction as a disease, with its psychologic, physiologic, metabolic, and social components, obviates the possibility of any simple attack. Such complexity in itself would not preclude the possibility of successful treatment, for other diseases of multifactorial origin and character have yielded to medical and public health attempts at control. It is our belief, however, that most treatment programs in the field of addiction have been developed on a base of expediency rather than on a rational philosophy oriented toward realistic goals of positive social value. Further, such expedient programs have often been discarded quickly, before there has been adequate time for careful evaluation, comparison with other types of program, or the establishment of base lines on which to build.

For the past 50 years in the United States narcotic addiction has been viewed by most people, including those in responsible, authoritative positions, not only as a crime, but as an *evil*, epitomizing moral degradation. The moral outrage provoked by addiction to the opiates is not matched by the response to other addictions, notably that of alcohol, in spite of the fact that the behavior of the alcoholic can be so much more devastating to himself, his family and society. As another example of the tolerance of our society for other types of damaging activity, I might refer to cigarette smoking. Although there is still disagreement as to whether or not smoking should be labeled an addiction, it has now been pointed out by public health authorities that bronchogenic carcinoma has assumed the proportions of an epidemic. Nevertheless, only recently have official steps been taken to bring the matter to public scrutiny, and no widespread programs yet exist to discourage cigarette smoking among young people.

It is wise to maintain some historical perspective when considering attitudes toward narcotic addiction, for addiction was not always considered as reprehensible as it is today. As Lindesmith has pointed out,[1] a respectable medical journal in 1889 carried a statement by a physician giving in considerable detail his reasons for believing that it was obviously better to be a drug addict than a drunkard and advocating that chronic alcoholics be cured by transforming them into drug addicts. One can only speculate on the reasons for the extremely punitive attitude toward narcotic addicts that has developed in the present century. Isbell[2] traces the roots of addiction and accompanying social attitudes in the United States to symptomatic treatment of various diseases, the Civil War, and importation of Chinese laborers to the West Coast between 1852 and 1870.

Whatever the reasons for this peculiarly punitive attitude, it is clear that the goal of most treatment programs—total abstinence from narcotics—is related to this attitude on the part of our society. This goal has proven unrealistic, if not impossible to achieve, in a large percentage of persons treated. The recognition of this failure has led to some attempts at changing treatment modalities, but to little serious questioning of treatment goals.

THE METROPOLITAN HOSPITAL TREATMENT PROGRAM

The program in which we are presently engaged at Metropolitan Hospital is distinguished from other treatment programs, first of all, by the enunciation of goals based on our belief that present-day narcotic addiction is a public health problem characterized primarily by social loss. This loss stems from the inability of most addicts to contribute constructively to society, not necessarily because of their addiction per se, but because of the type of life into which they are driven by the legal sanctions attached to the use and distribution of the opiates. With the acceptance of these fundamental considerations, the aims of efforts directed toward those who are already addicted then emerge as, first, social and medical rehabilitation of those addicts who are noncontributing citizens of the community, and, second, social integration into the community of those addicts who are already contributing citizens, since there is some evidence that there are persons for whom this may be possible. Abstinence from drugs is seen not as an end with great intrinsic value, but as one method, along with others, of achieving the goals of this treatment program.

The philosophical basis for such a treatment program has emerged with the development and operation of the male-narcotic-addict service at Metropolitan Hospital in New York City. The hospital is located in East Harlem, a neighborhood where narcotic addiction is endemic. This service, established in 1959, was from the beginning unusual in several ways. First, the service was established in an 1,100-bed municipal general hospital within the department of psychiatry. It differed in this respect from most previous inpatient programs which were established in specialized institutions, often serving a penal as well as a medical purpose, that is to say, serving as both jail and hospital. Second, the service was set up as a benign, voluntary program, oriented toward treatment of the addict as just another patient, albeit in need of specialized services, just as the cardiac or paraplegic patient is in need of specialized services. All the adult patients are voluntary admissions; none is under the jurisdiction of a court or committed by a court. This is also true of most adolescents, but a few who are on parole are admitted if consultation with their parole officers indicates they may benefit by the program. Third, the department of psychiatry of a medical school is actively engaged in the treatment of addicts and in research into the etiology and therapy of narcotic addiction. This medical school affiliation provides the resources of a large and active medical center.

Elsewhere [3,4] we have discussed in detail some of the advantages and difficulties in administering a narcotic-addiction service in a community general hospital. Briefly, the advantages stem, first, from the acceptance and treatment of the addict as primarily a sick person in need of specialized medical and psychiatric treatment. The acceptance of the addict-patient in this way tends to overcome the difficulties that ensue when the addict is committed to the specialized institutions such as Lexington or Fort Worth, where he is both patient and prisoner. Second, there are available within the general hospital the total range of services, medical and surgical, that may be necessary at some point in the treatment process. Third, the complexity of addiction as a disease, to which I have already referred, presents a challenge to the medical profession that calls for its most creative research efforts. In a large general hospital where clinical research is an accepted and ongoing procedure coexistent with treatment, the stimulation and possibilities for such research are greatly enhanced. Finally, the general-hospital setting provides an opportunity for interesting and involving the nonpsychiatrists in the medical profession in the problems presented by this group of patients.

The difficulties attendant on the treatment of addicts in a general hospital stem, first, from the resistance of nonpsychiatric professional personnel to working with *any* psychiatric patients. Such resistances are compounded in the case of narcotic addicts. Research on the attitudes of hospital staff members in our own program has been described elsewhere.[5] It is apparent from our preliminary studies that even among those persons actively engaged in a medically oriented program for addicts, popular stereotypes are still maintained and moral judgments on addiction are not wholly discarded. This not only applies to nonprofessional personnel in the hospital, as might be expected, but is also true of some of the professional staff. The administration of the hospital seems to have considerable anxiety and apprehension about the addict patients and is able to find incidents to justify this anxiety, e.g., the breaking of some furniture on the ward. Finally, the deceit and manipulativeness which characterize many addicts, and are considered by some authorities as a symptom of the disease, provoke a response, sometimes hostile or negative, in both professional and nonprofessional personnel that multiplies the problems involved in administering this type of program.

This is the general picture of the inpatient service; I would now like to deal more specifically with our experience and development in the past 3½ years. From the beginning this program was viewed as an opportunity for study and research on narcotic addiction; there were no illusions that because of its difference from other programs it would necessarily lead to a higher percentage of "cures." Originally two wards of 25 beds each were designated for the treatment of heroin addicts. The average anticipated period of hospitalization was 28 days, during which period withdrawal by means of methadon was to be carried out and the patient introduced to the aftercare program. Outpatient facilities were available for individual and group psychotherapy. Psychotherapists were, and are, in the main, board-eligible psychiatrists who have completed or are undergoing psychoanalytic training. Other staff members include social workers, psychologists, vocational counselors, and recreation therapists. A social club for discharged patients was established early in the program.

The treatment process was seen as part of a continuum which extends through initial contact with the patient, referral of the patient for admission, admission to the ward, detoxification, convalescence and therapy in the hospital, treatment preparation for aftercare, aftercare, follow-up contact by a research team, and evaluation of the program. Our hope was that this might be an action-research opportunity which would provide insight into the success or failure of the treatment process so that changes might be made where indicated and the program would remain a dynamic rather than a static one.

In keeping with this objective, there have been a number of revisions in the program since it was begun over 3 years ago. The first 22 months of operation, beginning in November, 1959, were characterized by efforts to apply to the problems of drug addic-

tion standard psychothcrapeutic practice. A member of the part-
time psychotherapy staff met the patient (who had numerous
contacts involving personnel other than the therapist) as soon as
possible after his admission for detoxification. It was hoped that
the personal relationship established with the individual therapist
would provide a bridge to participation in the aftercare program.
In order to make the program attractive, every effort was made
to make detoxification as free of discomfort as possible. Soporific
and tranquilizer drugs were prescribed freely in the aftercare
clinic, but prescriptions were written to carry the patient only up
to his next clinic appointment in order to reinforce motivation to
attend.

Of the 490 adults who comprised the group of 683 admissions
during the first 22 months, there were only 66 patients who were
attending the aftercare clinic in September, 1961. Another dozen
or so were regularly attending the social club. In the absence of
clinical tests to determine whether or not these patients were
currently using heroin, there were no reliable data on the percentage who had actually altered their pattern of drug use as a
result of contact with the program. Using aftercare-clinic attendance as a crude and really questionable gauge of effectiveness,
the program as it was then set up appeared meaningful enough
to warrant continued participation to only about one-seventh of
the patients. This discouraging picture, obtained as the result of
our interest in continuing evaluation of the program, was not
wholly unexpected. The primary therapeutic instrument of the
service as originally established was psychotherapy. Previous attempts at curing addiction with psychotherapy alone had already
been shown to be effective in relatively few cases. The nature
of our patient population, largely of minority-group status and
characterized by little education and much economic and social
deprivation, certainly contributed to the ineffectiveness of conventional psychotherapy.

In an attempt to improve that state of affairs, procedures were
revised in the fall of 1961. At that time there was established a
coordinated program with an existing neighborhood agency which
had been working with addicts and ex-addicts on an outpatient

basis for some years. This cooperative arrangement provided for the referral to the hospital program of addicts known to the neighborhood agency over a period of years. Priority of admission was offered to such patients, utilizing the neighborhood agency's knowledge of their life history and family history to facilitate screening. A full interagency sharing of information was inaugurated so that the follow-up potentialities of both staffs could complement each other. The staffs of both agencies attended meetings jointly, both professional meetings and meetings with groups of addicts. Provision was made for the psychiatrists to spend a portion of their time each week at the neighborhood agency, seeing prospective patients and ex-patients who would drop in informally to discuss their problems (or the possibility of admission) in this setting in preference to keeping appointments in the outpatient clinic.

Within the hospital, the two 25-bed wards, originally established as an adolescent and an adult ward, were changed to a detoxification and a rehabilitation ward. This change followed the observation that those patients who were still receiving methadon presented a severe challenge to those whose physiologic detoxification was completed. The restlessness engendered in the latter group seemed to precipitate an undue number of sign-outs against medical advice. The separation of the two groups therefore seemed a logical step, and all patients were consequently admitted to the detoxification ward for a period of about two weeks, to be followed by about two weeks on the rehabilitation ward. Some improvement did result. There was a reduction in tension, a reduction in the number of sign-outs, and a generally improved atmosphere, particularly in the drug-free rehabilitation ward.

The stated aims of the 2-week stay on the rehabilitation ward required for discharge with medical consent were:

1. To restore normal sleep patterns

2. To provide sanctuary from the temptations of the streets during the difficult period immediately following detoxification

3. To devise an aftercare treatment plan appropriate to the needs of each individual, including social work intervention in

the family situation prior to discharge, vocational counseling and placement, and pairing patients with individual psychotherapists if the staff judged the patient could utilize individual psycho-therapy profitably.

At present, there are three phases in the program for addict-patients—the preadmission period, the inpatient detoxification period, and the aftercare, postdischarge period. The final phase is now recognized by practically everyone interested in the treat-ment of narcotic addiction as a phase of primary importance.

The patient seeking services (often interested only in detoxi-fication) is given a screening interview with an intake psychia-trist, who assigns the patient to a staff psychiatrist and simul-taneously places him on a waiting list for admission. The waiting list at present usually consists of 40 to 50 applicants, and a 3- to 4-week waiting period is usual. In this preadmission waiting pe-riod, however, the patient is seen by his psychiatrist, who attempts to help him, utilizing both psychotherapy and pharmacotherapy. There are special problems during this phase arising from the fact that many of these applicants are losing their illicit supply of drugs and suffering some degree of withdrawal sickness.

After admission as an inpatient, the addict spends from 8 to 14 days on the detoxification ward, the length of time depending upon the level of his habit at the time of admission. Detoxification is routinized and presents no special problems. The subsequent 2-week stay on the rehabilitation ward is still oriented toward the goals originally established for this period. At any point in this process, from initial contact into and through aftercare, appropriate referrals are made by the psychiatrist to psycholo-gists, social workers, and vocational and recreation workers on the staff. At the time of discharge, the patient is given an ap-pointment for continuing therapy on an outpatient basis with the same psychotherapist whom he has been seeing on the ward. In aftercare the patient is considered an active case so long as he sees his therapist at least once in 3 months.

In the past 3 years there have been approximately 2,800 admis-sions to the inpatient addiction treatment service. Of this total, approximately 50 per cent have been first admissions. In other words, about 1,400 different patients have used the inpatient program in the past 3 years.

This treatment program, which to date has not achieved any revolutionary results in terms of cures, *is* distinguished from many others in the extent to which it is characterized by a thorough-going research effort. One of the great traditions of medicine has been the investigation of the pathogenesis of disease. Knowledge in this area can then be followed by rational treatment efforts. Viewing narcotic addiction as a public health problem with broad social implications, as we do, suggests the necessity for attaining some knowledge of the natural history of the narcotic addict as a prior condition to social control of addiction. It is this kind of effort which in our department has begun to bear some fruit. In addition to the study of hospital-staff attitudes and adjustments to working with addicts, to which I have already referred, there has emerged a preliminary report on social types of addicts.[6] These studies are being conducted in our division of community mental health by an interdisciplinary group under the direction of Dr. Richard Brotman. The data on social types of addicts were derived from the responses of 100 addicts to two lengthy structured interviews during their hospitalization. They provide a new classification of addicts based on their social adaptation to the world around them. The prevailing public stereotypes of addicts have varied from time to time, and although they have within them a kernel of truth, they nevertheless suffer from the fault that characterizes all stereotypes. They are *fixed* forms or notions, based to no small degree on prejudices, and of little value in devising treatment programs. Most scientific classifications of addicts have tended to focus on personality traits exclusively. Although this approach may have contributed to our understanding of the predisposing factors in addiction, it suffers from the limitations that attend an unawareness of the crucial role played by social policies and cultural restraints in the development and perpetuation of addiction.

The classification of "life-style adaptations" which we have developed is an attempt to introduce a realistic multidimensional social characteristic into the study of addiction. By emphasizing the concept of adaptation, we direct attention to the social and cultural environment as well as to the individual. In studying the pattern of an addict's social relationships and social attitudes with respect to major areas of living—his life-style adaptation— we are investigating his involvement with various conventional and deviant (most often criminal) social systems and subcultures. There is evidence in our preliminary data that our addict-patients vary in the extent of their involvement in the conventional and the criminal worlds, even though practically none of them belongs to the well-educated or professional classes. We have found that over a quarter of our sample of 100 addicts report that they have worked fairly steadily at a conventional job at least half the time during which they were addicted. This and similar findings contain implications of importance for a community mental-health approach to addiction. A project is now under way in conjunction with the present study of the life-style adaptation of narcotic addicts which will extend this approach in an effort to compare narcotic addicts with persons addicted to other substances, such as alcohol. Such research will, hopefully, contribute to the establishment of base lines on which realistic programs in this field can be designed.

The conviction that only a community-based program for addicts holds any hope for successful treatment and prevention of addiction has led us to project a model continuum of treatment, described in previous papers.[7,8] Such a continuum is designed to expand the range of services presently available to the patient applying for admission to include whatever forms of ambulatory treatment are necessary to help the patient become engaged in the treatment process. These might include a sheltered workshop program as well as a pharmacologic regimen and psychotherapy. The program in the inpatient facility would be followed by admission to a day-night center, located away from, but near, the hospital.

After an extended stay at the day-night center, the patient would return in gradual stages to his neighborhood under the continued supervision of a clinic which would be jointly operated by the hospital and the neighborhood agency. It would be expected that this clinic would have continual contact with the family of the patient from the point of initial contact through ambulatory care and detoxification, through the stay in the day-night center, and in the aftercare program at the local-neighborhood level. The patient would continue to be engaged in the process until rehabilitation and social integration were achieved.

A key aspect of the day-night center would consist of a program of public health education aimed at increasing the level of community understanding of narcotic addiction and of the community's role in helping to effect rehabilitation of addicts and former addicts and in helping them achieve integration into community life.

Research into the continuum of treatment would be under the supervision of the division of community mental health of the department of psychiatry which is responsible for the total program. The development of a day-night center is thus viewed as an integral step in the development of a model continuum of community care for the narcotic addict.

Such a community-based program obviously suggests that the department of psychiatry responsible for the treatment of narcotic addicts must address itself to the social institutions of law, housing, schools, and employment in the milieu where addiction develops. Further, although the psychiatrist is usually free to use drug therapy as well as his own skills in interpersonal relationships in his attempts to help patients effect behavioral change, the physician's freedom in this regard is sharply limited when the patient is a narcotic addict. There is a strong need for complete freedom for the physician to experiment with all types of treatment modalities, and legal obstructions to carefully designed and controlled experimentation should be removed.

CONCLUSION

The history of treatment efforts directed toward narcotic addicts in the United States during the past 50 years reveals the fundamental uncertainties and lack of knowledge surrounding both the patients and the disease. In the early part of the century addiction was viewed as a medical problem, and such treatment as was offered was available from general practitioners. The passage of the Harrison Act and the subsequent intimidation of physicians was followed by the ill-fated clinics and dispensaries also providing medical treatment under city health department auspices. With the closing of the last of the clinics in 1924, medical treatment gave way completely to the dominance of legal efforts at control. The opening of the Public Health Service Hospitals at Lexington and Fort Worth in 1934 introduced another attempt at a medical approach. Treatment has now developed into a largely psychiatric specialty. However, it is scarcely necessary to point out that the psychiatrist using conventional psychotherapeutic methods finds himself, in general, little more successful than other physicians—or even law enforcement officers—in coping with the problems presented by this group of patients. At present we seem to be entering an era characterized by the development of the exhortative, the cultist approach. Synanon, like Alcoholics Anonymous, is obviously providing for some patients a means of achieving abstinence. What it can *not* do, however, is move into the community for early intervention and thus provide the all-important basis for the prevention of this disease. As long as treatment remains a problematical and frequently unsuccessful procedure, addiction must be approached as other public health problems have been, and broad social efforts at primary prevention must be given high priority. This, of course, does not preclude simultaneous efforts directed toward the individual who is already addicted.

This dual approach is based on our belief that social manipulation, while of primary importance, is not the entire answer to the problem. The addict represents the end result of a combination of individual and social pressures. The ways in which present-day addicts differ from those of the late nineteenth and early twentieth centuries have been pointed out many times—the great increase in criminality, the differing social, economic, and ethnic classes, the changed ratio of males to females, the existence of an "addict subculture," the marked change in the number of persons who become "medically" addicted—all establish the vitality, if you will, or the adaptability of the disease. Many literate persons, having read or seen Eugene O'Neill's "Long Day's Journey into Night," have acquired a picture of a type of addict relatively common in O'Neill's youth, but not so today. Today we see evidence of change occurring in patterns of addiction. For example, heroin has become a focus of attention, particularly among law enforcement officials, because for some years it has seemed to be the drug of choice among those addicts who are most deeply involved in illegal activities. At the present time, however, we find addicts, preoccupied with drugs per se, moving from one substance to another. Such behavior, I believe, is evidence of more than social deviation. It is a general response to the pressures of the external and the internal environments. That general response is *addictive behavior,* not heroin or morphine or Demerol addiction.

The change in objective or sociologic characteristics of drug addicts does not alter the fact that some predisposition, psychologic or physiologic or both, must be present for the development of addiction in any one individual. This, too, must be dealt with.

The problems presented to our society by the whole field of mental illness have aroused tremendous interest and concern in recent years. With the issuance of the final report of the Joint Commission on Mental Illness and Health [9] in 1961, there came a mobilization of effort directed toward these problems. Recent legislative enactments concerning mental illness and mental retardation, which insure major Federal involvement in the improvement of community-centered treatment facilities, are providing impetus for much-needed action. However, in spite of all that is known at this time about the genesis and treatment of mental illness, a great deal remains unknown. Only the most rigorous, scientific approach to investigation of causes, selection of population, and evaluation of results of various treatment modalities can lead to progress in this field. Let me emphasize the need for experimentation with new types of therapeutic intervention. Conventional psychotherapy has proved to be so unrewarding with so large a proportion of present-day addicts that we should explore all possible methods of treatment for mental ills suggested by responsible investigators.

Narcotic addiction serves as a paradigm of mental illness and as such must be subjected to the same systematic interdisciplinary study required for other types of emotional and mental disturbance. This is the answer to the question, "What are we trying to do at Metropolitan Hospital?" We are not naive enough to expect to provide immediate solutions to a problem of such social, cultural, physiologic, and psychologic complexity. We are trying only to study addiction in the hope that we may thus provide for ourselves and others some guidelines along which steps may be taken on the road to control and prevention of a major public health problem.

An experimental program of the type in which we are engaged must be recognized as a form of demonstration project. It is worth examining the purpose and the value of demonstration projects in general, particularly when the specific project is in a field of operation historically characterized by failure. There is a value in demonstration projects, assuming that they are reasonably conceived and operated, which stems from their forcing the public, or at least interested professionals, to confront the deficiencies and gaps in existing programs. Even if the new program does not succeed in its enunciated goals, it does focus attention on such existing deficiencies and helps to mobilize efforts that stimulate experimentation and needed fundamental change. It provides a critical eye that may not otherwise exist or function. This general truth may be seen in the area of education, for example, where such experiments as enrichment programs for deprived children may bring to public attention the great lacks in conventional school systems for such children. However, we must not lose sight of the fact that a small demonstration project, operated for a limited group of people, may not necessarily succeed when it is enlarged or its scope is widened to include much larger groups. In the field of narcotic addiction, the private practitioner may meet with success with an individual patient, or some experiments may be successful with small groups or a limited number of cases. Such groups, however, may be self-selected, and the limits established by such self-selection must be remembered when plans are made to extend such programs to include *all* narcotic addicts in need of treatment.

To summarize the ways in which this program differs from most other existing programs, I would point out, first, that it is completely voluntary. Second, its goal is social rehabilitation of the addict, not just abstinence from drugs. Third, it is an action-research program, the essence of which is study. Treatment can be rationally undertaken only when there is some understanding of the whole addictive process and possible ways of ameliorating it. Fourth, we are concerned with the *total* addictive process which we see as a reaction to stress, both internal and within the community. Abstinence from one drug does not necessarily mean that addiction is cured. Finally, we are oriented toward the prevention of addiction. With some knowledge of the genesis and development of this disease we may be able to confront society and interested professionals with the critical issues that demand their attention if social control of addiction is to be achieved.

REFERENCES

1. Lindesmith, A. R.: "Opiate Addiction," p. 183, The Principia Press of Illinois, Inc., Evanston, 1947.
2. Isbell, H.: Historical Development of Attitudes toward Opiate Addiction in the United States, in S. M. Farber and R. H. L. Wilson (eds.), "Conflict and Creativity," p. 154, McGraw-Hill Book Company, New York, 1963.
3. Freedman, A. M.: Treatment of Drug Addiction, Presented at the Dedication Conference, Mount Sinai Hospital Psychiatric Institute, New York, Feb. 2, 1963.
4. Freedman, A. M.: Treatment of Drug Addiction in a Community General Hospital, *Comp. Psychiat.*, 4:199 (1963).
5. Brotman, R., Meyer, A. S., Freedman, A. M., Alksne, H.: Hospital Staff Attitudes and Adjustments to Working with Narcotic Addicts, Presented at the 40th Annual Meeting, American Orthopsychiatric Association, Washington, D.C., March 8, 1963.
6. Brotman, R., Meyer, A. S., Freedman, A. M., Lieberman, L.: A Community Mental Health Diagnosis of Narcotic Addiction: A Preliminary Report on Social Types of Addicts, Presented at the Meetings of the National Research Council, Ann Arbor, Mich., Feb. 15, 1963.
7. Freedman, A. M., Brotman, R. E., Meyer, A. S.: A Model Con-

tinuum for a Community Based Program for the Prevention and Treatment of Narcotic Addiction, *Am. J. Public Health*, in press.

8. Freedman, A. M.: The New York Medical College-Metropolitan Hospital Program, in *Proceedings, White House Conference on Narcotic and Drug Abuse*, Washington, 1962, p. 84.

9. Joint Commission on Mental Illness and Health: "Action for Mental Health," Basic Books, Inc., Publishers, New York, 1961.

*Lewis Yablonsky
and Charles E. Dederich*

12

SYNANON: AN ANALYSIS OF SOME DIMENSIONS OF THE SOCIAL STRUCTURE OF AN ANTIADDICTION SOCIETY

GENERAL DESCRIPTION OF SYNANON

SYNANON IS AN EXPERIMENTAL MODEL for the treatment of drug addicts. It must be emphasized that it is still in its experimental stages of development. It was founded in 1958 by Charles E. Dederich, a layman who had successfully worked through an alcoholic problem.* The informal, intensive group discussion sessions which he ran in his home in Ocean Park, California, attracted at first a group of Alcoholics Anonymous members and then some narcotic addicts. Dederich became impressed with the fact that some of the addicts attending these sessions reduced their use of drugs and in several cases completely stopped using drugs. This he attributed to the intensive group discussions and the community or extended-family living which began to develop around his home in Ocean Park.

A small community spontaneously emerged in the area. Most

* In this chapter coauthor Charles E. Dederich will be treated as a source regarding the workings and philosophy of the Synanon movement.

of the "members" of this informal collectivity were disaffiliated people, and they voluntarily moved into apartments and rooms in proximity to Dederich's club. There was and is no professional staff, although many professionals have taken a friendly but non-interfering interest. The organization was and is managed entirely by ex-addicts trained at Synanon, and it is supported, as it always has been, by goods and services contributed by friends from the community. The closest sociologic approximation of Synanon's early form was that of an extended family comparable to a primitive tribe. Dederich described the early organization in this way in an address to The Southern California Parole Officers Association in 1958:

> The autocratic overtone of the family structure demands that the patients or members of the family perform tasks as part of the group. If a member is able to take direction in small tasks such as helping in the preparation of meals, house cleaning, etc., regardless of his rebellion at being "told what to do," his activity seems to provide exercise of emotions of giving or creating which have lain dormant. As these emotional muscles strengthen, it seems that the resistance to cooperating with the group tends to dissipate. During this time a concerted effort is made by the significant figures of the family structure to implant spiritual concepts and values which will result in self-reliance. Members are urged to read from the classics and from the great teachers of mankind—Jesus, Lao Tse, Buddha, etc. These efforts have been successful to a rather surprising degree. The concept of an open mind is part of a program to help the addict find himself, without the use of drugs.

This family structure characterized the early framework of Synanon and remains as the emphasized ethos despite Synanon's growth in size.

Another early process which remains as a fundamental force in Synanon is the so-called "small s synanon," a kind of group psychotherapy in which all residents participate three times a week. Dederich describes it as follows: [1]

> Another device which has seemed to produce beneficial results is the "Synanon." The Synanon can be defined broadly as a kind of type of group psychotherapy. Synanon, which is a coined word, is used to describe a more or less informal meeting which ideally consists of three male patients and three female patients, plus one Synanist who is himself an addictive personality, but who has managed to arrest the

symptoms of his addiction for some considerable length of time, or seems to be progressing at a rate somewhat faster than his colleagues in the meeting. The Synanist acts as a moderator, and by virtue of an empathy which seems to exist between addictive personalities, is able to detach the patient's conscious or unconscious attempts to evade the truth about himself. The methods employed by a Synanist in a Synanon meeting may include devices or strategems which appear to be unorthodox, but such surprisingly beneficial results have occurred in an encouraging number of cases that we feel we must further explore the method.

The Synanist leans heavily on his own insight into his own problems of personality in trying to help the patients to find themselves, and will use the weapons of ridicule, cross-examination, hostile attack, as it becomes necessary. These Synanon sessions seem to provide an emotional catharsis and seem to trigger an atmosphere of truthseeking which is reflected in the social life of the family structure. The Synanist does not try to convey to the patient that he himself is a stable personality. In fact, it may very well be the destructive drives of the recovered or recovering addictive personality embodied in the Synanist which makes him a good therapeutic tool—fighting fire with fire.

There were several significant phases in the early development of the Synanon System which help to describe its structuring. Phase 1 consisted largely of participation in random and organized discussions, synanons, and group living. The next significant development was the emergence of a totally clean antiaddiction society, with no one affiliated with the organization using any kind of drugs. Next, when Synanon became a California corporation with a Federal tax exemption certificate, there was a concentration on developing and refining the organization. These phases were not clearly separate but developed in sequence.

After about a year of development under Dederich's direction, in 1959, about 40 ex-addicts with an antiaddiction ethos moved into a large three-story brick armory on the beach at Santa Monica, their current main headquarters. Here Dederich, and a "clean" [2] staff of eight ex-addicts, the "Board of Directors," began to develop the social system which comprises the current Synanon society. The current Synanon establishment includes a program involving the Synanon form of group therapy, noontime educational seminars, cultural activities of various kinds, and a work program.

As indicated, Dederich views the current organization as still in its experimental stages. His view is that it will take at least 10 years for the structure to be refined. Despite the experimental nature of the organization, the essential fact indicating that Synanon has achieved some measure of success is that there are currently (1964) affiliated with Synanon about four hundred ex-addicts, most with long criminal records, who are no longer using drugs or committing crimes. Most of these are living in the Santa Monica complex of eight separate houses within a 3-mile radius of the three-story converted armory. Thirty are living in their own community, and others are living in Synanon installations in San Diego, California; San Francisco, California; Reno, Nevada; and Westport, Connecticut. (See tables 12-1 to 12-7 which provide a breakdown of the Synanon population according to age, ethnicity, addiction background, and institutional factors, as of April 15, 1963. Since this analysis was made, the population has more than doubled. The tables provide a crude estimation and profile of the current Synanon organization.)

Dederich rejects the concept of recidivism as an adequate measurement of evaluation of the success of the Synanon program. He views as normal occasional relapse of many addicts in the early phase of their desire to quit drugs. Therefore, the first 3 months of an addict's living in Synanon is seen largely as a trial period. Although the data have not recently been rechecked, it was determined in 1962 that of those addicts who stay at Synanon longer than three months, more than 70 per cent are still residing clean in Synanon. A cursory appraisal reveals that Synanon's "holding power" has improved.

Dederich suggests a modified epidemiologic view point for the proper evaluation of Synanon. He developed what he refers to as the concept of "clean man-days." He describes this position as follows: [3]

There is a vast national drug addiction problem. Let us assume that the 50,000 to 60,000 figures on number of addicts published by the Federal Bureau of Narcotics is somewhat accurate, although I believe it is a minimal figure. Our goal is to remove as many using addicts from drugs as possible. We will take as many off the streets, who can respond to our program, as possible. Each addict affiliated with Synanon not using drugs for a day represents a clean man-day unit. We try to operate as a counter-epidemic force to drug addiction. If these clean man-days build up in one individual, this is fine; however, our goal as an organization is as many clean man-days as possible. As of March, 1964, we are achieving 400 clean man-days each day. In 10 years—I would predict—we will be producing thousands of clean man-days each day. The more clean man-days we achieve in Synanon, the greater our counter-epidemic force. Taking addicts out of the population into Synanon also decreases the contagious spread of the drug addiction epidemic.

If an addict uses on the average of $25 a day for his habit—keeping him clean in Synanon saves the community at least this amount which he would have to steal. (The addict usually has to steal $100 worth of merchandise to realize $25.) Using the 25-dollar figure as a base, keeping 400 addicts clean each day in Synanon saves society about $10,000 each day, or over $3.5 million per year. (Addicts do not take vacations from drug use.)

Dederich rejects the use of recidivism as an evaluative measure of success for several reasons. One is related to the assumption that many addicts will use known relapse rates to rationalize their "hope-to-die–addict" concept of life.[4] Dederich amplifies this view as follows: [5]

Addicts, like emotional children, won't gamble and want a sure thing. Let us assume that at Synanon there is a 60 per cent chance of success. Better than half of those who come to Synanon will never use drugs again. Many addicts will seize upon the 40 per cent failure rate and use it as a rationalization for continuing to use drugs. As of now the percentage of people who come here and remain is not published. I have the data but I won't release it to general public attention. It would present a situation for the newly arrived addict which might deter his potential success at Synanon.

Perhaps the reason why Lexington and other similar institutions have, as I understand it, a 90 per cent recidivism rate is that the addict goes there essentially to clean up. He does not believe he will fully quit using drugs as a result of the treatment. (There is a tone of failure rather than success that pervades these institutions.) Many addicts who have been to Lexington or to Fort Worth tell me the professional staff tells them "in front" that they are incurable.[6] Synanon, however, has set a tone of success, which is part of the method. Along with this we have of course been modestly effective in producing "clean man-days"—our measure of success.

Another reason why traditional recidivism and cure concepts do not apply to Synanon relates to the nature of the organization. Recidivism refers essentially to an institutional model. The institution process involves an addict going through a painful process of incarceration in a hospital or prison and then attempting to succeed on his own in the outside world. The institutional emphasis is on getting him "cured and out." Since life at Synanon is pleasant, involving many aspects of "club living," there is no great haste for many addicts to leave this way of life for the same pressures in our society which produced their illness.

Although some Synanon graduates return to the open community, others may wish to spend their lives in Synanon work as executives within the framework of the organization. The problem of defining a "cure" is complicated. Even if the individual remains clean for 1, 5, or 10 years at Synanon, it could be argued that he has not succeeded until he has left the "institution." As indicated previously, there is no special pressure to leave, and many ex-addicts find the Synanon way of life to be optimum for themselves.

Synanon members currently carry out their treatment approach in the Nevada state prison institutions with cooperation of officers of the institution.[7] This, combined with working with newly arrived addicts, has created a new social role and career for many ex-addicts. Perhaps Synanon can further help treat the problem by adequately training more Synanists. Donald Cressey [17] has described one aspect of this issue—when criminal *A* treats criminal *B*, criminal *A* may be helping himself. If in time we had thousands of ex-addicts and ex-criminals doing Synanon work, we would have made a substantial inroad into the addiction problem.

A COMPARATIVE ANALYSIS OF SYNANON AND OTHER TREATMENT STRUCTURES

There are, as has been indicated, 400 Synanon members currently leading constructive lives free from drugs and illegal behavior in 1964. They appear to be representative of narcotic addicts in the United States. Without presuming that Synanon is more or less effective than other facilities and methods for treating addiction, we can make some appraisal of structural differences in treatment between Synanon and other settings that may reveal the impact of Synanon on addicts who have failed in these other settings. Although, at best, this is a crude form of analysis, it may reveal how some of the known deterrents to rehabilitation in the traditional institution are handled either "better" in Synanon or at least differently. The purpose of this type of analysis is heuristic. An effort will be made to produce some propositions which might account for the differential impact of more traditional facilities and Synanon on the treatment of addicts.

The research problem inherent in cross comparing institutional treatment settings are tremendous. Even if we were to find significant differences in relapse or recidivism rates, the issue of accounting for the specific factors that produce the overall results are most difficult to delineate and measure. Some dimensions of the total complex of an approach, however, can be grossly compared, and this might be productive in developing relevant hypotheses for research purposes.

This appraisal is therefore a modest attempt to delineate and compare the gross variables operative in the traditional settings [8] (e.g., prisons and hospitals) for treating addicts and in the Synanon approach. In the following appraisal it is hoped that such a comparative analysis will, at a minimum, help to articulate some of the structural forces at work in Synanon, as well as in the other settings.

Ex-addict Staff and Indoctrination Procedures

Most addicts arrive at Synanon filthy, running from both ends (diarrhea and vomiting) with one shoe off—no underwear. They stumble in with their phony little story and say, "Dad, please help me." [9]

The indoctrination or initial interview establishes the "contract," or conditions, for Synanon's therapeutic intervention. At first some token road blocks are thrown in the way of the addict desiring to enter. He is given an appointment and made to wait. If he is late for the appointment, he is told to come back at some other specific time. In some cases money is requested as an entrance fee. An effort is made to have the individual fight his way in.

This is a new experience, since the addict is usually hauled into a prison or hospital.

> In his usual dazed condition, on arrival he feels more secure encountering a firm defined situation, which Synanon provides. Slobbering affection is something he can't bear at this time. His enormous guilt might activate him to run out the open door and smash himself once more.[10]

The firm hand of ex-addict "experts" is puzzling and attractive to the newcomer. Often the newcomer's curiosity is piqued by the spectacle of people with whom he shot drugs himself—as executives!

> I couldn't figure it out. I figured there must be a gimmick. I didn't really want to stop being a dope fiend. I wanted to rest awhile. First, I began to look for the connection in the joint. They laughed at me. I think I stuck around at the beginning cause I couldn't believe it was true. Live dope fiends not shooting dope—behind an open door, with no screws to keep them locked up! [11]

After he "kicks his habit," the addict is given a job commensurate with his limited ability at the time (e.g., washing dishes or mopping floors). This is intended to give him a sense of security, satisfaction, and participation.

> Before his mind can race too far in the wrong direction towards drugs, he is involved in group therapy, Synanons, where everyone laughingly points out all his silly little plots and devices as they hatch in his feeble brain.[12]

He is thus further confused and kept off balance by the experts.

Synanon views the newly arrived addict as an emotional infant, "encapsulated," that is, limited in his ability to communicate meaningfully. His confused verbosity is generally ignored for all practical therapeutic purposes. As one addict (now 3 years clean) at Synanon put it in response to a compliment on his current verbal ability (he had just lectured on Synanon to a group of parole and probation administrators),[13] "When I got to Synanon, I would begin a sentence in the middle and I didn't know which way the words would go, forwards or backwards." His old pattern had been to lie so much that he found it difficult to know when he was telling the truth.

The newcomer is usually physically sick. Some of Synanon's

volunteer medical staff (over twenty doctors and dentists) have concluded that many of the addict's physical illnesses are held in a state of suspended animation by his self-administered heroin medicine. The main Synanon "family doctor," Dr. Bernard Casselman, states: [14]

> When heroin is withdrawn not only does the addict suffer withdrawal illness, his teeth, liver and other vital organs begin to manifest a sickness and pain that was contained by the drugs. There is some evidence that heroin has the therapeutic effect of holding certain physical problems in check. When the addict's "medicine" (heroin) is withdrawn, he tends to reveal a variety of illnesses. Also, often a variety of psychosomatic symptoms emerge which to the addict may serve as a rationale for him to split. He may break out in a nervous rash, or complain of pain, which upon medical examination reveals no physical base.

Thus, at Synanon the situation is reversed from the way it usually operates in other settings.[15] The addict has to prove to the indoctrination committee that he truly seeks help and wants to change his behavior.

Some of the forces at work in the Synanon indoctrination are revealed in the following verbatim interview. The addict had come voluntarily for help, fresh off the streets of New York. Here he is presented with the Synanon contract by a Synanist and ex-addict himself. The following interchange occurred after the committee had decided they would accept the newcomer. (This indoctrination took place with a Synanon committee of three, headed by Jack Hurst, then Resident Director of the Westport Synanon House.) The "prospect" (a Synanon term) had been through jails and a variety of hospitals without success. Not all indoctrinations are this "tough." Possibly because this prospect had experienced failure in other settings, he came to Synanon with a "chip on his shoulder." He was met with firmness, in part to test his ability to "take" some of the "attack therapy" he would later receive in a larger measure:

J. H.: You'll be the new element in the family. You'll be kind of like the new baby. We'll talk in terms of family structure, it isn't bad. You'll be told when to get up, you'll be told what to do when you do get up. You'll be told when to go to Synanon, what kind of work to do, when to go to seminars. You'll be told when to talk and when not to talk. You will kind of be told what to do for a while. I guarantee you that if you go through the motions that we describe and prescribe for you you'll end up being a man, not the sniveling whining brat that you are now. You'll be a man!

Prospect: What makes you think I'm a sniveling brat? You only know me for five minutes and . . .

J. H.: You see, people that use drugs, people that live with their sisters, people that steal hubcaps, people that go in and out of jails, the people that go to nut houses for help, these are sniveling brats in my opinion and my opinion carries a lot of weight in this house. Get that gut level. My opinion is pretty Goddamn certain to be valid as a salad. Try to understand that, if you don't understand it, act as if you understand.

When you make a lot of noise in our environment it's not very nice to listen to. Arguments are something we save for Synanons. You can argue your ass off in a Synanon. When you're being talked to around here, and when you're in my office or in my dining room you kind of behave yourself and keep your big mouth shut. Listen to what's going on around you, you might learn something. Don't be so frightened to learn something. You see, you almost learned something a moment ago —the fact that you are a whining sniveling brat. But you fight it.

That's your big trouble with life, you fight information that could help you. If you could start to accept some of these things about yourself and learn to live with them, you know, you may outgrow it. I guarantee you, you will if you stay, there's no question about that in my mind. No question whatsoever. If you stay, if you listen, and if you do as we say—I guarantee it.

Now you're not going to be expected for a couple of, three–four months, to do our banking, for instance. This would be like asking a four-year-old child to carry a hundred-pound suitcase like a man. You're not going to be expected to do our shopping. You're not going to be expected to get into our car and go to Bridgeport to pick up donations. You're not going to be expected to make big decisions concerning what will be policy around here. We have other people to do this. What you're going to be expected to do is wash the toilets, wash the floors, do the dishes, anything that we feel that you should be doing. As you learn how to do these things *well, well* mind you, then you will gradually get to more and better things, or let's say, more responsible jobs. You'll graduate up the power structure, pretty soon you know in a couple of years, maybe even a year, you just might be a big shot around here—or Santa Monica or Reno.[16]

In summary, the addict enters voluntarily into a community of ex-addicts, who tell him in no uncertain terms that the only basis for his entering the institution is to clean himself up. He is expected to fulfill the "therapeutic contract" he accepts when he arrives. This situation is usually the reverse of the addict arriving in a jail or a mental hospital, where he generally is committed or ordered.

Caste and Stratification

It is well documented in published theory and research regarding prisons and mental hospitals that a patient or inmate subculture, or subsociety, emerges and exists within the overall structure.[17] This subsystem has norms, patterns of behavior, and goals different from, and often in conflict with, the inclusive institutional structure. Weinberg points up some of the problems of this structural situation: [18]

> The inmates and officials are two segregated strata whose relations and attitudes, like those of other castes, result from previously unresolved conflicts. Their relations are impersonal, and the individual members of the respective groups are considered as stereotypes. Modes of deference and obedience are expected by the officials, and expressions of authority are anticipated and tolerated by the inmates. Castes which are long subservient acquire inferiority feelings from traditional displays of deference, for groups in a less-resolved conflict situation, such as the prisoners, also consider the upper groups as out-groups: consequently, their respect remains superficial and external.

It is often conceded by correctional administrators that the inmate-administration relationship often contradicts, conflicts with, and impedes therapeutic progress with the inmate. The inmate subsystem often emerges to cope with the new set of problems that the patient or inmate finds in the institutional setting.

As indicated, the inmate system in prison militates against proper correction. The inmate tends to maintain his criminal, "tough-guy" behavior since this gives him status within prison. According to Korn and McCorkle, another prisoner pattern is "to reject the rejectors." Based on their extensive study of prison social systems they describe the problem as follows: [19]

> Observation suggests that the major problems with which the inmate social system attempts to cope center about the theme of social rejection. In many ways, the inmate social system may be viewed as

providing a way of life which enables the inmate to avoid the devastating psychological effects of internalizing and converting social rejection into self-rejection. In effect, it permits the inmate to reject his rejectors rather than himself.

The prison or mental hospital society is a type of a *caste system*. No matter what the patient or inmate does, he cannot rise in the hierarchy beyond his status and role of "patient" or "inmate." Therefore, he is essentially a member of a lower caste, in many ways comparable to an "untouchable," within the social system of the hospital or prison.

Synanon on the other hand presents the addict with an open-end *stratification* system. A full measure of upward mobility is available. (As Hurst states in the indoctrination, "in a couple of years . . . you just might be a big shot . . . here—or in Santa Monica or Reno.") Not only is there upward social mobility in the stratification system of Synanon, "status seeking" is heavily encouraged.[20] There is an assumption at Synanon, with some evidence to support it, that one's position within the stratification system is a function of social maturity, mental health, work ability, "social" ability, and a good understanding of the Synanon social system. One hypothesis operative at Synanon is that there is a significant correlation between one's position in the hierarchy and the scope of clear perception of the organization's dynamics. Another hypothesis is that social skills within Synanon are concomitantly functional within the larger society. (The reverse appears to be true of skills within the prison caste society.)

"Tough Guys" and Status

Synanon attempts to discourage the tough-guy criminal role as a means of approval and status. An effort is consciously made to smash the criminal tough-guy mold and its derivatives, which may have been useful in prison, but is not legitimized at all in Synanon. There is no symptom reinforcement of "criminal tough-guy" behavior at Synanon.

In a ridicule "haircut"[21] session Reid Kimball, a member of Synanon's board of directors, drives this issue home to a group of newcomers—10 young "gangsters" from New York. Reid was himself formerly an addict and "gangster" for 18 years. (He is currently clean since 1959 in Synanon and is resident director of the Santa Monica operation.) The group of "New York gangsters" was called in for this haircut for cursing excessively and acting "like punks." The following is only a portion of the more extended haircut. It partially reveals the Synanon attitude toward tough-guy behavior: [22]

R. K.: Some of you guys in here will make it, whatever that means. I guess on some level you want to quit being real nuts, lunatics, and locked up. It seems quite obvious that before that happens you will have to quit doing what you've been doing. If this place was San Quentin or Dannemora or Sing Sing, I would fully agree with your tough-guy act. In Dannemora or Sing Sing I suppose you have to let it be known that you were a hotshot on the street and that you're a bad guy inside the walls to get status. This is what you should do in prison. But think of how ludicrous it is when you come here to this place and you try to be tough guys or gangsters or something like that. Here you are in a place where if you make progress you can become an adult. . . .

I must have a Jimmy Cagney complex. If I saw a Jimmy Cagney picture late tonight where old Jim was taken after a terrific gunfight as a big-shot racketeer, he really had it made and was sent to the joint and he strutted around the big yard talking bad and commenting on the lames you know and everything, my heart would go out to him. There's old Jimmy boy ——ing those squares, that would make sense to me. But if Jimmy's mama mailed him there to make it and he was walking around wisecracking about the lames of society, I'd think why that silly son of a bitch.

The effort here is to demonstrate dramatically and graphically to the addict tough guy that he can achieve status and approval in Synanon only by good behavior—and not by the type of customary behavior in the subsociety of traditional settings. [23] It is pointed out to him that tough-guy behavior in Synanon is not encouraged or rewarded. In Synanon, if the individual does not behave properly, he may be "thrown out." The threat of ostracism, "30 days on the street" is the ultimate punishment. The Synanist believes that the addict would not "last on the street," and this is confirmed by considerable evidence. He uses drugs, becomes sick, and often returns to jail. In prison, punishment involves confinement from "the hole" to the straitjacket. At Synanon, punishment involves ostracism.

It is pointed out to the newcomer that he can achieve any role in the organization by *positive* behavior, and this is forcefully encouraged and demonstrated. Dederich in talking to a Synanon group once stated, "In here you have 150 doctors and you are a doctor to 149 others." The implication of his remark is that the Synanon member is not restricted to patient or inmate status. He can literally achieve a "therapist" or an "executive" role; and this is encouraged. This of course is not possible in the caste structure of traditional inmate-administration divided settings.

Identification with the Synanon Organization

Another factor that differentiates Synanon from the traditional institution is the fact that the addict at Synanon has the status or role of a *person* rather than "ward," "inmate," "prisoner," or "patient" in the organization.[24] He can identify with the constructive goals of the organization for which he works. He is, in fact, after he "kicks his habit," automatically an employee of the organization, and in this role he takes part in Synanon's management and development. He is encouraged to believe that he is in some measure able to control the program of which he is a part, and this of course is true.

In other settings the reverse is generally true. The organization is run by administrators over whom the individual inmate has no control whatsoever, and he feels helpless within the organizational structure. As indicated, hospital and prison administrators tend to be negative representatives of the "rejectors," and this sets up additional blocks to correction. At Synanon, there is no such split, and the administration consists of coworkers and colleagues.

Involvement in the Synanon organization may help to foster the empathic quotient of the addict personality. Often for the first time in his experience, he begins to identify with a constructively oriented group of his peers. He develops feeling and concern for the other members and the destiny of the Synanon totality, a reversal of his former sociopathic inclinations.

Involvement in the organization is a natural involvement. Work at Synanon comes closer to being "real" work than the often contrived work which takes place in prisons and mental hospitals. There is no "basket weaving" at Synanon. All jobs and work activities are tied in to the real needs of the organization. These include the "hustling of food," [25] an office staff, a maintenance and service crew for fixing the physical structure of the building, an operations crew for dispatching people, and a coordinating staff for handling incoming and outgoing phone calls and interaction with the larger society. Since its inception Synanon has been shorthanded for carrying out the many jobs necessary to its functioning.

Synanon constitutes a social organization, membership in which is of importance to the recovering addict and is clearly evidenced to him as necessary. Also at Synanon cultural activities tend to be in accord with the wishes and desires of the residents. There are no special rewards other than those the individual gets from the activity on a personal level. He participates in lectures, seminars, theatrical groups, semantics classes, and other types of activities which operate at Synanon. He is more apt to take part—of his own volition—since he is not, as he is in prison, the recipient of "good time" or earlier parole for being an active participant.

Although there have been attempts at self-government in some prisons and hospitals, the inmates in these settings recognize that final decisions on important policy issues remain with the administration. In Synanon, perhaps for the first time in his life, the addict assumes a significant role in controlling his own destiny. Leadership in a constructive situation is a new experience for him and appears to develop responsibility in a constructive fashion.[26] The residents at Synanon, unlike patients and inmates, are involved with the growth and development of their own organization. Because there is a generally held belief by the residents that "Synanon saved our lives," the *esprit de corps* and involvement in the organization is strong. Few inmates would give three cheers for "dear old San Quentin"; however, Synanon people seem to enjoy cheering for Synanon at every opportunity.

Group Psychotherapy in Prison and at Synanon

A major difference in the forms of group psychotherapy between Synanon and the other institutions is the fact that Synanon has no professional therapists other than the trained Synanist. As described earlier, by Dederich, the Synanist is a unique type of group psychotherapist.

There is some evidence that in prisons individuals participate in group psychotherapy with an eye upon the front door. Consciously and unconsciously the prisoner may produce insights and therapeutic progress in efforts to convince officials that he has changed and is ready for release.

At Synanon, the sessions are closely related to the "real life" problems which confront the member in the social system in which he resides. Given the lack of caste division, lines of communication exist throughout the organization. This, plus the "gold-fish bowl" atmosphere and expectations, are conducive to a total revelation of all behavioral and thought material. ("We tell all of our dirty little secrets.") The Synanon method makes an intensive effort to bring to the surface all possible data, since this is vital to the protection and growth of the organization. At Synanon, lying is considered reprehensible. The Synanon session is an emotional "first-aid station," where members must tell the truth completely.

The small s synanon performs another important function. Dederich has referred to the small s synanon as a "floating primary group," in part developed to help counteract Synanon's large growth in size and a drift toward bureaucracy. When Synanon was smaller, it seemed apparent that Synanon's therapeutic impact was related to a continuing primary-group situation involving face-to-face relationships, identity of ends, and a reciprocal concern. When Synanon grew in size from a small primary group to a large secondary organization of over one hundred people, there was a concern that it would lose its qualitative primary-group impact. This danger was anticipated and described by Dederich as follows: [27]

The small s synanon is the contrived constructed primary-group formula for the maintenance of the secondary organization. The two put together produce the most effective type of human organization. It has become axiomatic in Synanon that the triggering mechanism in the whole Synanon dynamic was, is, and always will be the small s synanon in its expanding form. The small s synanon started as being peculiarly suited to its time and place and is of course growing and expanding and taking on dimensions that it didn't have before. I guess the original invention, the innovation of Synanon, was not living together, it was not preparing meals together, the original innovation in the field of psychology and sociology was the devising of the so-called small s synanon. Preserving, adding to, and expanding the dimension of the small s synanon will of course have an effect which we trust will ameliorate some of the so-called "evils" that we associate with bureaucracy. The small s synanon concept is a floating kind of primary-group interaction that affects the whole secondary-group structure of Synanon.

Another result of Synanon group therapy is that the resident is in a position to test his therapeutic developments and growth. About two-thirds of Synanon residents enter into some daily activity with the outside community. Their social growth is testable. The hospital patient, or the prisoner, in contrast, is usually restricted to the artificial society of the institution of custody. He may feel he is "getting better"; however, the circumstances for testing his social growth are generally not available in this restricted situation.

Synanon in the Community

Synanon members have a qualitatively different relationship with the larger society than "prisoners" or "patients." According to Korn and McCorkle the isolation of the prisoner from the outside world is a major problem of correction: [28]

The total result of the interacting trends and processes described has been to isolate the confined offender from socially beneficial contact with individuals outside the inmate social world and to prevent the formation of relationship bonds which might redefine him as an acceptable member of the non-criminal community. This is the major dilemma of penology.

In a real sense, Synanon *is in* the community. It is visited weekly by hundreds of professional and other interested members of the community. Synanon residents interact with visitors in a manner entirely different from the patient's or the inmate's. Synanon members meet with members of the community on equal terms. The visitor, whether psychiatrist, sociologist, or a layman, is visiting his home. He is pleased to show him around and talk about Synanon. He is not being visited involuntarily as in a prison, where approval for the visit is given by an administration over whom he has no control. People who live at Synanon can and sometimes do eject individuals who do not behave properly in their home.[29] Given these circumstances, over a period of a year or two the Synanon resident has a significant experience in effectively interacting with a variety of members of the larger society in a situation of equality. Because of these important distinctions between Synanon and traditional institutions, the type of personal growth and development in Synanon is more apt to equip the Synanon person to function more effectively in the larger society.

SUMMARY AND CONCLUSIONS

The following propositions reflect the differences between Synanon and other types of institutions that exist for the treatment and rehabilitation of drug addicts. As further descriptive data on Synanon accrue, these propositions may be stated in the form of more concrete hypotheses in a design susceptible to systematic research. The following generalizations may serve as guides to the further development of such testable hypotheses.

1. There is a qualitative difference between indoctrination at Synanon and in other settings. The contractual arrangement for therapy and the addict's expectation of success as incorporated in the indoctrination process represent some of the differences. The indoctrination of the "prospect" by successful ex-addicts is a significant force which differentiates Synanon from other approaches. It provides the newcomer with a role model of what he can become.

2. Synanon provides an upwardly mobile stratification system for the ex-addict. Most institutions and hospitals represent social caste systems. Becoming a "Synanist," a new social role, provides a different type of incentive for modifying one's proaddiction motivation to antiaddiction motivation.[30] The Synanon resident can realistically achieve any desired role within the organization.

3. There is a qualitative difference between the small-s-synanon form of group therapy and the group therapy carried on in prisons and hospitals. This is partially a function of the overall social system within which the group therapy takes place and the functioning of the Synanist in the therapy session. Because of his continued voluntary participation in Synanon the resident has little to gain from "faking progress." He is encouraged by others who have traveled the same route to recovery to reveal and deal honestly.

4. The nature and ethos of the Synanon subculture is significantly closer to, and more connected with, the larger society than traditional institutional settings. The flow of members of the community through Synanon and, concomitantly, the entry of Synanon's members into the larger society in many respects place it closer to the "real life" situation of the outer world than the generally artificial community of the prison or the mental hospital. Moreover, the Synanon resident has an involvement with, and a commitment to, the Synanon organization which do not obtain in other settings. This provides him with a natural role training for living effectively in a constructive social system.

5. The forces at work in Synanon differ qualitatively from those in most other institutional arrangements. Better measurement of the particular variables most significant to understanding the differences will result from further studies. An inherent research problem lies in the fact that control settings have to be taken *in toto*. It would be difficult to vary certain factors at Synanon or in prison to carry out this kind of research. Necessarily the *total* process of the prison, the halfway house, or the hospital has to be measured against the *total* Synanon organization.

There is a natural resistance to "control-study" and statistical-analysis types of studies at Synanon. As indicated, one reason is that the Synanon system has not yet been defined.

Another is the emphasis on having Synanon residents viewed as *people* rather than as "addicts," "sociopaths," "prisoners," or "criminals." In the next several years as the Synanon organization becomes further delineated and its methodology becomes clearer through descriptive studies which provide a more adequate conceptual framework, increasingly formal research methods may be permitted into the environment without upsetting its equilibrium and thrust. According to Dederich, "It will be another five years before this situation obtains." In the meantime it is important that Synanon be understood in terms of its own defined conceptual framework. This would seem preferable to forcing it into theoretical and research constructs developed within the traditional therapeutic settings, which have had only a limited measure of success in solving the narcotics problem.

Table 12-1   CLEAN TIME AND LOCATION (as of April 15, 1963) *

Time clean at Synanon, years	Synanon Locations			Third stager (lives and works in community)	Total
	Santa Monica, Calif.	Westport, Conn.	Reno, Nev.		
Under 1	73	16	1	. . .	90
1–2	17	4	7	1	29
2–3	12	. . .	1	. . .	13
3–4	7	2	1	10	20
4–5	7	1	1	9	18
Total	116	23	11	20	170

Table 12-2   TOTAL CLEAN TIME IN SYNANON (as of April 15, 1963) *

Years	Number of residents	Per cent of total population
Over 1	85	50
2	51	30
3	38	22
4	18	15

Table 12-3   AGE DISTRIBUTION (as of April 15, 1963) *

	Below 20	20–24	25–29	30–34	35–39	40–49	50 and over	Total
Male . . .	2	18	26	23	18	12	5	104
Female .	1	11	14	8	2	1	1	38
Total .	3	29	40	31	20	13	6	142

Table 12-4   RACE (as of April 15, 1963) *

	Caucasian	Negro	Mexican	Puerto Rican	Unknown	Total
Male	75	18	8	2	1	104
Female . .	31	5	1	1	0	38
Total . .	106	23	9	3	1	142

Table 12-5 RELIGIOUS BACKGROUND OF FAMILY (as of April 15, 1963) *

	Protestant	Roman Catholic	Jewish	Unknown, mixed, other	None	Total
Male	13	35	17	22	9	96
Female ..	6	11	7	8	4	36
Total ..	19	46	24	30	13	132

Table 12-6 NUMBER OF YEARS SINCE BEGINNING OF ADDICTION
(as of April 15, 1963) *

	5 or less	5–10	10–15	15 or more	Total
Male	5	29	33	25	92
Female	6	14	11	4	35
Total	11	43	44	29	127

Table 12-7 INSTITUTIONAL BACKGROUND
(Jails, hospitals, etc., as of April 15, 1963) *

	Male	Female
	(N = 92)	(N = 35)
Institution Time Factors		
Total years of time............	254	44
Mean	2 years 7 months	1 year 5 months
No time served...............	16	2

* There was a grand total of 170 Synanon members when this analysis was made in April, 1963. (In some cases fewer are totaled in a particular area because the data were unavailable.) As of March, 1964, there were 400 residents in Synanon's five locations. If this rate of growth continues, there will be about 1,000 residents in Synanon when this book is issued. A crude assessment indicates that the only major shift that has taken place in the newer Synanon population profile, since these data were compiled, is that median age is decreasing.

REFERENCES

1. Dederich, Charles E.: Lectures delivered before graduate seminars of the School of Social Welfare, University of California at Los Angeles, in the fall of 1962.
2. The term "clean" in this report refers to freedom from the use of any drugs, chemicals, or alcohol and from involvement in any illegal behavior.
3. Dederich, *op. cit.*
4. The phrase "hope-to-die addict" is used by addicts to signify their acceptance that there is no cure and that "once an addict, always an addict."

5. Dederich, *op. cit.*
6. Almost all Synanon residents have attempted to quit using drugs in other settings—voluntarily and involuntarily.
7. For a more detailed analysis of the Synanist role in prison see Lewis Yablonsky: The Anticriminal Society: Synanon, *Federal Probation*, September, 1962. A book with the same title will be published by the Macmillan Company in 1964.
8. Hereafter, use of the term "traditional settings" will encompass prisons and narcotic treatment hospitals of various types, including Lexington, Fort Worth, and Riverside, New York. No reference is made to the halfway-house approach, since this method has only been operational for a short period of time.
9. Dederich, *op cit.*
10. *Ibid.*
11. *Ibid.*
12. *Ibid.*
13. Synanon residents have filled hundreds of speaking engagements with professional groups, college and university classes, church groups, high school assemblies, and other community organizations.
14. Personal communications.
15. For a detailed discussion of entrance into "total institutions," see Goffman, Erving: "Asylums," Anchor Books, Doubleday & Company, Inc., Garden City, N.Y., 1961.
16. Dederich, *op. cit.*
17. See especially the following: Clemmer, Donald: "The Prison Community," Holt, Rinehart and Winston, Inc., New York, 1958; Sykes, Gresham: "The Society of Captives," Princeton University Press, Princeton, N.J., 1958; Korn, Richard, and McCorkle, Lloyd: "Criminology and Penology," Holt, Rinehart and Winston, Inc., New York, 1958; Cressey, Donald (ed.): "The Prison," Holt, Rinehart and Winston, Inc., New York, 1961; Yablonsky, Lewis: Correction and the "Doing Time" Society, *Federal Probation*, March, 1960.
18. Weinberg, S. Kirsen: Aspects of the Prison's Social Structure, *Am. J. Sociology*, March, 1942.
19. McCorkle, Lloyd, and Korn, Richard: Resocialization within Walls, *The Annals: Prisons in Transformation*, p. 88, May, 1954.
20. A total set of indoctrination sessions at Synanon was devised for encouraging the resident to seek status and its "rewards" within the organization.

21. A "haircut" is a severe, caustic verbal attack on behavior considered "atrocious" at Synanon. The "offense" is caricatured, exaggerated, and severely ridiculed. It is employed as a standard therapeutic tool.
22. Dederich, *op. cit.*
23. See the following for an excellent discussion of the "prestige" implication of the "thief and convict" subculture in prison: Cressey, Donald, and Irwin, John: Thieves, Convicts and the Inmate Culture, *Social Problems,* 10:45, 1962.
24. Dederich was once asked what he called "Synanon inmates." He said, "We call them 'people.'"
25. "Hustling" involves the work of collecting donations of goods from contributors. Currently Synanon has a motor pool of 12 vehicles for this work.
26. Twenty-two-year-old Anita, clean since 1961 in Synanon, has the responsibility and power, as the Synanon accountant, to place the final authorized signature on all check payments for the Foundation. This involves the responsibility for the expenditure of several thousand dollars per month.
27. Dederich, *op. cit.*
28. Korn and McCorkle: *The Annals: Prisons in Transformation,* p. 97.
29. An interesting case in point is provided by the following incident. One Saturday evening, at Synanon's traditional "open house," a visitor, a well-known Hollywood movie producer, was engaged in an intense conversation with a Synanon resident. The discussion was cordial, until the producer revealed that he had a "pill habit." The situation changed dramatically. He was immediately brought into the coordinators' office, where he was severely told that "no using addicts could be permitted or tolerated in Synanon." He was firmly told to leave—and it was suggested that if he wanted to enter Synanon to deal with his problem, he would have to apply like any other "dope fiend." In another case a large financial donor attempted to visit one evening, slightly under the influence of alcohol, and was promptly asked to leave. There is no compromise with the use of any chemical in the building by anyone.
30. Lewis Yablonsky describes the basis for this modification in the September, 1962, article in *Federal Probation:* "Unlike most professional or ex-offender workers in the field the trained Synanist has three levels of experience which uniquely qualify him for work with other offenders.

"1. He has a lengthy history of criminal experience. He himself has made the 'scene.' He knows the crime problem in its many dimensions—at first hand.

"2. At Synanon, this individual has deeply experienced the emotional upheaval of rejecting one way of life for another. He has 'in his gut' gone through a resocialization process and knows something about the set of experiences and the pain involved in the transition.

"3. He knows the Synanon social system. He has a subconscious conception of the processes at work for helping others and he is himself a functional part of this organization. He has been trained at 'the Synanon College' for working with recalcitrant offenders. This triad of experience qualifies the Synanist uniquely for the task at hand."

Leon Brill | **13**

REHABILITATION IN DRUG ADDICTION: A REPORT OF THE NEW YORK DEMONSTRATION CENTER*

THE NEW YORK DEMONSTRATION CENTER was established in 1957 by the Community Services Branch of the National Institute of Mental Health. The Center's program was founded on the belief that an increased use of community resources would help rehabilitate narcotic addicts discharged from the Public Health Service Hospital at Lexington, Kentucky. Goals visualized were: eliciting the needs of Lexington dischargees and preparing them for referral to appropriate community agencies. The Center was to serve as an informational and consultative resource for the city as well.

Initial plans called for the Center staff to select for referral only the "best-motivated" patients in order to overcome agency reluctance to working with addicts; and to increase the likelihood of initial success, in the hope of encouraging their readier acceptance of addicts in time. Early understandings with agencies in-

* From "Rehabilitation in Drug Addiction," Mental Health Monograph 3, National Institute of Mental Health, Public Health Service, PHS Publication no. 1013, 1963.

217

cluded a number of difficult stipulations geared to the exceptional rather than "run-of-the-mill" addict—such as the requirement that he be totally abstinent, and have completed Lexington hospital treatment, among others.

Although it had been anticipated our most difficult problem would be enlisting the cooperation of agencies, this proved to be unfounded, with almost all agencies approached agreeing to extend their services to referred patients. In a number of cases, this required a revision of policy, which opened agency doors for the first time to Center patients, and eventually to other agency clients as well. It was later believed that the reassurances offered by the Center staff, the availability of its full-time professionally trained workers for consultation, and the good conscience of the community agencies involved were the major factors at work in reaching these agreements. In time, some agencies modified their original conditions, agreeing to accept irregularly relapsed patients as well. Liaison relationships were thus established by the Director of the Demonstration Center with the executives of many social agencies in New York City, including employment and vocational rehabilitation facilities, the Department of Welfare, and family agencies and mental hygiene clinics.

Although making available to the addict services previously withheld from him was an essential first step in efforts to rehabilitate him, it was soon clear this was far from the whole answer. It proved very difficult for the addict to make use of these community resources, especially those entailing sustained counseling services. Agencies which had reluctantly agreed to accept addict-clients and had anticipated being flooded with applicants, began to wonder about the small number of referrals from the Center. It soon became evident that assumptions regarding the addict's "referrability" were subject to considerable question.

With the steady stream of Lexington dischargees to the Demonstration Center (912 in all), the full impact of the "addict" and his behavior was soon perceived. The extent of his dependency, passivity, narcissism, low frustration-tolerance, suspiciousness and unrelatedness to others, his disregard of time, and irresponsibility, made it necessary to alter many staff preconceptions. Because the addict was so different from clients seen in other settings, it was quickly realized that modifications in traditional casework approaches and techniques would be necessary.

The first departure from traditional practice was in the area of appointments, which needed to be approached with great flexibility and patience in order to meet the addict's marked unrelatedness to time. Workers found, to their dismay, that most patients failed to return after one or two interviews. Knowledge gradually gained from direct contacts with the addict, from supervisory conferences and staff meetings, and individual and group conferences with the Demonstration Center's psychiatric consultant, was augmented by discussions with specialists in a variety of other disciplines, with reference to the sociological and cultural factors in drug addiction.

One of the outstanding problems in working with the addict stems from his pattern of looking to narcotic drugs for the solution of his problems, while viewing himself as the victim of a "monkey on his back." This use of projection and the "easy" solution of problems through use of drugs make work with addicts extremely precarious. The patient, vulnerable to constant relapse, has great difficulty using even the "concrete services" typically sought at the Center. In view of the tremendous individual gratification obtained from narcotics use, he is almost totally unrelated to psychological services involving the need for self-examination which the professional community believes he needs urgently.

A number of patients nevertheless used casework help in a limited way, following through on employment referrals with a good deal of support, remaining on jobs longer, and working out better ways of dealing with stresses in their familial and social relationships.

On the whole, while many patients were placed in employment, it was found that they seldom stayed on a job more than a few weeks, because of their relapse to drug use. One of the clearest findings to emerge from the project is that the addict needs contact with a resource which provides not only step-by-step support in following through on referrals, but constant supervision to help him sustain his efforts. In time, staff began to see the "concrete" services, viewed hitherto as incomplete, as valid services for addicts who neither sought nor could use help beyond simple support, combined with tangible assistance. It was frustrating to the Center staff to be unable to intervene more effectively in the addict's repetitive cycles of relapse and find ways of competing with drugs which offered nirvana.

Efforts were made to work with the families of addicts since it was early recognized that some modification in family attitudes was urgently needed in most cases if the patient was to have a chance to readjust. The destructive interactions in the relationship between addict and family made it difficult to effect such a modification. The mother's ambivalence, overprotectiveness and need to control, for example, fed into the addict's infantilism, passivity, and resentment.

Where the addict and/or his family evidenced even a minimal understanding of the problem, and some ability to keep appointments, every effort was made to refer the case to a counseling agency in line with our role as a referral service. Only a very small number of cases, however, met these requirements or followed through on referrals.

Community agencies, while initially skeptical about the possibility of working with addict-clients, soon became very interested and cooperative. They learned that, while the specific character of the addict's symptomatology and his perennial crises frequently engendered negative reactions in workers, the basic human problems were essentially the same as in their other clients. Through consultation and conferences with the Demonstration Center staff, experiences and ideas were shared to the benefit of all.

Preparation of even the few selected cases for referral to a counselling agency was a process that involved a good deal of patience and persistence, far beyond that usually required in other settings. The addict and his family strongly resisted transfer from the Demonstration Center, regressing repeatedly to denial of problem. The family especially proved recalcitrant since they wished to have the spotlight focused on the addict in the Demonstration Center rather than on themselves and family problems elsewhere. In some of the families who remained with the Center, help was offered in the form of attempting to modify their blatantly destructive and self-defeating behavior. It was learned this could be done in a limited way even with those families whose capacity for self-awareness was so vestigial as to make them unreferrable to outside agencies as currently structured. One of the more important conclusions drawn from work with these Center cases, often for extended periods of time, is that the addict himself and, often, his relatives as well, require a protracted period of "pretreatment" (which almost no agency today is prepared to offer), before they can in any sense be viewed as a "client." Family agencies have frankly expressed their reluctance to take on a "ten-year case," and have suggested that such cases are in the province of public agencies such as the Department of Welfare.

Experience with several "long-term" cases in which contact was sustained through some factor of compulsion, rather than true motivation—such as pressure from a probation officer, or the threat of losing a source of support—suggests that such initial structuring may help point the way for effective treatment of the addict.

In the course of its operation, the Demonstration Center fulfilled a number of secondary functions apart from its primary goals. It offered informational and consultative services to a wide number of interested individuals and agencies who were seeking information regarding various aspects of drug addiction, including available resources for treatment. The Center provided these services on a number of levels—starting with the close consultative relationship established with agencies to which our patients were referred; and extending to requests by individuals or agencies for help with individual situations, or exploration of some of the general aspects of addiction. These contacts in time constituted a substantial service, totaling many thousands in the years of our operation.

Requests from agencies were usually centered around a common theme: Where can we find help for a patient? To whom can we refer? Center staff was helpful in allaying agency anxiety, overcoming stereotyped thinking, suggesting resources and, in many cases, helping the agency retain a patient it had sought to refer once it could view the situation more calmly and cease looking for a nonexistent facility. The so-called "Brief Services"—involving contacts with non-Lexington patients to explore their problems and clarify with them how they could proceed to help themselves—also constituted a considerable service to the community during the years of our operation. As with Lexington dischargees, most of these patients' requests were for help with detoxification or financial maintenance and employment.

Consultation was also offered in terms of helping agencies plan public meetings and workshops or programs of their own for extending their services to addicts. Center representatives offered testimony at city, state and Federal legislative committee hearings. Other functions included lecturing, and publication of the Center's preliminary report on its work in the community.

RECOMMENDATIONS

1. Within the framework of our present knowledge, addiction needs to be viewed as a chronic illness, with limited goals the only appropriate and realistic ones. Helping the addict hold a job and abstain from drug use for even brief periods, with the hope of increasing these intervals in time, represents a worthwhile goal.

2. To counteract the addict's deep-seated dependency needs, passivity, poor motivation for change, difficulties in communication, and low frustration-tolerance, the casework approach needs to be active, directive and reaching out. Specifically:

   a. The worker should be flexible about appointment schedules since the addict lives from crisis to crisis and comes in, for the most part, only during such periods of crisis.

   b. The addict's reaching out for help during these periodic crises must be used dynamically in the hope of eventually establishing an ongoing casework relationship. Active assistance with emergency problems to the point of sometimes making decisions for him when he is immobilized may help the addict view the worker as a strong reliable person, interested in his welfare. Reaching-out efforts would include repeated home visits, the sending of follow-up letters when a patient fails appointments, making telephone calls, and being available in times of acute stress to reinforce the addict's image of the worker as a person committed and able to help him.

c. Addicts can best be reached and helped, at least at the outset, on the level of concrete and tangible services. Center workers believed these services to be the only appropriate ones to help ease pressures on the patient and family, build a relationship and ultimately involve the addict more meaningfully.

d. Helping the addict utilize appropriate community resources entails a "supportive" process and step-by-step guidance through each agency contact to insure that his characteristic impulsiveness and low frustration-tolerance do not push him back into his typical patterns of avoidance of assistance and relapse to drugs. Consultation and close cooperation with community agencies serving the addict are essential to obviate his "getting lost" between agencies.

e. The "action approach" appears to be the approach indicated for the addict, at least in the initial stages of treatment, rather than focusing on intrapsychic or interpersonal conflicts, attempting to "work through" problems, elicit feelings and develop insight.

f. The intensity of the relationship with the addict needs to be diluted. His inability to tolerate closeness may endanger his already precarious balance and stimulate further acting-out behavior, to which he is so prone.

g. Before any regular treatment can be initiated with the addict, a period of "preliminary-treatment" should be maintained for varying periods of time until a relationship can be built and the addict becomes a "client" who can assume some responsibility in planning to work out his problems.

h. The caseworker must constantly be aware of, and learn to control negative reactions to the addict since he poses greater problems than other clients in terms of unrealistic demands, self-defeating operations, testing the limits of the relationship and repudiating the social values and standards with which the worker is identified. Without condoning his antisocial behavior, the worker should try to remain nonjudgmental while coping with the constant drain on energies represented by the patient's dependency needs, apathy and continued acting-out behavior.

    i. In view of the addict's impulsiveness and strong resistance to change as evidenced in his unwillingness to seek out or sustain any rehabilitative endeavors, it is felt that the role of authority in relation to rehabilitation warrants further investigation. Attempts should be made to find the optimal balance of helping *cum* compulsion, which can sustain the addict in a rehabilitation program.

3. Work with the addict's family is a *sine qua non* in any efforts to rehabilitate him and halt the family's storm and stress. The family needs to be helped to view his addiction as a chronic illness and cease its endless destructive interaction with the addict, which reinforces and perpetuates his addiction. The family's passive orientation and defeatist attitudes can be challenged through active casework intervention, which offers them support in their struggle, and reduces their feeling of being alone with an insoluble problem.

4. Caseworkers charged with responsibility for rehabilitating addicts and their families need to increase their understanding of the diverse factors contributing to narcotics addiction, including also the sociocultural characteristics of urban lower-class society and the addict subculture. Knowledge of the addict's patterns of behavior, his life style, his values and ways of viewing and dealing with the world at large, should help to increase the worker's ability to identify with him, and possibly throw light on the many unknowns (e.g., the phenomena of "resistance," and/or "lack of motivation" predisposing him to use) which at present limit our effectiveness in work with him.

5. Narcotics addiction is a complex, multi-factored problem which has not responded to traditional rehabilitation approaches.

There appears to be a need, consequently, for experimental research projects geared to answer the outstanding questions; and for the coordinated efforts of community agencies to sustain the addict by offering him a spectrum of services on a number of levels. The use of an epidemiologic-ecologic approach would also appear to be indicated.

John A. O'Donnell | **14**

THE RELAPSE RATE IN
NARCOTIC ADDICTION:
A CRITIQUE OF FOLLOW-UP STUDIES

NARCOTIC ADDICTION is a controversial field. Conflicting views are current with regard to the extent of the problem, its etiology, treatment, the desirability of stricter or more lenient laws, whether addiction should be regarded as a crime or disease, and almost any other aspect of the problem one might isolate. There is, however, almost universal agreement, even among persons who strongly disagree on everything else, that the relapse rate among addicts is high—though "high" is rarely defined in numerical terms and may have different meanings for different people.[10,11,13,15,16]

Originally, the conviction that relapse rates are high seems to have been based on studies of addicts in hospitals and prisons, of those arrested, or, in a few cases, of addicts introduced to the investigator by other addicts. When histories are taken in such situations, they will usually contain references to previous periods of treatment, or at least of withdrawal, and of subsequent relapse. The only histories which will not show relapse will be those of patients who have used the drug steadily from the first time they were addicted, who, in short, have had no opportunity to relapse.

The conviction is also based on the experience of those who have had contact with addicts over some period of time, either as therapists or law enforcement officers. They find themselves treating again, or arresting again, many of the addicts they had treated or arrested years before.

Psychologically, repeated experiences of these kinds explain why so many feel that relapse is almost inevitable in any case of addiction. But logically, of course, such experiences do not justify that conclusion. The circumstances in which retrospective studies are done make it certain that they will find only histories of relapse. If it be accepted, as a logical possibility, that there are some addicts who do give up their drug use and never relapse, then obviously such addicts do not get into these studies, and they have no chance to be counted. Similarly, the fact of relapse is brought home to law enforcement and treatment personnel by those addicts whom they see again and again, and they find it easy to forget those whom they do not see again.

Not all succumb to the logical fallacy. Even 35 years ago, Kolb [7] called attention to the fact that many addicts sincerely try to abstain and implied that many must succeed. For years the late Dr. Kenneth Chapman called attention to the fact that current arrests and admissions of addicts in the older-age ranges fall far short of the figure we would expect if all the known youthful addicts of 20 or 30 years ago had continued to use drugs.

To this writer's knowledge, however, the literature contains only one statement that any sizeable, or specific, percentage of addicts can be expected to remain abstinent indefinitely or for a lengthy period of time. The one exception comes from Winick's use of Bureau of Narcotics files to check Chapman's suggestion, resulting in his conclusion "that addiction may be a self-limiting process for perhaps two-thirds of addicts." [19]

This suggestion is still highly tentative, however, as Winick is careful to point out, because of inherent limitations in the data currently available to the Bureau. The questions about relapse can only be answered by careful follow-up studies, studies which select a sample of persons who were addicted and withdrawn at some point in time and then, after some lapse of time, determine their subsequent history of drug use or abstinence. This paper will consider the 11 follow-up studies of American narcotic addicts, which are, as far as can be determined, all the studies which have been reported. Its purposes will be to summarize what has been learned from these studies, with some attention to the limitations of the studies and the generalizations which may be inferred from them, and to suggest improvements in the design of future follow-up studies.

One prefatory note is in order. There is much that can be criticized in almost all these studies, but nothing to be said here is intended to detract from the investigators. These are pioneering studies, and one should not expect of them all the rigor and technical sophistication to be expected in an established field of investigation. Most of the investigators were not primarily oriented to research, but to treatment or program administration. Most of the studies were conducted as part-time projects by persons whose primary responsibilities lay elsewhere. They deserve credit for the research they did accomplish and little or no blame for the flaws which were probably inevitable. Further, it will be the better, more adequate studies which are most criticized, because only such studies furnish the critic with the ammunition needed to attack them.

FINDINGS OF THE STUDIES

The studies are summarized in Table 14-1. It should be noted that although most of the studies used "relapsed" and "abstinent," or equivalent terms, as the major classifications for their findings, some used other classifications. In the column of findings, their classifications have been translated, when possible, into "relapsed" and "abstinent." This operation may have introduced some error into the table. The notes in the bibliography describe how these translations were made.

Perhaps the outstanding point to be noted is the wide range of rates reported, from a high of 90 per cent relapsed found in one study, to a high of 92 per cent abstinent reported in another. So great a difference points to the possibility of errors, biases, and major differences in definitions of terms. Such explanations must

Table 14-1 FINDINGS OF FOLLOW-UP STUDIES

Author	Sample size	Source of sample	Follow-up period	Findings (Percentage)				
				Relapsed	Irregular use	Dead	Unknown	Abstinent
Senate[17]	584	Committed patients, Spadra	2 years	85.1	...	...	...	14.9
Pescor[14]	4,766	Lexington	6–72 months	39.9	...	7.0	39.6	13.5
Knight[6]	50	Voluntary patients, New York Hospital	1–21 years	33.3	...	17.6	27.5	21.6
Kuznesof[8]	83	Lexington–New York probation	Not given	79.5				
Gerard[3]	247	Riverside	1 year	53.3	26.7	...	6.7	13.3
Jones[5]	30	California physicians	5 years	8.0	...	...	...	92.0
Trussell[18]	49	Riverside	2½–3 years	90 Relapsed, had police trouble, or both. 4 No relapse, no police trouble. 6 Insufficient information to classify.				
Diskind[1,12]	344	New York parolees	2–36 months	55.0	...	...	...	45.0
Hunt[4]	1,912	Lexington	1–4½ years	90.1	3.3	...	...	6.6
Lieberman[9]	389	Civil commitments to state hospitals	1–3½ years	18 Readmitted to a state hospital. 30 Arrested or convicted.				
Duvall[2]	453	Lexington	5 years	46.0	...	...	...	Vol., 25 Invol., 24

not, however, be assumed. It could be that each study is accurate and that the differences in their findings indicate that relapse rates vary widely, in association with factors to be inferred from characteristics of the samples studied.

One finding is well established by these studies; that is, when relapse occurs, it tends to occur quickly. Hunt reports that 90 per cent of the relapses which will occur take place within 6 months, and almost all of the rest within 2 years. The other studies which touch on this point confirm the finding, and none reports any evidence to the contrary.

The relapse rate of addicts, and the time within which relapse occurs, are of obvious importance in a practical sense, but the questions they answer are trivial, from the viewpoint of scientific theory. The questions which have theoretical importance—and equal practical importance—relate to the factors which distinguish the relapsed from the abstinent, and those who relapse quickly from those who abstain for fairly long periods. Such distinguishing factors, unfortunately, become difficult to identify when almost all of the subjects fall in one classification, and almost none in the other. Only a few of these studies even try to identify these distinguishing factors.

A few, however, are identified, and others can be inferred from the individual studies or from a comparison of the studies. The variables considered here are to be considered not as established predictors of relapse or abstinence, but as possible predictors, suggested by the 11 studies under consideration, which would be worth investigation in future studies.

1. Sex. Only half of the studies included women in the sample, and of these only Hunt and Duvall included enough for comparison to be meaningful. No difference in relapse rates by sex is reported by either, but certain differences by other variables held only for men.

2. Age. Hunt reports that, for men, those who were 30 years or older had lower readdiction rates than those under 30. This finding was again reported by Duvall. Diskind also reports tentative evidence that subjects over 25 abstained more frequently than the younger group. It may be noted that the two studies based on Riverside patients, whose median age was about 18, report higher relapse rates than most of the other studies, which used older samples. Age may play some part, therefore, in explaining the differences in relapse rates.

3. Voluntary Status. Hunt found that, among patients 30 years or older, nonvoluntary patients had lower relapse rates than voluntary patients. Pescor's findings suggest that it may be post-hospital supervision, rather than nonvoluntary status, which affects relapse rates. He also reported lower relapse rates for parolees as compared with probationers. It will be noted, on the other hand, that Knight's subjects were voluntary, and Lieberman's and Jones's, while under some legal compulsion, were not convicted of crime, and all three studies report low relapse rates.

4. Race. Hunt reports that, among nonvoluntary patients under 30 years of age, whites had a lower relapse rate than Negroes. Gerard also found whites doing better than Negroes, with Puerto Ricans doing still better.

5. Length of Hospitalization. Hunt reports that, among voluntary patients under 30 years of age, those hospitalized 31 days or more had a lower relapse rate than patients hospitalized 30 days or less. Knight reports an average duration of hospitalization of 5.4 months for his abstinent patients, against 3.3 months for all patients in the sample. On the basis of his findings, Pescor recommended a comparatively short period of hospitalization, from 2 to 5 months.

6. Social Class. The lowest relapse rates are reported by Jones, for a group of physicians, and by Knight, for an upper-middle-class group which included many professionals.

Other variables of interest are noted in only one study each. Trussell reports that the number of posthospital arrests, and the number of new admissions to Riverside, varied:

1. Directly with recorded prehospitalization offenses
2. Directly with length of drug use prior to first Riverside admission
3. Inversely with the age at which marihuana or heroin was first used

Knight implies, but does not clearly document, a lower rate

of relapse for patients whose personality study revealed a pre-
dominance of psychoneurotic traits. Gerard reports a better post-
hospital adjustment for patients who accepted a relationship with
a therapist, and a worse one for those who, without accepting such
a relationship, conformed to hospital regulations and expectations.
Further, of those patients who predict, at the time of leaving the
hospital, that they will remain drug-free, those whose reasons
show ego development have a better posthospital adjustment than
those whose reasons indicate repression, omnipotence, or denial.

One final hypothesis can be suggested on the basis of the 11
studies as a group. Six of them—Kuznesof, Hunt, Duvall, Trussell,
Gerard, and Diskind—were done in New York City. These report
six of the seven highest relapse rates or failure rates. This could
mean that relapse is more probable in New York than elsewhere.
In an unpublished pilot study done by this author a few years
ago, it was found that the failure rate was higher, to a statistically
significant degree, for parolees and probationer addicts in New
York City than in the rest of the country. We know that relapse
is triggered quite frequently by contacts with old addict friends,
and we might speculate that such contacts are more probable, the
larger the number of addicts in the community to which the subject returns.

DEFINITION OF RELAPSE AND ABSTINENCE

It is apparent from a close reading of these 11 reports that
there is some variation in their definitions of relapse and abstinence, but few formal definitions are given. Hunt and Duvall
use the classification of readdicted, irregular use, and abstinent,
and define them as follows: readdicted means that the patient is
using, or has used, narcotic drugs to the extent of at least one
injection per day, for a period of 2 weeks; in irregular use, the
patient used drugs to some lesser extent; abstinent means that he
is not taking, and has not taken, any narcotics. Diskind clearly
implies that a single use of drugs, preceded and followed by long
periods of complete abstinence, was sufficient to classify a parolee
as "reverted to the use of drugs." In those studies which relied,
in part, on information obtained by questionnaire, it is obvious

that the effective definitions of the terms used must have been those of the respondents, allowing for the possibility that definitions and therefore classifications varied within several of the studies, as well as between them.

One point, however, is clear from those studies which define their terms. "Abstinence" refers to the entire period of time from the beginning to the end of the follow-up period, while "relapse" refers to a point in time, or a very brief span of time, within the total follow-up period. This is most clearly exemplified in the Hunt report. There, to be classified as abstinent, the subject had to remain drug-free for a period of 1 to 4½ years, depending on when he entered the follow-up. The readdicted group, however, can contain (1) some who used drugs for the entire period of time; (2) some who remained drug-free for over 4 years and then relapsed for 2 weeks just before the end of the follow-up; and (3) some who used drugs for 2 weeks soon after release from the hospital and then were abstinent for years through the remainder of the follow-up period. These three patterns are chosen to exemplify the extreme possibilities; the number of different patterns which could be identified is much larger.

It is fruitless to argue definitions. An investigator has the right to use any classification he considers useful, though he should, as does Hunt, make it clear to his audience what his definitions are. It is legitimate, however, to ask if the classification chosen is as useful as others would be. The classifications used in most of these studies are questionable in that they conceal as much or more information than they reveal; they group together, and thereby make seem identical, great differences in behavior.

The point can best be made by an improbable, but legitimate, speculation based on the Hunt report. Most people would feel that its finding of 90 per cent readdicted is discouraging. There were almost 2,000 subjects in the study, and the average length of time between their discharge from the hospital to the end of the follow-up period was certainly over 2 years. We have, then, roughly 4,000 man-years to be accounted for in periods of abstinence and drug use. The 90 per cent readdiction rate could mean, then, that about 3,600 man-years were spent using drugs, an equally discouraging finding, if it were to be made. But taking the 2-week criterion for readdiction as about 2 per cent of the total follow-up period, the 90 per cent readdiction rate could also mean that as few as 72 man-years were spent using drugs, that over 3,900 of the 4,000 man-years were drug-free. Such a finding would be less discouraging.

The point, of course, is not to suggest that the true figure lies close to the latter extreme, nor that Hunt could have reported his findings in these terms. It is simply that this is a legitimate and useful question to ask of follow-up data, and future studies should make the attempt to answer it.

Addiction to opiates can be seen as a long and complex process, frequently involving alternating periods of use and of abstinence. The abstinence, in turn, can be broken into periods of enforced abstinence in institutions and periods of abstinence in the community, perhaps voluntary on the part of the subject and perhaps forced on him by circumstances. It is measures of these periods, in terms of drug-free months, or the ratio of this number to the months during which the subject could have been using drugs, which would be the meaningful variable in future follow-up studies.

This principle was first recognized by Gerard, who scaled drug use on a continuum so that, for example, use of marihuana alone or occasional use of heroin could be classed as improvement over previous addiction, and heavier use could be classed as deterioration. The later Trussell study is the first, however, to measure time on and off drugs, time on the street, and time in institutions. It then becomes evident that, even among those who relapsed, there are some who could be classed as much more successful than others.

Such differences tell us something at least as important as the fact that these subjects did relapse. In addition, they open up possibilities for research which are lost by the simple relapse-abstinence classification. Against them other differences, perhaps differences in treatment methods, can be measured, or predictions and theories can be tested.

Duvall carries the concept much further, by maintaining contact with the subjects for a full 5-year period and reporting addiction status at three points in time, at 6 months, 2 years, and 5 years after discharge from the hospital. This approach succeeds immediately in establishing a fact which the other studies were unable, or failed, to look at. Duvall reports that only 12 of the 453 subjects were voluntarily abstinent for the full 5 years. The group which was voluntarily abstinent from narcotics at these three points in time increased from 9 per cent at 6 months to 17 per cent at 2 years, and 25 per cent at 5 years. At the end of the 5 years the percentage abstinent, either voluntarily or involuntarily, was actually slightly higher than the percentage readdicted.

One other point remains to be made on the classifications used in follow-up studies of addicts. It would be well to avoid complex classifications, in which relapse is grouped together with other criteria, like arrest or conviction, as "failure." It cannot be regarded as wrong to do this, and indeed studies like those of Kuznesof and Diskind are almost forced, to be comparable with other probation and parole statistics, to use such a complex classification. But it is possible, as Diskind does, to report the types of failure separately so that we can isolate relapse for study.

The Trussell report, on the other hand, devotes about 80 per cent of its discussion of findings to the 139 subjects who were located and found to have relapsed. Twenty per cent is devoted to the entire group of 247 subjects, for whom it is reported that 90 per cent had continued difficulties with narcotics or the police or both. The net effect of reading the report is, again, discouraging. Yet it remains true that as far as the report tells us, only 139 subjects are known to have relapsed, and the relapse rate for the entire group of 247 may be 56 per cent. And 56 per cent relapse rate would be regarded as encouraging by many.

This question of arrest as an indicator of failure has other aspects. There is the fact, for example, that in the disposal of the arrests reported by Trussell, 14 per cent were dismissed. Legally, this means that the persons arrested were innocent of the charge, or at least not proved guilty of it. We could be in the position, therefore, of classifying a subject as a failure simply because he had been arrested for something he did not do.

Another aspect is the purpose for which subjects are classified. Suppose, for example, the goal is to measure the effectiveness of treatment of addiction. Two patients are treated, both abstain from drug use, one returns to his previous occupation as a physician, and the second to his previous occupation as a shoplifter. The first is clearly a success; it is not equally clear that the second is a failure. But there is no need to tackle the philosophical questions involved. If the facts are reported, both the shoplifting and the abstinence, the investigator and the reader of his report can use the behaviors separately or together as criteria.

METHODS OF CLASSIFICATION

Abstinence and relapse are not simply facts which can be observed and recorded. They are conclusions, judgments, based on evidence. Further, the relapse-abstinence dichotomy or continuum—it can be handled either way—has an interesting quality. It is relatively easy to get firm evidence of relapse in a large proportion of cases. The patient returns to the hospital for further treatment or is observed to show withdrawal symptoms, or is arrested with narcotics in his possession and fresh needle marks on his arms, or admits to the investigator that he has been using narcotics regularly.[20]

Equally firm and adequate evidence of abstinence is theoretically possible, if the subject is hospitalized under close observation in a drug-free environment and shows no withdrawal symptoms, or if he does not react positively to one of the antagonist drugs like Nalline, or if his urine tests negative for opiates. But none of the studies cited obtained such evidence of abstinence. A classification of abstinence in these studies, then, can mean only that the investigator has sought for evidence of relapse, is reasonably satisfied that he would have found this evidence if it existed, and has failed to find it. Proving abstinence becomes proving a negative, and this is notoriously difficult.

Further, most of these types of strong evidence of drug use or abstinence establish the classification for only a brief period of time. If the urine test is negative, it remains possible that the subject was using drugs up to a few weeks, or even a few days, before the date of the test. If withdrawal symptoms are observed, it may be that the drug use began only a few months, or less, before the date of the observation. It is much more difficult, therefore, to establish the pattern of use and abstinence over a long period of time. This may account, in large part, for the tendency in these studies to accept relapse at one point in time as the final basis for classification. If the subject has been out of the hospital for 5 years, and claims abstinence for the past 4 years, but admits use for the first year after release, the investigator can comfortably count him as relapsed and have no worries about what kinds of confirmation he would need to accept the claim of abstinence for 4 years.

Although firm evidence of relapse may be available for a fairly large proportion of the sample, there will also be many cases in which it is not found, and the investigator will have to base his classification on more tenuous evidence. Such evidence is exemplified in the signs of relapse noted by Diskind: ". . . the partaking of sweets and soda, blood stains on shirt sleeves and in the bathroom, drinking ice water to excess, powder or salve on arms, irregular employment pattern, and difficulty in waking the parolee in the morning. . . ." [1]

Those who have worked with addicts will agree that such signs do, or can, indicate relapse. They will also agree that the signs vary in value, with bloodstains on sleeves, for example, indicating somewhat more than drinking ice water or sleeping late in the morning.

There is an obvious possibility of error in classifying a subject as relapsed on the basis of such evidence. The classification of abstinence or relapse, then, is not analogous to a reading from a calibrated scale by a white-coated scientist in a laboratory. It much more closely resembles the process by which a physician makes a diagnosis, taking into account a wide variety of symptoms and signs, and giving to each the weight which his experience suggests. It even more closely resembles the process by which a juryman votes "guilty" or "not guilty" on the basis of sometimes conflicting testimony, some of which he chooses to believe, and some to discount.

In short, the classification of subjects as relapsed or abstinent is subject to question. It is a problem of measurement, and the usual questions of the reliability and validity of the measurement may be raised. In terms of follow-up studies of addicts, the questions we may ask include at least these:

1. What kinds of evidence of use or abstinence did the investigator obtain?

2. When different degrees of evidence were available, in what proportion of cases were strong and weak evidence used for the classification?

3. What procedural steps were taken to move from the evidence available to the classification as relapsed or abstinent?

4. What steps were taken to measure the degree of reliability of the classification?

5. How valid, how correct, is the classification?

A major flaw in almost all of these studies is that they give the reader little or no information to answer these questions. This lack of information is disturbing because it may imply that the investigators were not aware of the legitimacy and importance of the questions and, therefore, did not take the necessary precautions to insure against errors and bias.

On the point of the data available to the investigators, there is a very wide range. At the one extreme, Diskind's parole officers saw their subjects weekly for 9 months, and twice a month after that, plus interviewing family members regularly, and probably employers and other informants. In addition, they received notice automatically if the parolee was arrested. Kuznesof's contacts were of the same type, though less intensive and frequent. At the other extreme, Jones gives no information on what data he had, and Lieberman got only reports of arrests and rehospitalizations, and those only from one state, with no firm knowledge that his subjects had remained in that state.

The remaining studies all obtained information from sources of varying value, but do not tell us in how many cases they had strong evidence and in how many it was more dubious. In Pescor's study, for example, it would be helpful to know in how many cases his classification is based on readmission to the hospital, in how many on detailed reports from probation officers, and in how many on questionnaires alone. In the study reported by Hunt, many of the subjects were interviewed and some of them regularly over a period of years. In other cases, however, there may have been no more than one or two telephone contacts with a relative or other source of information. The findings of the study will obviously carry more weight if most cases fall in the first, rather than the second, category.

Hunt was aware of the importance of this point. The first of the three major questions he lists as the purposes of the study is "Can contact be achieved?" with the study subjects. But the only answer he gives is that "some degree of contact was achieved with 1,881, or 98.4 per cent." [4] This is not a satisfactory answer. What we should be told is how much contact was achieved with how many patients.

After the data are gathered, the possibility of error exists in the process of using them to classify the subjects. In this step, Lieberman had no problem. His data consisted in reports of arrest or hospital admission, and no judgment was involved in classification. Trussell gives no specific information on the classification procedure, but seems to have found both rehospitalization and admission of drug use for almost all subjects he classified as continuing to use drugs, and on the others he used the fact of arrest as the basis for classification. Gerard alone describes how the judgment was reached, including the use of formally defined scales, with examples of where subjects should be placed, and training of raters. Diskind does not specifically discuss the problem involved in reaching a judgment, but does mention a program in which project personnel were trained to deal with the problem.

These four studies, then, either had no classification problem or took steps to handle it, and the reader can probably assume that the reliability of their classifications is high, even though not formally measured. The remaining studies are more difficult to evaluate in this respect, because they give no information on the point. To the extent that they based classification on questionnaire responses, the reliability of the classification is probably high, but its validity more dubious. To the extent that other data were used, the validity may increase, but the reliability suffer.

Among the seven other studies, only Hunt touches on the question of classification of data. Efforts were made to weight the various kinds of information obtained, to array them

> . . . in a series with consistently increasing validity. All of these attempts proved fruitless and were abandoned. . . . During the final years of the study, the chief of the follow-up team reviewed the records of all patients and was responsible for determining the final classification of each patient in the study. If there were any doubts about the diagnosis of readdiction, the patient was classified as an irregular user or as abstinent.[4]

Here, then, the problem was recognized, and it would have been prudent to have the classification made independently by one or more additional judges. Then their agreement could have been measured. Instead, the reader is asked to accept on faith what could have been based on measurement. Since the Duvall study made use of the procedures described by Hunt, the same criticism applies to it.

A measure of validity implies a comparison with an independent criterion. In these studies, no such criterion was available. A practical procedure, however, and one which might be followed in future studies, would be to break down the classifications by the weight of evidence on which they are based. The report could show, for example, how many classifications were based on strong, moderate, and weak evidence, and give examples for each group. The reader would then be in a position to evaluate the findings in terms of his agreement or disagreement with the investigator's judgment.

SUGGESTIONS FOR FUTURE FOLLOW-UPS

The major points made above may be summarized, and a few minor points added, in terms of suggestions for future follow-up studies.

More attention should be paid to the problem of what evidence is sufficient to classify the subjects. A useful tool would be an objective index of use at the time contact is made with the subject. The use of Nalline testing, in California and Illinois, and of urine testing for parolees, in Colorado and Wisconsin, will be extremely valuable. In these programs, the subjects can be required to submit to the testing, and we may not be able to generalize from these studies to voluntary patients. In a study we are conducting in Kentucky, however, only 1 subject of the first 81 located refused to give a urine specimen, and the early experience with a similar study in Puerto Rico suggests that the refusal rate there will also be low.

The validity of findings will also be greatly increased by repeated contacts with subjects, as in the parole programs mentioned above. This would pose practical problems, however, for studies which cover a longer follow-up period. The design of such studies is almost automatically limited to a one-contact approach. The problem of what evidence to accept for classifying patients as abstinent over past periods of time is a serious one, and one which we are not sure we can solve in our Kentucky study, which covers a 25-year period for some subjects. The way these problems are handled, however, can be described in the report, so that readers can credit or discount the findings to the extent they consider justified.

The relapse-abstinence dichotomy should be replaced by an emphasis on identifying periods of use and abstinence and the circumstances associated with these. It will be useful to identify those addicts who gave up drug use for long periods of time, even though they may later have relapsed, and see if the factors which account for these periods can be isolated. Their adjustment in other areas while abstinent should also be studied. If an addict gives up narcotic use, does he automatically become a good husband, father, and citizen, or does he perhaps shift to alcohol or barbiturates, or become a more efficient criminal when the pressures and dangers of drug use are avoided?

A new point to be made is the importance of reducing the number in the "unknown" category to the absolute minimum. In Pescor's study, for example, 40 per cent are classed as "addiction status unknown." But it was known that none of these had returned to the hospital, and it was known for those subjects who had been prisoners or probationers—73 per cent of his sample—that no notice of subsequent arrest was received from the FBI. The number of later arrests for this group, therefore, must have been low.

So, for most of the unknowns in the study, for about fifteen hundred individuals, we actually know two facts which do not establish abstinence, but are consistent with it. If a patient left the hospital determined to give up drug use, and broke away from his old ties to help him do this, where would he be classified? He would not return to the hospital, he would not be arrested, and a questionnaire sent to his old address might well not reach him. He could fall only in the unknown category. It may, therefore, be that the very subjects who are hardest to locate and classify are those most likely to be abstinent.

That this is more than a possibility can even be demonstrated from the Trussell report. Slightly under half of the subjects were easily located, because they were institutionalized again, and almost all of these had relapsed. The few exceptions had probably not been addicted on their first hospitalization. About 90 per cent of the subjects were identified in an intensive search of records, and of these, almost all could be classed as having continued difficulty with narcotics or the police or both. Twenty-nine subjects, however, were not located by these means. They could have been written off as "unknown." But by virtue of an extra effort, sufficient data for classification were obtained on 19 of these, and 11 of the 19 were found not to have relapsed, though two of them had police difficulty without drug use. In short, the relapse rate in this hard-to-locate group was much lower than in the easily located subjects, and indeed almost all of the known abstinent cases in the study are accounted for by this group.

CONCLUSIONS

What, then, can we say we have learned from these follow-up studies? Most of them do seem to establish that high percentages of their samples relapsed to drug use, but this is true only for a highly restricted definition of relapse. If one believes that most addicts, after a period of treatment or enforced abstinence, relapse to drugs and continue to use drugs, or that addicts spend most of their time outside of institutions using drugs, this may be true, but not one of these studies establishes it as true, or even indicates that it is probable. They offer us no evidence on this, except for the Duvall study, which points in the opposite direction, to less use of narcotics as more time elapses.

On the face of it, these studies indicate a wide range in relapse rates. It would be possible to take those at one extreme, for example, those that report low relapse rates, and by legitimate criticism show that so many sources of error are possible that the low relapse rates need not be accepted. But the same criteria would bring the high relapse rates reported in other studies equally into question. It would seem safest to accept all of the studies at face value, as indicating variations which are not yet explained. Whatever the definition of relapse one prefers, and whatever the rates of relapse may be, these studies strongly indicate that there are differences in relapse for different subgroups of addicts.

Many readers of these reports have uncritically accepted them as painting a discouraging picture, as indicating that past and present programs for addicts have been ineffective. This, it would seem, is a dangerous conclusion, not so much because it might discourage those who are now working with addicts, but because it might make experimental programs, using slightly different classifications as criteria, seem more effective than they actually are. The safest general conclusion is that far more knowledge of relapse, and the factors associated with it, is needed than we have obtained from the studies done to date.

REFERENCES

1. Diskind, M. H.: New Horizons in the Treatment of Narcotic Addiction, *Federal Probation*, p. 56, December, 1960.
2. Duvall, Henrietta J., Locke, Ben Z., and Brill, Leon: Follow-up Study of Narcotic Drug Addicts Five Years after Hospitalization, *Public Health Rept.*, *U.S.*, 78:185 (1963). The percentages in Table 14-1 are taken from p. 187, but, more than in any of the other studies cited, an injustice is done to the wealth of significant data reported by reduction to these bare figures.
3. Gerard, D. L., Lee, R. S., Rosenfeld, E., and Chein, Isidor: Posthospitalization Adjustment: A Follow-up Study of Adolescent Opiate Addicts, Research Center for Human Relations, New York University, October, 1956. (Dittoed.) The percentages reported

are computed from table 11, p. 26, and the coding instructions on p. 59. These show that 16 boys returned to daily use of opiates, 8 used alcohol to excess and/or used marihuana, and perhaps used narcotics irregularly, 4 used no opiates, and 2 were unknown.

4. Hunt, G. H., and Odoroff, M. E.: Follow-up Study of Narcotic Drug Addicts after Hospitalization, *Public Health Rept., U.S.*, 77:41 (1962).

5. Jones, L. E.: How 92% Beat the Dope Habit, *Bull. Los Angeles County Med. Assoc.*, 19: 37 (April, 1958).

6. Knight, Robert G. and Prout, Curtis T.: A Study of Results in Hospital Treatment of Drug Addictions, *Am. J. Psychiat.*, 108:303 (1951). The percentages used in Table 14-1 are computed from the table on p. 306, ignoring the barbiturate addicts. The 51 other addicts include 50 narcotic addicts and one benzedrine user (p. 303), so some error is introduced. The authors report that 10 subjects were "relapsed and unimproved," and 7 were "managing better." The latter phrase is not defined, but in previous work on alcoholics, the classification used was "drinking, but managing better." It is therefore assumed that the addicts in this classification were using some drugs, and they are counted as "relapsed," as they would have been in most studies considered here. For the classification used for alcoholics, see Wall, J. H., and Allen, E. B.: Results of Hospital Treatment of Alcoholism, *Am. J. Psychiat.*, 100:474 (1944).

7. Kolb, Lawrence: The Struggle for Cure and the Conscious Reasons for Relapse, *J. Nervous Mental Disease*, 66(1):22 (1927). With minor changes, the paper is reprinted as chap. 6 of Kolb, Lawrence: "Drug Addiction: A Medical Problem," Charles C Thomas, Publisher, Springfield, Ill., 1962.

8. Kuznesof, Morris: *Probation for a Cure: An Analysis of 85 Drug Addict Cases Committed to the United States Public Health Hospital for Treatment as Part of Probation*, U.S. Probation Office, Southern District of New York, September, 1955. (Mimeographed.) Reprinted in U.S. Senate, Committee on the Judiciary, *Hearings before the Subcommittee on Improvements in the Federal Criminal Code, September 19, 20 and 21, 1955*, Part 5, Exhibit No. 30, 2091–2110. The finding of 79.5 per cent relapsed is based on the statement that "drugs were believed to be involved in 62 of the 67 violators," (p. 8) and that relapse is indicated (p. 9) for 4 of the other 16 subjects. It is not clear how many of the others can be classed as abstinent, or should be classed "unknown."

9. Lieberman, D.: Follow-up Studies on Previously Hospitalized Narcotic Addicts, paper read before Meeting of American Orthopsychiatric Association, March, 1962. This study was based on 389 patients, of whom at least 83, and possibly as many as 149, were not narcotic addicts. The findings are not related to the drug used, so it is not possible to compute percentages for the narcotic addicts separately.

10. Lindesmith, Alfred R.: "Opiate Addiction," Principia Press, Bloomington, Ind., 1947.

11. Meyer, Alan S.: "Social and Psychological Factors in Opiate Addiction," Bureau of Applied Social Research, Columbia University, New York, 1952.

12. New York State Division of Parole: *An Experiment in the Supervision of Paroled Offenders Addicted to Narcotic Drugs: Final Report of the Special Narcotic Project,* undated. The findings reported are taken from table XIV, p. 65.

13. Nyswander, Marie: "The Drug Addict as a Patient," Grune & Stratton, Inc., New York, 1956.

14. Pescor, Michael J.: "Follow-up Study of Treated Narcotic Drug Addicts," *Public Health Rept., U.S.,* Suppl. 170, (1943).

15. *Proceedings, White House Conference on Narcotic and Drug Abuse,* p. xviii, 17–18, *et passim,* 1962.

16. Schur, Edwin M.: "Narcotic Addiction in Britain and America," Indiana University Press, Bloomington, Ind., 1962.

17. Senate Interim Narcotic Committee: A Critical Analysis of Eight Years' Operation at Spadra, *Report on Drug Addiction in California,* 57–60, 77–78, State Printing Office, Sacramento, Calif., 1936.

18. Trussell, R. E., Alksne, H., Elinson, J., and Patrick, S.: A Follow-up Study of Treated Adolescent Narcotic Users, Columbia University School of Public Health and Administrative Medicine, New York, May, 1959. (Mimeographed.) Percentages in Table 14-1 are taken from p. 42. A summary of this study is available in *Proceedings of Conference on Post-Hospital Care and Rehabilitation of Adolescent Narcotic Addicts,* Under Joint Auspices of the Governor's Task Force on Narcotic Addiction, The New York State Interdepartmental Health Resources Board, and the New York City Board of Hospitals, Albany, New York, Jan. 8 and 9, 1960.

19. Winick, Charles: "Maturing Out of Narcotic Addiction," *Bull. Narcotics, U.N. Dep. Social Affairs,* 14(1): (1962).

20. None of the studies gives in detail the bases for classifying sub-

jects as relapsed, but it is probable that most of them classed at least some subjects as relapsed solely on the basis of the subject's admission of drug use.

At least two subjects in the Hunt study, however, on later admissions to Lexington, told staff members they had reported relapse to research staff earlier than it actually occurred, as a quick and easy way to get rid of the researcher. Whether this is true is unknown, but it clearly represents a possibility. Even when the investigator has the admission of drug use, therefore, it would be desirable to have some confirming evidence before classifying the subject as relapsed.

Part 5

GOVERNMENTAL PROGRAMS

Harold Meiselas | **15**

THE NARCOTIC ADDICTION PROGRAM OF THE NEW YORK STATE DEPARTMENT OF MENTAL HYGIENE

THE NEW YORK STATE DEPARTMENT OF MENTAL HYGIENE program in narcotic addiction had its formal inception with the opening of a 55-bed research unit at the Manhattan State Hospital in New York City in August of 1959. It was further expanded in 1961 and 1962 by the establishment of the Central Islip and Utica State Hospital service units consisting of 80 and 20 beds respectively. This phase of the program, which provided a considerable range of operational experience, recently entered a transition stage shaped by a new law passed during the 1962 session of the state Legislature. The following seeks to acquaint the reader with this statute, which reflects the suggestions and recommendations of many individuals and groups, both public and private, who in the course of their daily endeavors are confronted with one aspect or another of the drug addiction problem. The initial steps which have been taken to implement its provisions will then be discussed.

THE METCALF-VOLKER ACT

Although narcotic addiction is not a new problem, for many years it fell from the view of most professionals working in the fields of medicine, psychiatry, social work, and psychology. The writer shall not attempt to explore the reasons why this should have happened. However, he would like to emphasize that following the Second World War, there were few professionals in the New York area with actual and up-to-date experience with this clinical entity. It is not surprising, therefore, that in the face of a resurgence of the narcotic problem, considerable disagreement existed about its extent, its true nature, and the role psychiatry and ancillary fields should play in the search for a solution. To say that these disagreements have been completely resolved would be incorrect. But for some years now, a growing attempt on the part of many members of the community to face up to this pressing issue has made for a body of experience and an interplay of positions out of which the new law has emerged, a law which, in acknowledging the human suffering and social and economic loss associated with narcotic abuse, attempts to provide a basis upon which a psychiatric approach to this disorder might be pursued.

More specifically this statute,[1] commonly referred to as the Metcalf-Volker Act after the State Senator and Assemblyman who sponsored its passage, calls upon the commissioner of mental hygiene to formulate a comprehensive plan for the long-range development of adequate services and facilities for the prevention and control of drug addiction and the diagnosis, treatment, and rehabilitation of drug addicts through the utilization of Federal, state, local, and private resources; and, within the appropriations made available for this purpose, to promote, develop, establish, coordinate, and conduct unified programs for prevention, diagnosis, treatment, aftercare, community referral, and rehabilitation in the drug addiction field. In addition, it empowers the commissioner, within the amounts made available by appropriation, to direct and carry on basic, clinical, epidemiologic, social-science, and statistical research either individually or in conjunction with

other agencies; to provide education and training in the prevention, diagnosis, treatment, rehabilitation, and control of drug addiction for medical students, physicians, nurses, social workers,
and others who work with the drug addict; to disseminate information relating to public and private services which are available
in the state for the assistance of drug addicts and potential drug
addicts; to gather information and maintain statistical and other
records relating to drug addicts and drug addiction in the state;
to establish special facilities for the treatment, training, and rehabilitation of adolescent drug users under the age of 21 years;
and, within the monies made available for this purpose, to make
agreements with public and private agencies to do or cause to be
done those things which would be consistent with the purposes
and objectives of the act. To aid the commissioner in this effort,
the law provides for the establishment of a division of narcotics
within the State Department of Mental Hygiene to be directed
by a special assistant to the commissioner and for the creation
of an advisory council on drug addiction to consist of the commissioners of mental hygiene, health, the industrial commissioner,
the attorney general, the budget director, the chairman of the
parole board, the director of the division for youth and nine members from outside of state government. The latter members are
appointed by the Governor and with the exception of the initial
appointees, whose terms vary to allow for a staggered turnover,
serve for 3 years. Finally the statute describes four ways in which
narcotic addicts may be admitted to mental-hygiene facilities.
These are admission as a civilly committed arrested narcotic addict, voluntary admission, admission via commitment as a condition of probation, and admission on court certification.

Civil Commitment for Arrested Narcotic Addicts

Of the four modes of admission listed, the opportunity to commit
an arrested narcotic addict to a mental-hygiene facility represents
a relatively new procedure, which first became available January
1, 1963. Defining as a narcotic addict an individual who at the
time of his arrest is dependent upon an opiate, The Arrested Narcotic Addict Commitment Act calls for the court, correctional, or

other detention official or facility that is customarily charged with the care and custody of arrested persons to medically examine such individuals and make available a physician-supervised course of detoxification if this is found to be necessary. This is to be done only if the arrested addict does not object to such examination and treatment. Further, a defendant's request for detoxification and the statements he makes to the medical authorities may not be used against him in the criminal proceedings. If such examination reveals an arrested person to be a narcotic addict as previously defined, he becomes eligible for civil commitment. However, since the law seeks to disqualify the serious criminal offender from such consideration, he may *not* be committed when charged with a narcotic crime if:

1. There is pending against him a prior charge of a felony and either such prosecution has not been finally determined or the individual has not completed his sentence on such charge

2. There is a record of two or more felony convictions

3. He has been civilly committed under the act because of his narcotic addiction on three prior occasions arising out of three separate arrests

4. The amount of drugs he is alleged to have possessed is substantially greater than would be necessary to support his own narcotic habit

5. Or the court does not consider it to be in the interest of justice to proceed with a civil commitment

In addition, when charged with a nonnarcotic crime, this procedure may *not* be followed if:

1. There is a history of a prior conviction for a capital crime

2. The individual in question is being held on a felony charge for which a mandatory minimum term would have to be imposed on sentence if he were convicted

3. He is charged with a felony which because of a prior felony conviction could result in a statutory mandatory minimum term

4. The district attorney objects to the use of the commitment procedure

Finally, the court may *not* civilly commit the arrested narcotic addict without first obtaining certification from the commissioner of mental hygiene that he is agreeable to the acceptance of the individual in a facility which has been certified as having a special unit for the care and treatment of drug addicts. The commissioner in so certifying is expected to give consideration to the individual's ability to benefit from treatment and to whether a place is available where the prospective patient may be received.

When an arrested narcotic addict is not barred from civil commitment for the reasons stated, the law calls for him to be transferred to the care of the department of mental hygiene for a maximum period of 36 months, and for the criminal charge that led to his arrest to be held in abeyance. Such criminal charge is dismissed and inpatient and aftercare supervision terminated in advance of the maximum expiration date of the commitment upon notification to the court that the defendant's condition warrants his discharge from aftercare. Apart from such dismissal, if the criminal charge held in abeyance was a misdemeanor and the individual in question had not been previously convicted of a felony or committed under the act on a prior occasion in conjunction with a separate arrest, the charge is automatically dismissed following a period of 1 year of continuous treatment. In all other cases, the criminal charge is automatically dismissed if the individual is still under treatment at the conclusion of 3 years.

After his release from inpatient care the civilly committed arrested narcotic addict is required by the statute to report to a department of mental hygiene aftercare clinic at such intervals as are specified by the commissioner and is subject to reasonable regulation of his conduct. If during this period of posthospital supervision it is established that he has returned to the use of narcotics or is in imminent danger of doing so, he may be recommitted for inpatient care. On the other hand, if it appears that he cannot be further treated as a medical problem because of his apparent incorrigibility or nonresponsiveness to medical treatment, he may be returned to the court from which he had been civilly committed, in which case the criminal proceedings that had been held in abeyance are reactivated. The latter step may also be taken during the hospital phase of treatment. Further, if the addict leaves the hospital facility to which he has been committed without permission to do so or disappears from aftercare supervision, his civil commitment is terminated, the court is notified of his status, and a warrant is issued for his arrest. Addicts who are returned to the court in this fashion receive full credit against any sentence which may be imposed for time spent in the hospital. No credit is given for time spent subject to aftercare supervision.

Voluntary Admission

Although the procedure just described is a relatively new one in our hands, the voluntary method of admitting narcotic addicts represents a process with which the department is quite familiar, this technique having been utilized in well over fifteen hundred cases since the opening of our first unit in 1959. However, its inclusion in the current law does not reflect any great success we have had with this method. In fact, in proceeding along these lines, it soon became clear that the addict who voluntarily seeks hospitalization all too frequently does so without any real desire to participate in a long-term treatment program. The reasons that brought patients to the hospital were, for example, an interest in cleaning up before making a court appearance, a desire to make one's wife eligible for welfare payments or for an apartment in a public housing project, threatened or actual abandonment by parents, and the growth of habits beyond the point at which they could be supported. Thus, we found in an analysis of some one thousand voluntary admissions at the Manhattan State Hospital [2] that few patients, probably less than 15 per cent, had presented themselves as candidates for a program of rehabilitation. Instead, 41 per cent signed out of the hospital by the eighth day, another 33 per cent by the fifteenth day, and by the twenty-fourth day over 80 per cent had elected to return to the community without any recommendation by the hospital staff that they do so. By the twenty-fifth day, an additional 8 per cent, having satisfied the minimum terms of their voluntary application, terminated their hospital stay. Similarly, there was little interest demonstrated by this group in participating in outpatient treatment. Patients who were given appointments as they left the hospital usually did not keep them. When asked to call, in most instances they failed to do so. Many of those who did establish outpatient contacts appeared to be primarily interested in maintaining their eligibility for readmission. Usually such contacts were sporadic and of short duration.

On the other hand, our experience would suggest that a small percentage of patients who seek treatment on a voluntary basis do involve themselves in what can be described as meaningful relationships in an effort to strive towards better health. Such individuals often require a considerable amount of support and direction, and although few are capable of participating in insight therapy, some have been able to gain a greater understanding of the grosser aspects of their functioning, making it possible to pursue limited treatment goals while providing ample opportunities for social work service, vocational guidance, and job placement. In response to such efforts, most of these individuals have been able to function relatively well in the protective atmosphere of the hospital, and although a few have faltered on moving in the direction of the community, others have continued to grow in strength. The importance of making service available to such people is clear, and it is with this in mind that the department will continue to make use of the voluntary admission procedure.

Admission as a Condition of Probation

The admission of narcotic addicts as a condition of probation was also utilized as a mode of receiving patients prior to the 1962 legislation. However, this formerly was a rather loose arrangement, with the court and probation department simply standing behind a voluntary admission. Under the provisions of the new law, this procedure is formalized by allowing a court, which has competent criminal jurisdiction to commit a narcotic addict to a drug unit within the department of mental hygiene upon receiving the written consent of the commissioner. This may be done as a condition of any term of probation or of suspending sentence. Cases committed in this fashion are placed under department of mental hygiene jurisdiction for a time interval which is coterminous with the maximum period of probation. But if the drug addict is felt to be recovered or, if not recovered, is found to be unsuitable for further treatment, he may be returned to the jurisdiction of the court. The inclusion of this admission procedure in the law serves to broaden the opportunities for arrested narcotic addicts to enter the department's program, when this appears to be in the best interest of the individual and the community, by allowing people who, for one reason or another, are not eligible under the arrested drug addict commitment act to be given such consideration.

It should be noted that under the first three modes of admission described, screening by the department of mental hygiene to determine a prospective patient's suitability for participation in a treatment program is permitted. Furthermore, the department in each instance may remove from its facilities those patients whose unsuitability becomes manifest subsequent to entering the hospital. The right to proceed along these lines does not represent an attempt by the law to allow the department of mental hygiene to erect an artificial barrier to individuals seeking treatment; nor does it reflect an unwillingness on the part of this agency to understand the source of, and to deal constructively with, such individual problems as feelings of inadequacy, low self-esteem, marked dependency, low frustration tolerance, inability to give of oneself, lack of initiative, impulsivity, stubbornness, tendencies to procrastinate—in short the personality disorder which the addicted man or woman so frequently brings to a treatment situation. Rather, it represents a recognition of the need to include in a treatment program a method by which limits on patient behavior may be set without predisposing the patient-staff relationship to constant struggle. In first selecting those patients who genuinely appear to be interested in making use of the department's facilities and services and then separating out the uncooperative individual—who repeatedly violates basic hospital regulations, intimidates employees in an attempt to control the environment, utilizes physical prowess to dominate his fellow patients, destroys hospital property, or fights without provocation —management problems are greatly reduced, trends which make disordered behavior the rule rather than the exception are reversed, and a therapeutic milieu can be established.

Admission on Court Certification

On the other hand, this issue tends to make the final admission procedure to be discussed—namely, court certification—a most ineffectual way of attempting to approach the treatment of addicted men and women. Essentially a carryover from previous legislation passed in 1960 and amended in 1961 to allow for the discharge of a patient after the tenth hospital day if he is not a suitable candidate for treatment, this section of the law permits a narcotic addict who is without psychosis and over the age of 21 to be certified for admission, with the consent of the hospital director involved, to an appropriate department of mental hygiene facility on his own application or the application of his father, mother, spouse, brother, nearest relative, or the person with whom he resides. The usual safeguards, as they are included in certification procedures applying to the mentally ill, are spelled out, and a 12-month interval is defined as the maximum period of time the individual may be kept under department of mental hygiene supervision. The question of constitutionality aside, these provisions seem fine. However, in practice, a state of affairs exists with which a treatment facility in the absence of a criminal charge is really unable to cope, as it does not have a capacity to detain involuntarily large numbers of individuals who are without psychosis and capable of significant antisocial behavior.

The point in question is not simply one of how much "muscle" a narcotic unit must include in its structure to obstruct elopements. Rather, it once again becomes a matter of whether under such circumstances a therapeutic milieu in which a hospital rather than a prison environment prevails may be established. Our experience would suggest that all too frequently the court-certified narcotic addict, who without further legal involvements is sent to a hospital for a period of confinement which exceeds his own desires, soon finds a pattern of behavior which is inconsistent with the treatment goal. In doing so he precipitates his release and thereby defeats the certification procedure. If released to aftercare under such an arrangement, he not infrequently is lost to contact. Needless to say, we do not plan to use this section of the law to any great extent but instead will seek to build a civil commitment program on the two procedures previously described.

IMPLEMENTATION

As has been implied by the comments which have been made thus far, the provisions of the Metcalf-Volker Law do not represent a complete departure from the activity in which the New York State Department of Mental Hygiene had been participating prior to its passage. In fact it should be emphasized that the experience of the three units which had evolved since 1959 to no small degree allowed the department representatives who participated in the development of this law to contribute meaningfully to the creation of its provisions. Thus, the importance of pursuing a course of clinical and basic scientific research had been recognized with the establishment of the department's first narcotic unit at the Manhattan State Hospital. Some addicts were admitted under their own volition; others apparently were under strong pressure to enter from the state division of parole and local probation services. It is thus possible to study differences in treatment response due to mode of entry. Furthermore, representatives of these facilities had made themselves available for the education of nurses, social workers, physicians, and psychologists by participating in formal training programs and scientific meetings. Similarly they had participated in planning sessions with the representatives of other agencies, both public and private. They had conducted an aftercare program, had explored the state of present knowledge concerning causative factors of narcotic addiction and what constitutes appropriate treatment modalities, were aware of the kinds of facilities which are required to treat the addict, were familiar with the social and legal issues which surround this problem, and in general had acquired a fundamental understanding of drug addiction as a clinical entity.

However, to suggest that following the passage of this law, much did not remain to be done to implement its provisions would be incorrect, as it called for a much broader field of action than had been previously initiated. Therefore, it was necessary to take those steps which would allow for the development of a more comprehensive program. These included:

1. The appointment of a special assistant to the commissioner to direct the newly created narcotic office established by the law within the state department of mental hygiene

2. The appointment of nine citizens at large to serve on the advisory council on drug addiction

3. The creation of a male and female adolescent unit

4. The establishment of a facility for adult females

5. An increase in the number of beds available to adult males

6. An expansion of the department's aftercare facilities

7. The employment and training of an expanded personnel force

8. The development of a screening staff familiar with prison methods whose function it would be to select arrested addicts suitable for inclusion in the program

Movement toward the initial goals of the department's expanded program began shortly after the close of the 1962 legislative session, at which time a division of narcotics within the state department of mental hygiene was established and a director appointed to coordinate the department's operation in the narcotics field. Simultaneously, a study was initiated within a major New York City detention facility so that some impression could be gained of the numbers and types of cases a source such as this would be likely to yield under the provisions of the Arrested Narcotic Addict Commitment Act. This allowed for a random sampling of some four hundred individuals, who were interviewed over a 5-month period following their arraignment in magistrates' court and classified by the detention facility as narcotic addicts. The techniques utilized by this institution in the processing and management of addict defendants were also reviewed, and an opportunity to familiarize hospital personnel with these methods was provided. As a result the development of administrative procedures to be followed by local correction departments under the provisions of the new law was facilitated, and an opportunity to train personnel in the screening of arrested drug addicts was made possible.

The establishment of a unit for the treatment of the male adolescent addict was also begun shortly after the passage of the law. Thus, at the Manhattan State Hospital, where the clinical research facilities and basic science laboratories have been maintained in temporary quarters pending the completion of extensive reconstruction of the building which will house them, plans were laid to redesign still another building to be used in the treatment and rehabilitation of the adolescent drug user. This structure, which is anticipated to serve 135 patients, will include space to meet the educational, training, and recreational needs of this group. Pending the completion of construction changes, temporary quarters were made available, and this acquisition allowed the Manhattan State Hospital to begin treating patients under the age of 21 in October, 1962, thereby permitting this institution to run a short-term pilot project designed to test the operation of its program prior to its formal entry into the field of narcotic addiction treatment of adolescents on January 1, 1963. Some 55 of the 135 planned adolescent beds have been added thus far to the 55 adult beds which previously existed at this hospital, and it is hoped that the remainder can be added shortly.

The appointment of nine members from outside of state government to the newly created council on drug addiction in 1962 represented another step in implementing the program. Designating the executive vice-president of the state medical society as the council's chairman, the Governor appointed to the council a group of qualified and interested persons including a psychiatrist, a judge, the executive director of a social agency, a prosecuting attorney, and three clergymen, two of whom have worked actively in the drug addiction field. The entire council is presently meeting on a monthly basis in the pursuit of its work.

In September of 1962 three sites were selected to expand the department's inpatient facilities for adult males and to establish a unit for the treatment of adolescent and adult females. These new facilities, representing a total of 165 beds, are distributed as follows: 25 adult male beds at the Buffalo State Hospital, 35 beds for females at the Middletown State Hospital, and 105 beds for adult males at the Pilgrim State Hospital. These units began receiving patients on January 1, 1963, and should be completely phased in by July 1, 1963. It is anticipated, therefore, that with the 20 beds at the Utica State Hospital and the 80 beds at the Central Islip State Hospital the total bed capacity of the department will number 455 by this latter date.

A further step in the evolution of the program was taken later in the year with the decision to establish the first separate aftercare clinic detached from an institution with a drug unit in the city of New York's borough of Manhattan. This clinic is scheduled to open shortly and will supplement the work being done at the Manhattan State Hospital's outpatient department. As with the previously existing units, all of the new facilities offer aftercare services to those patients who come from nearby areas. However, we draw the overwhelming majority of our patients from New York City, and it is anticipated that at least a second clinic will be required in this municipality as the program develops. All of this indicates the emphasis we will place upon following patients once they have returned to the community. It is our hope that this work will be facilitated by the committed status of many of our patients and will allow for a coordinated use of community resources in an effort to assist them to higher-level functioning.

The matter of meeting the personnel needs of our program has also been actively pursued. Experience has taught us that the number of people required to deal effectively with the drug-addict patient far exceeds the usual staffing patterns as they are applied to the general state hospital population. This is particularly true of the ward personnel, among whom a significant number of individuals must be of high caliber and equipped to deal with the characterologic problems which the addict presents. We also need recreation workers, vocational-training personnel, occupational therapists, and teachers who are able to lead a patient group lacking in initiative and direction. An adequate number of psychiatrists, psychologists, and caseworkers must be available to plan with the addict in anticipation of his return to the community and to provide him with the support and supervision he requires after he leaves inpatient care.

The training of new personnel began at the Manhattan State

Hospital during the spring of 1962. A nucleus of people from each of the new units was subsequently included in this training program, and they, in turn, are providing instruction to those individuals who have been added to their staffs. This is an ongoing process, which will not be completed overnight, but it is our hope that in this manner a group of workers will be developed upon whose shoulders this program can securely rest.

CONCLUSION

The New York State Department of Mental Hygiene's Narcotic Addiction Program, which began in August of 1959, is presently in a transition stage as it moves in the direction of a broadened and more active role in the drug-addiction field. The department's program as it is presently envisioned seeks to meet the need for a coordinated psychiatric effort in the narcotic addiction field on the state level and will provide an opportunity for long-term treatment to voluntary and civilly committed patients while pursuing an active course of clinical and basic scientific research in an effort to improve treatment results. As such, it should not be expected to eliminate the drug addiction problem, but rather should be viewed as adding another dimension to the treatment of a complex clinical entity which leans toward chronicity and tends to resist intervention.

REFERENCES

1. N.Y. Mental Hygiene Law, art. 9, § 200–216.
2. Meiselas, H.: A Report of Some Early Clinical Experiences from the New York State Department of Mental Hygiene's Narcotic Research Unit, Presented at the 24th Meeting of the Committee on Drug Addiction and Narcotics, National Research Council, New York, Jan. 29, 1962.

Richard A. McGee | **16**

NEW APPROACHES TO THE CONTROL
AND TREATMENT OF DRUG ABUSERS
IN CALIFORNIA

C ALIFORNIA'S NEW APPROACHES to the narcotics problem—if they
can really be called new—began very quietly at a meeting of
the state board of corrections in the fall of 1957. The board, made
up mainly of the state's correctional administrators and parole
board members, was concerned because of the increase in commitments on narcotics charges. An outgrowth of this concern was
that the board of corrections, which has the statutory authority
to study all phases of crime, set up a committee to get the facts
about the extent and nature of the problem. Funds were obtained
and staff was recruited. Study findings and board recommendations were published early in 1959.

Several of the recommendations were subsequently imple-
mented. One of these was the creation of what we called the
narcotic treatment control project in the department of corrections. This pilot, experimental program with an assessment com-
ponent built in was designed to control, supervise, and treat the
prisoner with a history of narcotic addiction released on parole.

This project continues in operation. It works this way: A substantial portion of the men and women in California's prisons were found to have a history of narcotic addiction. Some had come in on narcotic charges, but about half were committed for other offenses. The experimental project did not alter or modify prison treatment, but when release time came, inmates going to specific geographical areas were randomly assigned to experimental and control field parole units.

A field unit consists of experienced parole agents who are trained specialists in supervising former narcotic addicts. They supervise only former addicts. Their case load is small, each agent supervising only 30 parolees. This is in contrast to the mixed group of 75 or 80 parolees supervised by the regular agents.

This small case load permits the project agent to provide intensive supervision—to know the man, his movement, his activities, and his associates. It permits the agent to work more closely with the parolee, to help him solve his problems without a return to narcotics. It permits the agent to encourage the parolee to make maximum use of constructive community resources.

As a part of this more intensive supervision, each parolee is required to undergo frequent medical examinations. This medical examination consists primarily of the nalorphine antinarcotic test.

A halfway house designed to further strengthen the parole supervision program was opened in October, 1962, in Los Angeles. The house is a joint project of the state of California and the United States Department of Health, Education and Welfare's National Institute of Mental Health. The halfway house is designed to provide a constructive-living atmosphere for parolees during the initial period after their release from state correctional institutions. The house provides a headquarters for parole agents supervising 200 narcotic addict parolees, a supervised residence for up to 35 selected parolees at a time, individual and group counseling for parolees and their families, coordination of community resources in job and home placement and educational activities, and increased parolee guidance and control through closer, more continuous contact with parole agents. Parolees are required to accept gainful employment to pay for their own support and that of their families.

As in the entire narcotic treatment control project, there is a strong emphasis on research. The research phase of the program is directed by a professional team headed by Dr. Gilbert Geis, professor of sociology at Los Angeles State College. Besides the research staff headed by Dr. Geis, plans call for cooperating professional people from Loma Linda University, Los Angeles State College, and private agencies to be associated with various aspects of the research program.

If the parole agent learns, or the medical examination discloses, that the parolee has started to use narcotics, the parolee may be immediately confined in a detention-treatment unit. He may be held there for up to 90 days. Either he may be returned to parole in the community after treatment if he appears to respond or, if not, he may be returned to prison.

Treatment in the detention unit is primarily psychologic. Possibly the greatest emphasis is on the promotion in the unit of a climate in which the inmates actively support each other in their efforts to understand and overcome the problems that induce them to use narcotics.

Concern over the narcotics problem continued to mount, and in 1960 another recommendation of the board was effected with the appointment by the Governor of a special study commission on narcotics. It reported to the Governor and Legislature in 1961.

As a consequence two major legislative bills were enacted. One of these drastically increased penalties for narcotics traffickers. The other established a procedure for the compulsory treatment of narcotic addicts. Drafting of the treatment legislation actively involved the Governor, the attorney general, the narcotics commission, the department of mental hygiene, law enforcement, the judiciary and the department of corrections. The legislation as finally enacted provided a civil commitment for treatment; establishment of the California Rehabilitation Center; a mandatory aftercare program including reduced case loads, chemical testing to determine narcotic use, and authorization for a halfway house; and a mandate for research into the rehabilitation of narcotic addicts.

After the experience gained here and elsewhere was carefully weighed, the program was made compulsory, and a long period of legal control was provided. There were several reasons for this, which took into account the needs of both the individual and society. First, without a legal, enforceable commitment a very large percentage of addicts will not undertake treatment. Given the opportunity, an extremely high percentage of addicts will leave treatment against medical advice. Then, too, without a legal, enforceable commitment there is no way postinstitutional treatment can be ensured. The lack of such treatment has been widely blamed for high rates of readdiction. Finally, we sought to provide a measure of public protection. Our legislation preceded the United State Supreme Court decision in the case of *Robinson v. California,* but it is thoroughly in accord with the view expressed by Associate Justice Stewart that "in the interest of the general health and welfare of its inhabitants, a state might establish a program of compulsory treatment for those addicted to narcotics" just as, he went on to say, it might for the unfortunate victims of mental illness, leprosy, or venereal disease. It is the author's view that the addict is no more entitled to determine himself whether he should undertake treatment than the tubercular is entitled to make such a determination.

The legislation adopted in California placed the responsibility for treatment and postinstitutional supervision on the department of corrections. This was done after great deliberation and was based upon the following factors. A large proportion of narcotic addicts are delinquently oriented. An even larger share of those who come to official attention have a long history of antisocial activity. They are not only addicts, but in most cases, they are also thieves, burglars, forgers, or narcotic pushers. Some are hostile, rebellious, and assaultive. A great many will go to any length to try to continue to get narcotics during the treatment period or to escape from treatment. The point is simply that as a group they pose a management problem not unfamiliar to correctional authorities, but one which clashes with modern, progressive mental-health concepts of open hospitals and patient freedom. Another factor was the existence within the department of corrections of a highly developed, professional aftercare service with extensive experience in the postinstitutional treatment of narcotic addicts.

I would like to emphasize that putting a particular departmental label on the administration of a program does not by itself make a program either therapeutic or punitive. This has long been recognized in California. The department of corrections has for many years shared responsibility for treatment of sex psychopaths and psychopathic delinquents with the department of mental hygiene. It treats tuberculars under arrangement with the department of public health. Under statutes held constitutional, the department of mental hygiene is empowered to transfer some patients needing "care and treatment under conditions of custodial security which can better be provided within the Department of Corrections" to corrections facilities. Corrections, in turn, transfers some of its felony prisoners to mental-hygiene facilities when this is appropriate. Thus, use of the most appropriate facilities for individual treatment is obtained.

The civil proceedings under which the addict may be committed may be initiated in three different ways: The addict or any other person who believes that he is addicted may report his addiction to the district attorney. The district attorney may then petition the superior court for the addict's commitment. Any person convicted of any crime in a municipal or justice court may, if the judge believes he is an addict, be sent to superior court for determination of that issue. Or, with some exceptions, any person convicted of a crime in superior court may be tried on the issue of addiction. In such cases, imposition of the criminal penalty is suspended.

The commitment proceedings are essentially those employed for the commitment of the mentally ill. They insure that the constitutional rights of the person sought to be committed are protected. They provide, for example, that he shall be taken before a judge and informed of his rights, that he be examined by two qualified medical examiners, that he shall be given ample opportunity to produce witnesses in his behalf, that he shall be personally present in open court and shall have court-appointed counsel if he is unable to employ his own. He may, under some circumstances, demand a jury trial on the issue of his addiction.

Once the person is committed, he is committed for a definite period, even though he may have actually volunteered himself for treatment. The law now provides for a 5-year commitment in some cases and a 10-year commitment in others. The first 6 months must be spent as an inpatient. The former addict may then be placed in outpatient status. If he abstains from the use of narcotics for 3 consecutive years, he is discharged from his commitment and the criminal charges against him, if any, may be dropped. The law provides return to inpatient status upon detection of narcotic use. It also provides that if the person is ineligible for discharge from the program, he shall be returned to court for imposition of the original sentence or, perhaps, for recommitment to the program.

The compulsory treatment bill was signed into law by the Governor on June 24, 1961, and went into effect September 15, 1961. The department had announced its readiness to accept the first commitments on that day.

There were, of course, many administrative problems in making the program operative. The biggest problem was that acquisition of the surplus facility we had expected to use for the California Rehabilitation Center was delayed for nearly a year. As a result, we were forced to develop the program in several different locations, shifting staff and patients from place to place and splitting the operation. Although we have now secured the former Naval Hospital at Norco and placed it in operation as the rehabilitation center, we have not as yet been able to consolidate all operations there. Throughout the difficult initial period of the program, however, we had excellent cooperation from the courts and from law enforcement.

In assisting with the drafting of the legislation and in planning the treatment program, the department drew upon its experience with the narcotic treatment control project, and also upon its own experiments with community-living groups. With the help of Drs. Maxwell Jones and Harry Wilmer we endeavored to adapt the therapeutic community concept to the correctional environment.

When the addict is committed, he is received at a special section of the southern reception guidance center of the department of corrections. Females are received at the California Institution for Women. The initial diagnosis is undertaken currently at the reception center. A variety of tests are administered, including intelligence, educational achievement, vocational aptitude, and personality tests. Social and criminal history is compiled. In each case the counseling staff makes a special effort to develop the history of narcotic use. From this material the staff structures a recommended treatment program, and a case summary is compiled, which accompanies the patient and to which information is added as appropriate.

An important use of these case summaries is for research purposes. An analysis of the first 500 cases shows:

1. The median age for all is about 4 years below that of felony offenders committed to correctional institutions, 25 as against 29 years.

2. More addicts are under 21, 14 per cent as opposed to 9 per cent, than persons in the general population of the department of corrections.

3. Most men and women committed are California "problems," 58 per cent having been born in the State and 90 per cent having lived in California 10 years or more.

4. Forty-three per cent, or 173, of the men had begun use of narcotics during their fifteenth, sixteenth, or seventeenth years. Eighty per cent, or 322, of the men had begun use of narcotics before reaching their twentieth birthday.

5. Twenty-eight per cent of the women had begun use of narcotics during their fifteenth, sixteenth, or seventeenth years. Forty per cent of the women did not start the use of narcotics until they had reached, or passed, their twentieth birthday.

6. Sixty-nine per cent of the men and 67 per cent of the women left school between the ages of 15 and 17 inclusive. Twenty-six men commenced the use of narcotics prior to reaching their teens.

After the diagnostic study is completed, the patient is transferred to the California Rehabilitation Center or one of the branch centers that are now operating.

Here the program is one primarily of group centered activity—

of community living. A large group meeting is held daily, 5 days a week, which involves all the patients in a ward, optimally about 60, together with the staff assigned to that ward. This hour-long meeting tries to work through the intragroup problems of living and working together. Problems of antisocial behavior, such as pilfering and informing, are discussed. Individual relationships with other group members and with families and friends outside the institution are considered, and the inmate's feelings about himself and others are brought to light.

This large community group meeting is followed by a meeting of the staff together with about three or four of the patients. The purpose here is to provide the staff a chance to evaluate what went on in the group, and it also serves as a means of staff training. The inmates are used as a communicating link between staff and group, particularly in feeding back to the group the staff's interest in, and involvement with, the group.

Two or three times a week, the big 60-man group is split into four groups of 15 men each, for an hour of more intensive group psychotherapy. On the days when small-group psychotherapy is not scheduled, the patients are encouraged to visit with their families, to meet individually with staff, if this is indicated, and to participate in organized recreation. The emphasis is on team play —pitting one dorm or ward against another when possible.

The second half of the day is devoted to what might generally be classed as work therapy. So far as possible the correctional officer assigned to the ward supervises the members of his group assigned to a work detail. Twenty persons is about the limit he can supervise. But others of his 60-man group are assigned to school or to vocational training. There is a full academic program through high school. Vocational courses taught are those in which competence can be obtained in a relatively short time. They presently include upholstering, building maintenance, landscape gardening, general shop, house painting, cooking, and baking. Music, arts, crafts, public speaking, and other forms of self-expression are encouraged in off-duty hours.

This institutional treatment program attempts a corrective experience for the addict, who is often socially immature, and who displays dependent, impulsive, and egocentric behavior.

The institutional treatment is only the first phase of the total program. The test of its success comes in the community and only in the community. The field staff becomes involved with the patient soon after his commitment. The caseworker contributes an extensive review of the patient's home environment, family feelings and attitudes, work record, and prospects to the case history while it is being compiled at the reception center, and he may at this time make his first contact with the patient. When the institution staff feels the patient is ready to leave, he is contacted by the caseworker to whom he will be assigned in the field. Together they work out release plans and begin to build a constructive relationship.

The caseworker is specially trained to work with addicts, and his case load of 30 are all addicts. The group work continues after release to the community. Each caseworker meets weekly with his case load as a group. Counseling attendance is regarded as particularly important for those patients who are unemployed. Use is also made of the parole and community services division's outpatient psychiatric clinics. The caseworker meets individually with each patient weekly at the patient's home or at his job. He also contacts others in a position to evaluate the patient's progress —his family, his employer, the police.

Efforts are under way to establish one or more halfway houses of somewhat the same type already established for parolees under the narcotic treatment control project.

In addition, each patient is chemically tested for relapse to narcotic use five times a month for at least the first 6 months. Four of these Nalline tests are given on an irregular basis, and one is a surprise test. If all the indications are good, this test schedule may be cut to two surprise tests a month after the first 6 months. Test failure or other indication of relapse results in return to inpatient status.

Realistically we anticipate relapse. Failure may in some cases be necessary to the eventual solution of the patient's problems. In talking to some of those men that returned, it was apparent that they went out convinced they "had it made" and then encountered unexpected problems and reverted to narcotics use. I was impressed with their attitude on return. Instead of the bitterness and blaming of others one might expect, I found a new appreciation of the problems involved in their rehabilitation and a new determination to overcome them.

Thus far, too few patients have been returned to the community to afford any measure of the program's effect. Needless to say, those released also have been the better prospects. And most of them have not been out very long.

There are about eighteen hundred persons in the program at present—about sixteen hundred of them inpatients. Of the men released, about 120 are still out and 14 have been returned—only one of these involved in criminal activity. There are approximately 100 women in the community, and 16 have been returned. Some of the women have been out since June, 1962, and some of the men have been out since July, 1962.

We are collecting a great deal of information from the addicts committed, which we hope will be helpful in research into the causes of narcotic addiction and which may provide some new clues for its treatment. We plan medical, pharmacologic, sociologic, and virtually any kind of research that is appropriate. We hope to have the assistance of foundations and universities in this endeavor.

So far, the new California approaches to the narcotics problem that I have been describing all deal with the end product, that is, the addict. If there was ever a situation in which an ounce of prevention is worth a pound of cure, it is in the field of narcotics. Too often in the past such small efforts at prevention as have been made have accomplished little because they were founded on myth instead of fact, have been directed at the wrong target, or were wholly superficial.

The administration of Governor Brown in California is backing new and promising basic efforts which will, I believe, as a part of their total effect, go a long way toward preventing narcotics addiction as well as other deviant behavior. I refer to such measures as those aimed at eliminating discrimination in private housing and in ending *de facto* school segregation. I refer also to measures to take bold new steps to help the culturally deprived child before he becomes "unschooled, unskilled and unemployable." One of these would provide funds to furnish special services such as smaller classes, more remedial help, and more intensive counseling of children and parents in schools composed of children from underprivileged homes. Another would provide for those children affected by special learning or behavior problems. These bills recognize that some children are just as much handicapped by background or emotional problems as others may be by physical defect. The Governor also has asked passage of legislation to study, improve, and expand vocational training. And for those for whom these programs come too late, he has proposed a youth conservation corps for the out-of-school, out-of-work youth.

This is the new direction—the new approach—to the control and treatment of drug abusers that must ultimately prevail.

CONTROL AND TREATMENT OF
DRUG ADDICTION IN HONG KONG

T HE NARCOTIC PROBLEM in Hong Kong is a very serious one and is a consequence, in large part, of the peculiar economy of Hong Kong. Hong Kong is a free port and the economic well-being of Hong Kong is dependent upon the free flow of commodities through Hong Kong. To encourage this, it has been the policy of the Hong Kong government to exercise a minimum of control over the movement of goods in and out of Hong Kong. International traffickers in narcotic drugs have exploited the liberal trade regulations and port facilities of Hong Kong to make Hong Kong one of the more notorious centers for narcotic traffic and abuse.

Since 1959 the Hong Kong government has intensified its efforts to combat narcotic addiction. The three main objectives have been to eliminate the source of narcotic supplies, and to cure and rehabilitate those who have been victimized. These various activities are the responsibilities of several agencies that are coordinated by the Secretary for Chinese Affairs, who also acts as Chairman of the Narcotics Advisory Committee. This committee makes major policy recommendations to the government, and its membership, other than the Secretary, is made up of leading non-

274

government citizens appointed by the Governor. I would like to discuss some of the complexities and difficulties of the narcotic problem in Hong Kong and some of the measures that the government of Hong Kong is taking to combat this problem.

INCIDENCE AND TYPES OF ADDICTION

The magnitude of the problem in Hong Kong is reflected by the high incidence of narcotic addiction in the Colony. Although it is not possible to obtain absolutely accurate figures, a rough estimate can be made from prison statistics. A government report in 1959 suggested the figure of 150,000, but with the information that has been made available since then, some of the authorities guess that 100,000 would be a more reasonable estimate of the number of narcotic addicts. The estimate is based on the annual number of narcotic convictions, which run in the neighborhood of ten thousand. Roughly 60 per cent of the prison inmates are drug addicts. If the assumption is made that the number of repeat narcotic convictions is balanced by an equal number of addicts who are not sent to prison because they are fined instead or because they succeed in escaping arrest, then the number convicted annually would represent the number of new addicts for the year.

A figure of 100,000 would mean that approximately one out of every eight male adults in Hong Kong is a drug addict. Such a ratio can be easily calculated from the population and prison statistics of Hong Kong, which are considered to be reasonably accurate. The population of Hong Kong is 3.5 million, and of the total male population about one-half are of the age 20 years and over. The prison records indicate that addiction in males under 20 is rare and that addiction in females is considerably less than in males, the incidence in females in 1961 being about one-thirtieth that in males. If we neglect these two groups, which combined probably represent no more than 5 per cent of the total addict population, there would be 100,000 addicts among the 800,000 males of 20 years or older in Hong Kong.

The largest number of addicts are in the 35 to 50 age group, and the next largest number in the 20 to 34 age group. The incidence in the 16 to 19 age group consistently runs less than 0.5

of 1 per cent of the total addict population. The vast majority of the addicts come from three main occupational classifications— laborers, street vendors, and skilled workers (tailors, carpenters, barbers, etc.). Most of the female addicts are prostitutes, but it is not known accurately whether they entered their profession before or after they acquired the drug habit.

Various reasons are given by the addict to explain how or why he became addicted. Curiosity is the most common motive mentioned. Undoubtedly this motive is closely linked to sociability or social pressure, inasmuch as narcotic use is believed to be almost universal among certain segments of the population. Many probably were unwittingly corrupted, although the authorities have made concerted efforts to educate people with respect to the harmful consequences of addiction. Polling the known addicts from the coolie-laborer or street-vendor class with respect to the incidence of drug addiction results in the general opinion that the vast majority of their cohorts are drug addicts, and, although not all may be physically dependent, everyone at their social level has used narcotics at one time or another. To combat fatigue is a fairly common motive. In general, conditions under which the worker is subjected to pressure and long arduous hours appear to be conducive to narcotic use. Tailors with 24 hours to complete a suit, construction workers with hazardous assignments, and coolie laborers fall in this category. Need to relieve pain or insomnia is also often given as a reason for narcotic use. In order not to take the time for, and assume the expense of, competent medical advice, many of the low-income group resort to self-treatment with narcotics to stay on their jobs. A few claim to use narcotics for producing euphoria, and some state they started on narcotics solely for the purpose of prolonging sexual intercourse.

The majority of the addicts (about two-thirds) are consumers of heroin; about one-third are users of opium. Addiction to the synthetic surrogates of morphine is almost nonexistent. The popularity of heroin is undoubtedly attributable to pragmatism. The increased effort of the Hong Kong government to suppress opium smoking has resulted in the unfortunate consequence of drug traffickers and addicts turning to heroin, which is much easier to smuggle and conceal. Then, too, the development of drug tolerance to opium has necessitated many addicts to resort to the more potent heroin for sustaining their increased needs.

The narcotic drugs are used in many ways. Opium is generally smoked with a special pipe, and the intake is preceded by a ceremonial heating process to prepare the opium for smoking. There are also a few who swallow, rather than smoke, opium. Heroin can be injected intravenously or intramuscularly, as is so popular in the United States, but more generally the effects of heroin are obtained by inhalation, and the addicts have their own parlance to describe the different modes of inhalation. The mildest form is by "ack ack" or "firing the antiaircraft gun," a procedure whereby the lighted end of a cigarette is dipped into heroin (powder or small granules), and in order to keep the heroin from falling off, the cigarette is smoked with the head tilted slightly backwards. A variant of ack ack is smoking cigarettes containing heroin concealed within the tobacco; many addicts claim that they were unknowingly introduced to the habit in such a manner.

The more "sophisticated" ways to inhale heroin are by "chasing the dragon" or by "playing the mouth organ," methods which may have been introduced to Hong Kong from Shanghai prior to the Second World War. Both processes are basically similar. Several granules of heroin in granular form and generally dyed red ("red chicken") are mixed with several parts of barbital on a piece of tinfoil folded longitudinally. The mixture is heated gently with a lighted match or taper, and as it melts, the molten mass is made to run slowly up and down the tinfoil by alternately tilting each end. The barbiturate and the heating process serve to prevent the rapid decomposition of heroin. As the molten mass rolls slowly back and forth, the addict inhales the fumes which evolve. The fumes take the shape of the undulating tail of a dragon, hence, "chasing the dragon." The fumes may be inhaled without the aid of an instrument, but generally a straw, rolled paper, or bamboo tube is used. If the fumes are inhaled through a matchbox cover, this is called "playing the mouth organ." Each variant requires considerable skill to prevent irritation from the fumes and waste of the material. The process generally can be completed within a few minutes, but some of the more adroit inhalers maintain that they can chase the dragon for hours at a time. Dragon chasing usually begins when tolerance to opium or to the ack ack method develops and often ends when the addict drifts to heroin injection to sustain his cravings. However, many dragon chasers have been satisfied with this mode of taking heroin and have maintained this particular habit for several years without need to resort to heroin injection.

The mode of narcotic use is largely dependent upon the earning capacity of the addict. When his daily income is used entirely to sustain his need for narcotics, either the addict is content to maintain his habit at this level or he shifts to taking heroin by another procedure which gives greater effects.

The heroin taken by injection or by ack ack is not the adulterated material seen in the United States. The "no. 4 powder," or "white powder," in Hong Kong is high-grade heroin hydrochloride that is generally more than 90 per cent pure, and the "red chicken" for dragon chasing is usually about 65 per cent pure. The heroin is dispensed in small packets containing 40 or 80 mg of heroin and costs respectively 18 cents and 35 cents per packet. If the material is for dragon chasing, another packet containing 100 to 200 mg of barbital is generally furnished without additional charge. Most addicts use 100 to 500 mg of heroin daily, taking one or two packets three or four times a day. The daily cost of their habit is usually 60 cents to $3, with most addicts spending a little less than $1.50 per day.

CONTROL

The Hong Kong government, through the United Kingdom, is a signatory to the various conventions and agreements adopted by the international bodies for the control of narcotic traffic. It reports annually to the Commission on Narcotic Drugs of the United Nations on various aspects of drug control. Relevant segments of the international conventions and agreements have been incorporated into municipal laws under the Dangerous Drug Ordinance. The cultivation of opium and manufacture of narcotics, the possession of drugs unless authorized by the Director of Medical and Health Services, and the consumption of opium or heroin are liable to maximum penalties of $17,000 fine and imprisonment for 15 years. However, the maximum penalties are seldom set for these offenses for various reasons, and usually with good cause. In many instances those arrested for the manufacture of heroin are refugees from the mainland of China committing their first offense, and the big operator behind the scenes, who may well be masking as a respectable member of the community, is seldom apprehended. To arrest and vigorously prosecute the mere users would flood the prisons and overtax law enforcement officials and existing facilities. In general, those who are charged with possession of narcotics have sufficient amounts on their persons or premises to indicate that they are peddling or manufacturing narcotics. These people are dealt with more harshly, and the punishment is roughly proportional to the amount of evidence seized and the number of previous convictions. Repeated offenses are more likely to be among those who peddle heroin, because many peddlars are also addicts.

Hong Kong is not an opium-producing area. If any is cultivated, it is rare and certainly not of commercial significance, so that the opium consumed in Hong Kong is smuggled in. While much of the heroin consumed locally is manufactured within Hong Kong, the main ingredient for its manufacture, morphine, is smuggled in from Yunnan, Laos, Burma, Thailand, and Viet Nam. The geographic situation of Hong Kong, coupled with its free-port facilities, makes Hong Kong an ideal transit center for narcotics throughout the world, and the traffic is particularly heavy between Hong Kong and Bangkok. Some of the smuggling occurs through the mail and by aircraft, but most of the smuggling is by sea. The control of this illicit traffic in narcotics in Hong Kong is under two government agencies, the Preventive Service and the Hong Kong Police.

The interception of smugglers and their contraband is undertaken by the Preventive Service of the Commerce and Industry Department. During the year the Preventive Service routinely searches nearly four thousand oceangoing vessels, over twenty thousand small local boats, nearly fifteen hundred aircraft, and nine hundred land vehicles. A vigilant watch is maintained on about four hundred oceangoing vessels, and approximately one thousand searches are conducted on the ferry steamships plying back and forth daily between Macau and Hong Kong. About two or three seizures are made a month. The amount seized varies widely. Roughly about 1,000 to 3,000 lb of opium, 100 to 300 lb of morphine, and less than 100 lb of heroin are seized within a year.

The police force handles narcotic violations occurring within the Colony. The amount of heroin seized within Hong Kong is generally higher than that seized in transit, but the amount of opium seized is far less. This may be explained by the fact that virtually no opium is grown locally and large amounts of smuggled opium are consumed, whereas facilities do exist for the manufacture of heroin from morphine. Arrests for narcotic violations number about forty each day. Successful raids on manufacturers or traffickers run about one or two a month. The intelligence work is done by the Narcotic Bureau of the police force, and the Bureau also coordinates the activities of the Police Preventive Service and Interpol. Most seizures are made after routine surveillance and search, but many raids are made after reliable tips from informers.

TREATMENT

There are several institutions where the drug addict can be treated. Some give excellent care, but in general the available facilities are inadequate to handle the large addict population. As a consequence many addicts seek treatment on an ambulatory basis from private physicians. Although it may not be illegal for physicians to treat addicts on an outpatient basis, should the evidence indicate that a physician is maintaining rather than treating addiction, he can be censured, and his license to practice can be revoked. An inventory of all narcotic purchases in Hong Kong is kept by the Hong Kong government, and if the amounts purchased by a physician appear excessive, the Director of Medical and Health Services can warn the offender or bring him before medical council. Such incidences, however, are rare. More likely when the addict is treated on an outpatient basis, the practitioner is a quack with an illegal source of narcotics.

Most of the convicted addicts are physically withdrawn from narcotics at the various prisons of the Colony, under medical supervision. After this withdrawal they enter the usual prison routine for the duration of their sentences. Many inmates convicted for offenses other than narcotic violations often become unknowingly withdrawn from narcotics while waiting for trial or sentencing. However, some may become withdrawn in prison. As has been said earlier, approximately 60 per cent of the prisoners are drug addicts, and since they are permitted to see visitors, it is extremely difficult to maintain maximum security conditions with respect to preventing narcotics from entering the prisons. In isolated instances prison guards have been convicted for passing narcotics to the inmates.

The Commissioner of Prisons, aware of these problems and of the fact that many of the prisoners convicted solely for drug violations and other minor offenses presented problems and had needs different from those of the other types of inmates, proposed the creation of an open-air prison especially for drug addicts. As a consequence Tai Lam Prison was established near Castle Peak late in 1958.

Tai Lam Prison

Tai Lam Prison in the New Territories is part prison and part hospital. Since its inception, over eight thousand addicts have been treated there. Between 1,500 and 2,000 prisoners are admitted and discharged from the prison annually, and the average daily population is maintained at about 700. The inmates are, in large part, those who have been imprisoned for narcotic offenses, but many other prisoners sent there were convicted for other crimes and were found to be addicts after their incarceration. The prisoners selected for Tai Lam are considered to have a reasonably good chance for rehabilitation. Generally speaking, prisoners with a sentence of not less than 6 months are accepted, since all sentences may be reduced by one-third for good conduct and 4 months is considered to be the minimum period for effecting a cure.

The addicts at Tai Lam are hospitalized and withdrawn upon arrival; some may already arrive partially withdrawn. Withdrawal is done under the supervision of a medical officer, who generally uses only chlorpromazine and psychotherapy for the alleviation of abstinence signs. After a few days the withdrawn addict is given light outdoor work and subsequently heavier work, the assignment being based on his physical condition, age, and experience. The work includes afforestation and construction work on roads, buildings, and fire barriers. Upon discharge there are four full-time social welfare officers following up selected cases. Aftercare is generally provided also for those prisoners who voluntarily indicate that they wish to be supervised for 12 months after their release. About 5 to 10 per cent of the prison population receive aftercare and are contacted at least once a month, more frequently if necessary. The follow-up statistics with respect to the program reported recently by the Commissioner of Prisons states that of the 160 ex-convicts who submitted voluntarily to 12 months of supervision, only 20 relapsed. In addition, although individual aftercare was not provided the other prisoners, 68 per cent of the addicts, who passed through Tai Lam from 1958 until the release of the report at the end of March, 1963, have not been reconvicted. The success of the program, however, cannot be fully assessed unless detailed follow-up data are obtained on all prisoners.

Shek Kwu Chau and SARDA

In 1959 the Society for the Aid and Rehabilitation of Drug Addicts or SARDA was formed by a group of civic-minded individuals in Hong Kong for the purpose of aiding the government in combatting the drug addiction problem. The leading members include physicians and attorneys, as well as other professions, and business men and government servants.

Since its inception, SARDA has been concerned primarily with providing a suitable institution where drug addicts can volunteer for treatment and rehabilitation. SARDA members were particularly disturbed by the fact that, at the time, any addict wishing to be cured on his own would have to go to prison first. The society undertook to raise funds for the construction of a hospital and related facilities from private individuals and organizations and the government as well. This proved to be a successful venture, and the society then proceeded to assume the responsibility of supervising the planning, construction, and staffing of the institution.

The facilities are located on a small island, Shek Kwu Chau, a little over 10 miles from the business center of Hong Kong. On the island about a quarter mile above the landing pier, the administrative area has been set up to include a 20-bed hospital, administrative facilities, and living accommodations for four staff members. About a mile above this site, facilities for housing and dining 250 patients have been erected, and this will be subsequently enlarged to accommodate 500 patients. Professional staff members include a medical officer, two medical orderlies, and a welfare officer. The program will be patterned after the one established at Castle Peak Hospital, described below. Drug withdrawal will be carried out at Castle Peak Hospital over a period of 4 weeks, following which the patients will be transferred to Shek Kwu Chau for occupational therapy and rehabilitation. The program is actively endorsed by the Hong Kong government, and this is apparent by material support that the administration has given in the construction of the facilities and staffing of the personnel. At the present writing the program is still in its infancy, and there will undoubtedly be some growing pains with respect to the details of management, but I feel that the citizens and the government of Hong Kong have taken a very positive step forward in providing suitable installations for the withdrawal and rehabilitation of drug addicts.

Drug Addiction Treatment and Rehabilitation Center, Castle Peak

Castle Peak Hospital is an institution with 1,000 beds set up by the Hong Kong government in 1961 for the treatment of mental diseases. It is located a little over 20 miles from the heart of Hong Kong. A building with two wards of 30 beds each has been set aside for treatment and study of male drug addicts, and, if necessary, each ward can accommodate 60 patients. However, with the existing staff of three nurses and seven orderlies, who divide their time on the admission and convalescent wards, it has been necessary to limit the total patient load to 60 patients in order to maintain proper discipline and morale.

There has been, and still is, a long waiting list for admission to the Castle Peak narcotic addiction facilities. With the exception of the first 60 cases, patients have been carefully screened for admission at the addiction clinic in the Hong Kong Psychiatric Clinic through an intensive interview of the applicant and on occasions his wife and relatives also, by an almoner (medical-social worker) and a psychiatrist.

The criteria for selection included the following:

1. Good family relationships
2. A good work record
3. Evidence of a genuine desire to be cured
4. Promise of employment after cure
5. Evidence of contributing to family support
6. Freedom from serious physical or other mental disease
7. Absence of a serious criminal record
8. Evidence of a reasonable degree of emotional stability

The patient must consent to sign a formal agreement of his willingness to remain for treatment for a period of 6 months. The treatment consists of withdrawal and rehabilitation under complete medical supervision. Withdrawal from heroin may be immediate or gradual, depending on the severity of the abstinence syndrome. If the signs are severe after immediate withdrawal, the patient may be given small doses of methadon for 2 or 3 days to decrease their intensity. Adjunctive symptomatic treatment is also given to alleviate distress. This period of treatment lasts 1 to 2 weeks, and patients generally are ready for physical activity after 10 days.

After withdrawal the patients are gradually brought into an active program of occupational and recreational therapy. The former activity consists of domestic work, tailoring, woodwork, shoe repairing, and gardening, generally with some incentive pay. Recreation takes the form of sports, card games, classes in music and English, and occasional movies, walks, and car drives. During the rehabilitation period contact between the social worker and the patient is maintained by weekly visits of the social worker.

These visits establish rapport between the two and pave the way for future follow-up work. The social worker attempts to reduce the patient's anxieties about his home to a minimum. Wives and mothers are advised to approach the social workers first with their problems. In the cases of disturbed relationships between the addict and his family the social worker attempts to help the family have a better understanding of the addict and his problem. At the end of 5 months the patient is given a 2-day probationary leave, and upon his return he is tested for narcotic usage by the nalorphine pupil test. If the test is negative, 1 month later he is given a second trial leave of 7 days, and after he returns and there is no evidence that he has used narcotics, the patient is discharged.

Patients after being discharged are instructed to visit the social worker once a week for 3 months, after which the visits can be reduced to once a month. If the patient obtains employment and is unable to keep his appointments, his wife or relative is asked to report to the social worker in his place. Rehabilitation for the addict is not easy during this period inasmuch as many ex-addicts are asked to prove themselves before they will be assigned jobs commensurate with their abilities. During this trial period the addict may be required to work long hours at a job which he considers below his standards. This apparently is the crucial period when the addict leans heavily on his relationship with the social worker. The discharged patient is encouraged by the social worker to meet weekly with other discharged patients who have formed a club for mutual support and help.

An active research program is maintained at Castle Peak to study the etiology of drug addiction in order that more effective means can be developed for the prevention and treatment of the disease. To this end the epidemiology of drug addiction is being studied to identify situations in which high rates of incidence are found. Socioeconomic data are being gathered to ascertain the degree of social deterioration that may attend addiction. Psychiatric studies are being conducted to assess the personality of the addict, to determine the initiating factors of addiction, to study the stabilized narcotic users as opposed to addicts, and to assess aversion treatment for preventing relapses. Pharmacologic studies are being made to develop and evaluate methods for detecting narcotic usage and to study the efficiency of different modes of drug intake. One of the most important projects is the intensive follow-up study in progress which should reveal much information concerning the success of the existing program.

The results of the follow-up study to date, although preliminary in nature, yield some information of interest. Of a total of 116 patients who have been discharged for over a year, 37 (32 per cent) have not felt the need to resume their habit. This figure is even more significant when one considers that this series includes the first 60 admissions, which were unselected cases, many of which would have been rejected by present selection criteria as poor risks. Of the 198 patients who have been in the program, 80 per cent were able to abstain from narcotics for a period of at least 3 to 6 months. Included among the relapse data are reports of at least 7 patients who have abstained voluntarily from narcotics for over 6 months after relapsing. These patients prior to their admission to Castle Peak had a long history of narcotic addiction. It would appear, therefore, that an early or occasional relapse does not necessarily mean a treatment failure and that institutional care does yield benefits which cannot be measured by the number of relapses on a short-term basis. Clearly then, follow-up figures should still be kept on individuals beyond their period of relapse, and perhaps a 5-year period of aftercare would give a more realistic assessment of any treatment program.

The Pui Sun Fraternal Association—"Addicts Anonymous"

One of the organizations in Hong Kong with an abiding interest in the welfare of the drug addict is the Lutheran World Service. Members of this group are keenly aware that the crux of the problem of curing an addict after his medical discharge lies chiefly in his rehabilitation to his social environment. Under their sponsorship, and with the encouragement of Castle Peak authorities, a society of ex-drug addicts was organized in December, 1962, with the object of helping addicts help themselves. The membership of Pui Sun is composed of approximately one hundred discharged patients from Castle Peak Hospital. The members meet for discussions under the supervision of a social worker from Castle Peak. Any member suspected of having relapsed is given the nalorphine pupil test, and if the test is positive, he is discouraged from attending further meetings. The headquarters of the society in Kowloon has been provided by the Lutheran World Service.

CONCLUSIONS

Hong Kong has a very serious narcotic problem, pointed up by the high prevalence of addiction to heroin and opium chiefly among males of age 20 and over. In recent years the government of Hong Kong has taken some positive steps to improve the medical and institutional rehabilitation care of the addict by providing excellent facilities for such purposes. On the whole the program in Hong Kong appears to keep the problem in proper perspective and reflects a realistic and sensible attitude toward the drug addict that is generally not matched by governments in the rest of the world. However, despite the progressive measures taken in Hong Kong to solve the problem, there are certain aspects that can be further modified.

The coordination activities of the Secretary on Chinese Affairs could be expanded. There is a need to obtain a more accurate picture of the extent of the narcotic problem, and the enumeration of data on sex, age, residence, and profession is highly essential. A central registry file and tabulating unit would be invaluable in this respect, and, in addition, the registry could keep permanent records of the addict after his discharge. A quantitative assessment of any project in narcotic addiction can be made only when complete and precise records of the addict are kept.

Adequate facilities for the treatment of the female addict are needed. At present the female addict is treated in the prison, and she has no special opportunities to rehabilitate herself as her male counterpart has. Although it is true that the number of female addicts is small in comparison to the number of male addicts, still the number runs in the hundreds. Moreover, if the female happens to be married and her husband is also an addict, the husband will usually be rejected for voluntary cure, because it is thought to be unwise to treat one member of the family and not the other.

Finally, interest in the research aspects of drug addiction need to be maintained, encouraged, and expanded at Castle Peak Hospital. The facilities and personnel for carrying out research there are unique, and the potential of Castle Peak to become a leading research center for addiction studies is not matched by any other institution. At present, however, there is no full-time medical officer on the program, and the professional staff, especially the junior members, lead a somewhat isolated existence. A better atmosphere for research can be maintained over a long period only by providing proper intellectual incentives for the staff.

The biggest improvement can be made in the follow-up care of the addict. The first 6 months after discharge from an institution appears to be a crucial period for the addict, and if he is able to resist temptation during this period, his chances for permanent rehabilitation appear to be reasonably good. At present the only institution in Hong Kong with an aftercare program anywhere near adequate is the Castle Peak Hospital, but even there, the two caseworkers are overburdened by their tasks of interviewing and selecting new admissions, maintaining rapport with hospitalized patients, and maintaining follow-up care with discharged patients. However, since the purpose of the program at Castle Peak is essentially that of research, the number of patients handled there is very small in comparison to the load at the other institutions, such as various prisons, the special open-air prison for addicts at Tai Lam, and the island at Shek Kwu Chau for addicts volunteering for treatment. The provisions for aftercare with these latter institutions at present are minimal, and clearly many more almoners need to be recruited for this program. A centralized bureau for supervised aftercare of all addicts would be desirable, and a program using the nalorphine test for detecting narcotic users would facilitate the work. The assistance of civic volunteer organizations, such as SARDA, for educating the public and for the rehabilitation of the addict in his community environment would be a tremendous asset.

REFERENCES

1. The Problem of Narcotic Drugs in Hong Kong, A white paper laid before the Hong Kong Legislative Council November 11, 1959, Government Press, Hong Kong.
2. Hong Kong Narcotics Advisory Committee: Progress report by the Secretary for Chinese Affairs, Chairman, November 1959–October 1960, Government Press, Hong Kong.

INDEX